WHY STUDY LITERATURE?

WHY STUDY LITERATURE?

Edited by
Jan Alber, Stefan Iversen, Louise Brix Jacobsen,
Rikke Andersen Kraglund, Henrik Skov Nielsen
and Camilla Møhring Reestorff

AARHUS UNIVERSITY PRESS |

Dorothy J. Hale's article
Aesthetics and the New Ethics:
Theorizing the Novel in the Twenty-First Century
is reprinted by permission
of the Modern Language Association of
America from PMLA (May 2009).

ISBN 978 87 7934 551 5

Published with the financial support of
The Aarhus University Research Foundation

Aarhus University Press
Aarhus
Langelandsgade 177
DK – 8200 Aarhus N

København
Tuborgvej 164
DK – 2400 København NV

www.unipress.dk

INTERNATIONAL DISTRIBUTORS:
Gazelle Book Services Ltd.
White Cross Mills
Hightown, Lancaster, LA1 4XS
United Kingdom
www.gazellebookservices.co.uk

ISBC
70 Enterprise Drive
Bristol, CT 06010
USA
e-mail: ian@isbookcompany.com

CONTENTS

HUMANITY

INTRODUCTION

WHY STUDY LITERATURE?

The editors

"Why study literature?" is an important question that continuously needs to be asked and framed. This book aims to provide a range of answers that takes into account the current status and challenges of literary studies. The book is thus one step on the road towards a theoretically well-founded basis and explanation for what might presently be considered a relatively unfounded historical fact: that literature and the teaching of literature hold a privileged place in many educational institutions in fields of study otherwise defined or outlined geographically or by language, as for instance in the departments of English, French, German, and Scandinavian that are still common in both Europe and the United States. We hope that the question "Why study literature?" will provide new ways of thinking about the historical, epistemological, and institutional role of literature.

In this introduction, we will outline first some often reiterated but probably untenable defences of literature, and some equally common and – we believe – equally untenable attacks on literature (or arguments in favor of the death of literature). Secondly, we will present earlier books and approaches that address the question of "why study literature?". Notably, almost all of these studies focus on literature itself rather than on the question of *why* it should be studied within the educational system. Thirdly, we will present a range of reasons why people should *study* literature, and finally we will outline the structure of the present volume as well as each of the contributions.

REFRAMING LITERATURE

"Literature is under pressure" has become a recurring mantra for both those who welcome and those who dread a decline of literature. Why is that? Is it true? And if so: in what sense? At the very least the omnipresence of the feeling or its expression suggests that the study of literature is no longer an auto-legitimizing enterprise. And indeed, there is a level at which the study of literature lacks legitimization. It seems to be the case, as suggested by Gregory Jusdanis (2010), that the pressure on literature and literary scholars to define the necessity of the literary field has muted the proponents of literature. It is a fact that even though billions of kroner in Denmark, and billions and billions of euros, pounds, yens and dollars etc. worldwide, are spent in educational systems from lower schools to universities on the teaching of literature, we know very little about its advantages and disadvantages, e.g. with regard to reading skills and general learning competences. Historically the study and teaching of literature has held and still holds a privileged position, but the historical reasons for this are contested today in several ways. Even if historical reasons are not necessarily invalid, they cannot in themselves justify the comparatively large amount of time and money spent on the teaching of literature in educational systems worldwide. Historical reasoning, such as the knowledge of a national literary canon, must therefore be replaced with other arguments: arguments that are not limited to a particular historical reason but take into account the contemporary conditions of the global knowledge society.

Literary scholars and critics have during the previous decade written quite extensively on the reasons why literature matters, producing or re-producing one or more of the following characterizations of literature:

- an exercise in empathy; the reader gains insight into lives and thoughts of other people
- an encounter with otherness and/or singularity
- a scene where one can encounter friendship and guidance in life through a mirror of society or history; because of what one conceives as the solitude and singularity of the individual reader literature supposedly holds up a mirror in which every reader sees something different
- a privileged medium for studying points of view (a perspective which has since been adopted by a series of other fields and disciplines)
- a means of improving the ethical judgments of readers
- a place of beauty and aesthetic experiences

These reasons for the necessity of literature and the study thereof are obviously valid, but a recurring starting point is nevertheless that they and the study of literature as such are threatened. In both historical and contemporary accounts for and defences of literature the hotly-debated notion of the death of literature recurs; to some this notion holds true while others find it greatly exaggerated. The death of literature is often described as an effect of the rise of new media. This perceived threat from, e.g., visual media is humorously exemplified by a scene in an episode of the TV series *The Simpsons*. Springfield library takes up the battle against visual media by proudly announcing on a large banner:

OLD SPRINGFIELD LIBRARY: WE HAVE BOOKS ABOUT TV

And when the library conducts a used books sale, Homer wonders: "A library selling books? If I didn't want 'em for free why would I wanna pay for them?"

In fact it has often been suggested that the "new media", "new forms of documentary", "technology", or even "the world wide web" either present a threat to literature or have already caused its death. This suggestion is often followed by statements about today's students being lazier and less prepared than their predecessors (whether at the high school level or the university level) and showing little interest in literature – all of which is supposedly caused by their preference for movies and video games. This notion of a general lack of "Bildung" within the school system has also been put forward with regard to general literary interest in Western societies.

However, there is very little empirical evidence to confirm these conclusions. On the contrary, actual numbers do not seem to confirm a turning away of consumers from the book market. When examining the statistics of book sales in a country such as Denmark during the last thirty years it is evident that the sales figures have not decreased dramatically since the beginning of the 1980s but have rather remained at a stable level. This does not indicate that the processes of globalization and the global media system do not alter the public uses of literature, but rather than wiping out literature, they transform it as a medium. The access to and use of literature has simply changed due to global media and communication technologies. We buy paper books, but we also access novels as well as theoretical texts online, or we buy them via our iPhones, iPads, or Kindle Readers. Reading literature is no longer, if it ever was, merely a question of individual immersion in one text. Reading literature can also mean browsing through one's iPhone while waiting at a bus stop, and the traditional book is to a great extent becoming the object of a fan culture of a type previously limited to film and TV. Online communities thus emerge around the reading of books, and it is not merely books that are adapted to the screen, such as *Harry Potter* and *Twilight*, but also authors like Bukowski, Dostoyevsky, Dante, and Joyce that have become the centre of ongoing online communities and debates. Literature is included in the global culture industry, and books have become objects in what Henry Jenkins calls the "convergence culture": "Welcome to convergence culture, where old and new media collide, where grassroots and corporate media intersect, where the power of the media producer and the power of the media consumer interact in unpredictable ways" (Jenkins 2006, 2). One of Jenkins' arguments is that the convergence of modes is blurring the lines between different medias and their uses. Conversely, a service that was provided in the past by a single medium – as for instance literature – is now provided in several different ways. Therefore the one-to-one relationship between a medium and its use is being eroded. Due to the process of globalization, literature is being remediated. According to Jay David Bolter and Richard Grusin, the term 'remediation' denotes both the ways in which new media absorb old media and the ways in which old media are modernized in order to answer the challenges of the new media (Bolter and Grusin 1999). Hence, books are remediated when they are adapted to the screen, but the screen and the Internet also partake in the moderniza-tion of literature that extends its territory when entering everyday digital units, such as our mobile phones, Kindles, or iPads. The effect of the global media environment or the convergence culture on literature is thus twofold. It can be understood as a dialectic between deterritorialization and reter-ritorialization (Tomlinson 1999). Deterritorialization basically describes how the conceptual ties between cultures, identity, and geographic and social territories are dissolving or at least thought of as being dissolved. Globalization deterritorializes literature in the sense that it dissolves the relation between the literary content, a single medium, and the reader. Yet this deterritorialization is met by numerous reterritorializing processes, in which the literary field gains a renewed importance by being remediated. By means of remediation, literature maintains its social importance, even though its characteristics as a medium are radically transformed.

Thus this book does not empathize with the notion that the global media environment causes the death of literature; rather, we argue that the literary field is being transformed. This poses new arguments for the continuing study of literature: we have to investigate the ways in which literature, as a medium, is altered as a response to societal developments. Furthermore, the remediation of literature calls attention to the fact that the lifeworld of human beings is always undergoing transformations which appear in lit-erature; we must therefore investigate and study the ever-changing human lifeworld as it manifests itself in literature.

So if literature is under pressure, it is hardly from globalization or from emerging new media. Rather, it seems that the external pressure on the study of literature is mainly the need it shares with most sciences of art to legitimize itself in a political era of utilitarianism. An internal pressure occurs when literary studies simultaneously refuses to answer the most urgent questions about its *raison d'être* and its eagerness to make itself useful in anything but the study of literary works – ranging all the way from medicine and ethics to the oil industry.

In this book we want to counter the feelings of resentment implied in the notion of the death of literature by not only welcoming, but also emphatically posing the question "Why study literature?". The question also stems from a desire to actually and eventually acquire knowledge of some of the most basic and interesting questions about literature and its study:

- What is the difference between statements that are true, statements that are false, and statements that are fictional?
- Why do we care about what happens to fictional characters?
- What are the differences and the potential overlaps between prose, drama, and poetry?
- Why is even a three-year-old child able to see that there is a difference between a fairy tale about dragons and a realist story about a horse?

Questions like these are so basic that we forget even to ask them, although their consequences for our understanding and interpretation of literature and the reasons for its study are of great importance.

WHY LITERATURE?

During the previous decade several monographs, anthologies and articles have raised and attempted to deal with the question of the role and function of literature in present day society. As a means of framing the more specific question of this anthology – "why study literature?" – we will in the following dwell on some of the recent work done on the broader question "why literature?". A quick glance at the long list of titles on this subject indicates that a substantial number of writers have felt the need to perform legitimating actions on behalf of literature: from *Why Literature Matters: Theories and Functions of Literature* (Ahrens and Volkmann 1996) to *Why does Literature Matter?* (Farrell 2004), *Why Literature Matters in the 21st Century* (Roche 2004) and *Why We Read Fiction: Theory of Mind and the Novel* (Zunshine 2006), the role of and need for literature has quite manifestly been questioned, though in most cases by literary scholars keen on providing positive answers. This is not the place for a full survey of the fairly diverse work and the many different answers produced in response to the question of the value of literature today. In lieu of a complete map of the field we will now briefly examine two works, both of which offer contemporary and ambitious answers to the question of the function of literature, but do so using different scientific paradigms. Distinctive in their own right, taken together they may serve as signposts in the current state of the field and thus be useful for situating the suggestions and discussions presented by the articles in this particular anthology.

The main goal of *Why We Read Fiction: Theory of Mind and the Novel* (2006) by Lisa Zunshine is to combine theories of the novel with insights from cognitive science in order to shed light on our intellectual and emotional reasons for engaging with fiction. She takes her point of departure in what is known as Theory of Mind, a key notion in many subfields of cognitive sciences. It claims that humans, in order to make sense of the desires and beliefs of other humans, are equipped with a theory of how humans are supposed to think and act and that this ability, referred to by some as mindreading, is what enables us to understand or "read" the motivations and wants of other people. Zunshine's basic idea is that fiction functions as a privileged place for vicariously engaging our Theory of Mind, as a sort of epistemological fitness centre: "Intensely social species that we are, we thus read fiction because it engages, in a variety of particularly focused ways, our Theory of Mind" (Zunshine 2006, 162). Literature holds a special place among fiction's set of training gear since literary narratives, according to Zunshine, are privileged when it comes to depicting extreme cases of what she calls socio-cognitive complexity, that is instances of multiple embedded readings of states of minds (as in "I know that you thought that I knew what he had in mind"). Thus, in this take on the question of the function of fiction, we use literature to perform a cognitive "workout" (164); it satisfies our "cognitive cravings" (4) as well as enticing them further, while keeping our ability to understand the desires and beliefs of other people fit. While the cognitive viewpoint on the relevance of fiction has many justifications, questions and possible objections can be raised. In the present context one could argue that there is more to literature than mind-reading and that mind-reading may be practised using other media than literature, though perhaps not in forms quite as complex as literature allows for.

The idea of attributing value to fiction and/or literature on the basis of its ability to facilitate vicarious experience was not invented by cognitive studies. A similar though differently phrased argument can, among other places, be found in Wolfgang Iser's short but rich contribution to the anthology *Why Literature Matters: Theories and Functions of Literature* (Ahrens and Volkmann 1996). The anthology does not carry a question mark in its title but according to the contribution by Wolfgang Iser it might as well. In 1995 Iser finds literature "relegated to the fringes of society" (Iser in Ahrens and Volkmann 1996, 13). Because of the advent of other media (especially visual media), literature is no longer taken for granted as the one medium capable of covering everything from entertainment to information and documentation. Rather than making literature obsolete, this process of marginalization has endowed literature with "unexpected importance" (16) and Iser gathers his thoughts on what he finds to be the continued relevance of literature under political, systemic, and anthropomorphic headings. Since it is the anthropomorphic relevance that most strongly resembles the Theory of Mind approach, we will begin with that.

Literature's relevance in an anthropomorphic setting hinges on its ability to function as "a stage for human self-enactment" (22). This aspect of literature relates to the ways in which literature mirrors what Iser calls "human plasticity", arising from the distance between being a self and having a self: "The impossibility of being present to ourselves makes it possible for us to play ourselves out to a fullness that knows no bounds" (19). Literature is a privileged medium when it comes to staging this playfulness of the self. On the one hand "staging allows us […] to lead an ecstatic life by stepping out of our entanglements" and on the other hand "staging reflects us as an ever fractured whole […]. Precisely because cognitive discourse cannot capture the duality adequately, we have literature" (19).

The political relevance, according to Iser, is to be found in the fact that literature remains a remarkably strong cultural capital, as evidenced and enforced by the many heated debates on literary canon formations. Finally, the systemic relevance comes from literature's insistence on being a "perturbing noise" (16) in technocratic modernity. Drawing upon Paulson's *The Noise of Culture. Literary Texts in a World of Information* (1988), Iser highlights the meeting between the reader and the always to some degree noisy system of the literary work as what enables reflection not only on the work of art but also on all such meetings or couplings between different systems in culture at large. This is what gives literature a cultural meta-reflectivity and what enables it to carve out "a space for unpredictability and invention" (18).

Both the systemic and the anthropomorphic relevance may be said to suffer from the same problems as Zunshine's Theory of Mind: one can claim that far from being defining traits of literature they do not *only* apply to literature and do not apply to *all* literature, but mainly to certain literary genres. And while the political relevance by necessity is closely tied to literature, it is an external, sociological truth that cannot in itself carry the weight of the question that informs this anthology. That question will be the centre of the following section.

SOME POSSIBLE ANSWERS TO THE QUESTION "WHY STUDY LITERATURE?"

As literary scholars, teachers of art, or researchers in the humanities, we are with increasing frequency asked to justify what we do and to say what might be the purpose of it. On the one hand, it is not totally unjustified to think of questions like these as the expression of untimely utilitarianism and poor understanding of the context and subject of literature and art. On the other hand, we can also wonder why politicians and other decision makers have been so long-suffering in this case. In a sense it is surprising that it is only recently that we have been asked exactly what we are doing and why anyone would want to pay us to do it.

The question is not whether there should be literary research and literary studies. Research is done in all the phenomena of the world: algae in brackish water, calcium depositions, large primes, etc. But not as *much* research is done. So when the argument is put forward that because a thing exists, it should be studied, and that literature therefore obviously should be studied, it doesn't even begin to justify the degree to which literature is studied from elementary school, via high school, to the university. Is there a middle way between utilitarianism and uselessness, then? Probably a need exists for reasons in many different contexts and registers and usefulness is one, but only one of these. If we who study literature don't answer the question, others will. So why should literature be studied on such a large scale?

From the outset several of the recent arguments for studying literature can be contextualized in terms of an opposition between sociological/cultural arguments and formal arguments. Focusing on sociological aspects in particular two arguments are of great importance. Firstly, there is the very down-to-earth fact that reading is an indispensable societal skill across almost all disciplines and job functions and that literature has proved an excellent way to exercise reading skills. It is probably hard to overestimate the importance of the *Harry Potter* series for the improvement of reading skills in large parts of the world; but also on a smaller scale reading skills are some of, if not *the* most important meta-competence needed to engage with a complex world and its written signs, and for many – though definitely not for all – the reading of literature is the most enjoyable way to acquire these skills. Secondly, when studying literature on a professional basis we examine the cultural production of our society; this tells us a lot not only about the literary works but also about predominant thought systems and culture. Studying literature is an investigation of different aspects of human life and of the possibilities of humanity through language as a semiotic form. Literature, then, is conceived of as a facet of social life closely connected to other facets of social life and hence as a significant aspect of major issues in social scientific research.

For cultural arguments, emphatically represented by Dorothy J. Hale, the formal study of literature is threatened above anything else by movements from within. In *Social Formalism* Hale argues that the turn toward cultural studies of many literary critics has had the unfortunate result that theorists tend to dismiss novel theory while still paradoxically using novels to describe historical and social realities – only now without theoretical rigour and relevant methods. Hale thus warns against a tendency within literary studies to demote the novel by using it mainly on contingent occasions to talk about something else, happily relinquishing literary theorists' status as experts.

However, the notion of not demoting the novel must take into account the formal perspectives in which the traffic and exchange between fictional and non-fictional genres have been increasingly emphasized over the last years. It has been argued that literature is able to contain valuable experiences and at the same time become a place for, say, testimonies of atrocities and concentration camps after the deaths of the last witnesses. Literature, then, can be studied in its capacity to contain, maintain, and create human experience.

Similarly there has in recent years been a turn in narrative studies to emphasize and even privilege the role of experience over the role of plot in narratives. This is especially so for Monika Fludernik and her concept of experientiality, but also for David Herman, who includes "what it is like" as one of four basic elements of narrative. This emphasis sheds new light on old questions about the importance of the medium specificity of literature and its ability to provide the reader with access to different points of view and the minds of different characters. If experience is central to narratives (and Herman even goes on to say that the reverse is also true – that there can be no experience without narrative) and if fictional narratives are paradigmatic carriers of experientiality and exemplary containers of "what it is like", then fictional narratives effortlessly provide access to the stuff narratives are made of.

If it is true that narratives are everywhere, and that they play significant roles in our lives, then literature (particularly when studied) is a useful corrective to the prevalence of non-complex, un-strange narrative fictions. In an era that disrespects expert knowledge, literature is a welcome arena for complexity. There is no doubt that the study of literature should examine all the ways in which literature is in the world and about the world, but it should do it critically, not obsequiously. Critical reading is what literary teachers and theorists do best. Close reading, the thorough investigation of the meaning of complex written signs, has to be learned and practised.

Slow reading, immersion, suspicion, thought access, lyricality etc. all have to be carefully negotiated in the study of literature. Surely none of these practices and tools, nor literature itself, turns anyone into a better person, but they do make students and other trained and skilled practitioners more aware of the covert and explicit messages and ideologies in all kinds of texts and narratives.

The sociological, cultural, and formal reasons for studying literature are argued for in *Why Study Literature?* through an exploration of the literary characteristics within three main sections 1) Mediality, 2) Locality & Temporality, and 3) Humanity.

MEDIALITY

The contributors in the mediality section focus on literature as a medium among and compared to other media. What are its characteristics? Can we talk of a distinctiveness of literature? And what are the implications for the *study* of literature?

In her contribution *Meaning as Spectacle: Verbal Art in the Digital Age* Marie-Laure Ryan asks what the computer has done for literature. The New Media development and digital technology in particular challenge the distinctions between traditional art forms. Ryan opposes the view of "technology as enemy" by emphasizing that although less time seems to be spent on reading literary works, digitalization has also fostered new and intriguing forms of textuality. Since digital texts mainly use language as a material substance that creates meaning in the sensory domain, it makes more sense to think of them as a new art form with different properties from print-based texts. Thus digital literature is used to pinpoint and defend literature's "distinctive power of expression". The new "hybrid forms of expression" are then an expansion as well as a narrowing of the qualities of traditional literature. Introducing the concept of bi-mediality, Ryan shows the possibility of combining print with the properties of digital media. This both points towards a new potential in literature as such, and also underlines the singularity of the print-based text and its irreplaceable features.

Werner Wolf shares the claim of distinct literary properties and he uses this stance to argue for the *study* of literature in its distinctiveness hence the title *A Defence of (the study of) Literature or: Why (the Study of) Literature Cannot Be Replaced by Cultural Studies or Film (Studies)*. According to Wolf, the current tendency in academia in general is to undermine the relevance of literature. The emergence of new media has to some extent suppressed literature as the object of study, and scholars participate in a "general and media-historical trend". Wolf's defence of literature, and especially the study of it, begins with a set of general functions of literature, and he explains why literature in its specificity cannot be satisfactory explained by the inclusive field of Cultural studies. Wolf discusses whether it is possible to pinpoint distinct literary qualities that not only justify the quality of literature in general, but also the purpose of the study of it. Many of these qualities can also be attributed to other discourses, but it is possible to describe a quality profile that adheres to no other discourse than the literary. This implies that literature (like film and other art forms) is irreplaceable and therefore that literary, film, and cultural studies cannot replace one another.

The mediality section is completed with Morten Kyndrup's contribution *Mediality and Literature Literature versus literature*. In a twofold argument Kyndrup shows the importance of both interdisciplinary or intermedial studies and of literature in its distinctiveness. The claim is that every art form is a distinct mediality and although literature still holds a privileged place in academic studies, this ever-increasing centrifugal orientation has caused the specific mediality of literature to be neglected. Morten Kyndrup lists a number of constitutive parameters for mediality: time, space, sign system, fictionality, and mode of speech. Literature may share these characteristics with other art forms, but the literary combination of these features is unique. The study of literature in a transmedial context will thus reveal the distinct character of literature and at the same time prove that literature still needs to be studied in its distinctiveness.

In this section the contributors ponder upon the physical and mental geography of literature. What and where are its places and spaces in time, and what does a diachronic view of literary history mean for the study and teaching of literature?

In *Literature as Global Thinking* Svend Erik Larsen argues that the importance of the study of literature can be directly linked to the increased focus on globalization. Literature is a necessary model of global thinking; it works as a model for understanding the cultural conditions of globalization. Larsen uses language and translation as his main argument to state that literature actively participates in the incomplete process of globalization. Languages get intertwined when they meet across the limitations of the language users. He argues that we express the boundary between the local and the global every time we speak, and that this implies that literature is working with a "broad linguistic and cultural palette". Since literature is based on language it is at the heart of basic cultural processes and for that reason literature and culture "engage independently in the changes of culture". When the boundaries of literature change, the culture can change and this can affect the way we study both current and older literary texts. This is his main argument for studying literature, and it justifies not only the study of the new and innovative cross-boundaries-literature, it also urges on a rereading of existing literature. Larsen states that we can use literature regardless of its time and space to take into account the "global and fractured cultural processes we are currently experiencing".

Sune Auken's contribution *Not Another Adult Movie. Some Platitudes on Genericity and the Use of Literary Studies* focuses on the study of literature as a gateway to knowledge about generic structures. Auken argues that generic categories are always present in meaning-making regardless of whether we are interpreting a work of literature or making sense of an every day situation. This builds on the assumption that we can only understand our own culture if we understand generic structures. And since literature can be seen as based on genericity and because literature holds a historical central place in genre studies, the study of literature can help us cope with the culture surrounding us.

In his contribution *Models and Thought-Experiments* Brian McHale also recognizes literature as a way to gain access to models of reality. A literary text is constructed from cultural models, which they in turn help to maintain and circulate. This means that literature can be seen as a means for learning about world-making in our culture. He further argues that not only can literature preserve our culture, it also possesses the potential to renew it. Literature can serve as a model of reality, but its essential quality is the innovative power of modelling *for* reality or *for* other possible worlds. McHale introduces the notion of thought experiments and he uses the genre of science fiction to illustrate the world-creating potential of literature. Science fiction is a world-building genre and thought experiments are always foregrounded in this particular genre's production of alternative reality models. The thought experiments of science fiction shed light on the properties and potentials of literature in general. Literature is indeed capable of conducting thought experiments and producing innovative world models, and therefore it can make us reflect on our own real life world models.

In *Literary Studies in Interaction* Anne-Marie Mai focuses on the history of both literature and the study of it. She describes how literature has undergone major developments and how this innovative status calls for a renewal of the study of literature. Mai states that since the definition of literature can be seen as less linked to a particular form of discourse, the answer to the question of "Why Study Literature?" is likewise complicated. The reaction against high-modernism in the 1950s and early 1960s caused literature to expand in new directions. Traditional boundaries were broken down and literature spread into new media and genres. In this diverse literary landscape the function of the author is changed and literature is deeply involved in a performative turn. Mai argues that this development calls for an interdisciplinary collaboration because "Literature studies have a future when they enter into a new oscillation between academic disciplines".

HUMANITY

Under the heading of 'humanity' the contributors think about the consequences of reading and studying literature. Many questions are posed such as whether literature can be seen as a training ground for innovation, for understanding the other, for ethics, or for originality.

In his contribution *On the Difference between Reading and Studying Literature* Magnus Persson directly addresses the relationship between reading and studying literature. Using the work of John Guillory he describes the gap between inside and outside academia as the difference between on the one hand studying literature or professional reading and on the other hand reading literature or lay reading. Persson argues that this distinction, which according to Guillory can be adhered to the difference between the concepts of reflection and desire, must be weakened and problematized. Since desire and reflection do not nescessarily preclude one another, and since they cannot only be included under spare time and the formal teaching of literature respectively, Persson argues for a third way of reading. Taking his point of departure in Hillis Miller's arguments for a fusion of the naïve and the critical reading, Persson introduces his multidimensional concept of "creative reading". Creative reading explores the boundaries between the two tendencies and it focuses both on the subjectivity of reading or the interplay between text and reader and on the singularity of literature with its otherness and unique experience. Reading is not only about the production of meaning, and we must give up the conviction that there is only one legitimate way of reading.

With his contribution Magnus Persson touches upon the ethical dimensions of both reading and studying literature, which are the core points in the two following contributions by Dorothy J. Hale and Jan Alber. In *Aesthetics and the New Ethics: Theorizing the Novel in the Twenty-First Century* Dorothy J. Hale argues that a renewed and general interest in ethics in literary theory can lead to a new understanding of novelistic aesthetics. For the new ethicists (e.g. Hillis Miller, Judith Butler and David Attridge), literature's ethical value "lies in the felt encounter with alterity that it brings to its reader". Hale argues that the novel is a privileged genre in this new turn of discussion of literary value, because the narrative structure of the novel has the potential to stage the conflict between social alterity and aesthetic discourse. She introduces the concept of "binding" as the precondition for ethical knowledge and choice. The reader participates in the same binding-process that she also performs in everyday life on people she knows, and this means that the reader can also have an emotional reaction to and make ethical judgements on the actions of the characters in the novel. Drawing on the work of Martha Nussbaum and Judith Butler, Dorothy J. Hale describes how the novel can help us make the right ethical judgments and moral decisions, because literature simply enables the reader to engage in the "sheer difficulty of moral choice".

In his contribution *The Ethical Implications of Unnatural Scenarios* Jan Alber argues for the study of literary fiction because it makes us capable of experiencing scenarios that would be impossible in reality. Like Brian McHale, Alber considers literature to be an important platform for thought experiments. In a second step, he argues that our encounters with the projected storyworlds in literature can create a new perspective on our own lives in the real world. Alber analyses a number of texts that project unnatural (i.e., physically or logically impossible) scenarios, and he points out that regardless of the degree of unnaturalness, the literary text is always part of a purposeful communicative act. Thus, intentions and motivations will always be a part of the production of the literary work in question and this involves the ethical dimension. "When reading literature, we enter the realm of the ethical through the experience of otherness". Unnatural texts are by their very nature particularly suitable for exploring different types of strangeness, and therefore they also in particular urge the reader to make ethical judgements.

Richard Walsh completes *Why Study Literature?* with his contribution *The Force of Fictions.* Implementing a cognitive approach to the study of narrative, Walsh argues how the study of literature can be seen as participating in the negotiations of cultural value. In the realm of the concept of emergence, Walsh discusses how the mechanism of narrative culture can be described as a "representational recursiveness". Narrative sense-making, and thus narrative fiction, has, according to Walsh, always been split between the concepts of saying and doing. Every time we need to describe something, it happens through a relation between what Walsh renames the value and force of literary fiction. A work of literature's saying or its value is an expression of our sense of the human, and the doing or the force of fiction is its ability to act or create. This is what creates the recursive effect, and thus "literary study also, necessarily, participates in the negotiations of the cultural value it describes; it acts, it has force".

REFERENCES

Ahrens, Rüdiger and Laurenz Volkmann, eds. 1996. *Why Literature Matters: Theories and Functions of Literature.* Anglistische Forschungen 241. Heidelberg, Germany: Winter.

Bolter, Jay David and Richard Grusin. 1999. *Remediation. Understanding New Media.* Cambridge, London: The MIT Press.

Farrell, Frank B. 2004. *Why does Literature Matter?* Ithaca: Cornell University Press.

Fludernik, Monika. 1996. *Towards a "Natural" Narratology.* London: Routledge.

Hale, Dorothy J. 1998. *Social Formalism: The Novel in Theory from Henry James to the Present.* Stanford: Stanford University Press.

Herman, David. 2009. *Basic Elements of Narrative.* Singapore: Wiley-Blackwell.

Iser, Wolfgang. 1996. Why Literature Matters. In *Why Literature Matters: Theories and Functions of Literature.* Anglistische Forschungen 241, eds. Rüdiger Ahrens and Laurenz Volkmann. Heidelberg, Germany: Winter.

Jenkins, Henry. 2006. *Convergence Culture: Where Old and New Media Collide.* New York and London: New York University Press.

Judanis, Gregory. 2010. *Fiction Agonistes: In Defense of Literature*. Stanford: Stanford University Press.

Roche, Mark William. 2004. *Why Literature Matters in the 21st Century*. New Haven, London: Yale University Press.

Paulson, William. 1988. *The Noise of Culture. Literary Texts in a World of Information*. Ithaca, London: Cornell University Press.

Tomlinson, John. 1999. *Globalization and Culture*. Oxford: Polity.

Zunshine, Lisa. 2006. *Why We Read Fiction: Theory of Mind and the Novel*. Columbus: Ohio State University Press.

MEDIALITY

MARIE-LAURE RYAN
Meaning as Spectacle: Verbal Art in the Digital Age

WERNER WOLF
*A Defence of (the Study of) Literature or: Why (the Study of) Literature
cannot be Replaced by Cultural Studies and Film (Studies)*

MORTEN KYNDRUP
Mediality and Literature. Literature versus literature

MEANING AS SPECTACLE: VERBAL ART IN THE DIGITAL AGE

Marie-Laure Ryan

Why study literature? Though formalists and structuralists did not explicitly address the question, we can imagine what kind of answer would derive from their conception of literature as a language within language and as the product of cultural conventions. In a much celebrated book, Jonathan Culler attributes the ability to understand and enjoy literary texts to a specialized "literary competence":

> To read a text as literature is not to make one's mind a *tabula rasa* and approach it without preconceptions; one must bring to it an implicit understanding of the operations of literary discourse which tells one what to look for. Anyone lacking this knowledge, anyone wholly unacquainted with literature and unfamiliar with the conventions by which fictions are read, would be, for example, quite baffled if presented with a poem…He would be unable to read it as literature… because he lacks the complex 'literary competence' which enables others to proceed (Culler 1975, 113-114).

Borrowing a concept from Jurij Lotman, Culler conceives of literature as a "second-order semiotic system, which has language as its basis" (113-114). We don't learn this system as we learn our first language: if literature is the product of semiotic and cultural conventions, its appreciation must arguably be taught, studied – or slowly acquired through the reading of many texts.

A counterpoint to this position was delivered by Mary Louise Pratt in her 1977 critique of the Russian formalist conception of literary language as separate from ordinary language. She championed a view of literature (and of verbal art) as continuous with the spontaneous practices of conversational storytelling and witty uses of language. Verbal art is everywhere – it is part of our basic social and linguistic competence. More recently, evolutionary approaches (Dutton 2009, Boyd 2009) have stressed the adaptive advantages to be gained through the practice of the arts in general and of literature in particular. Against the view that literature is entirely the product of culture-specific conventions, this school emphasizes the cognitive universals that make us appreciate the stories and poems of foreign cultures, and it postulates the idea (sacrilegious to postmodern theory) of a "human nature" shaped through hundreds of thousands of years of adaptation to environmental conditions which are basically the same for all of mankind. The differentiations that culture imposes upon the human mind are only the tip of the iceberg, compared to the common features determined by evolution. We learn the ability to understand literature (especially narrative fiction) from the storytelling of mothers, from life experience and from social interactions; there is no more a need to teach people how to appreciate stories, poetry or drama than there is a need to learn our mother tongue from a Berlitz course.

While this position rests on sound premises, too literal an interpretation can lead to an interpretation as fallacious as the attempt to justify the study of literature by claiming that we need a specialized competence to process literary texts. Even if the appreciation of literature comes naturally (at least to most of us), it does not follow that this faculty of the human mind is unworthy of critical or even scientific study. To the curious mind, everything in nature and culture is worth studying, literature included. As long as we place stock in the humanities, we can rely on the Roman playwright Terentius for a reason to study literature: *Homo sum: humani nil a me alienum puto*. But in this argument, literature is no more or no less worth studying than any aspect of culture, whether high or popular, and it loses the privileged pedagogical status that it has enjoyed so far. We would not ask the question "why study literature" if it weren't for a sense that literature has become an endangered species and reading an obsolete activity.

There are two culprits of this sense of decline: one theoretical, the other practical or social. The theoretical culprits are the critical fashions of the past twenty years. Literature has not (yet) disappeared from academic programs, but what is being done in these programs is often not the study of literary texts as a form of art and entertainment. The close reading of texts has been replaced by the study of a particular brand of philosophy, known as "critical theory", that uses the literary text as a springboard for its own self-centered activity; by the study of historical contexts, known as New Historicism; and by the study of cultural attitudes, a project that uses literary texts as documents of social realities and puts them on par with any text used by historians: statistics, testimonies, letters, newspaper articles, and so on.[1] The approaches that are currently most popular tend to be interested in everything that surrounds the literary text but nothing in the text itself, and they disregard the reasons why we read literature. What is lost in these critical schools is the *pleasure* of the text.

The social culprit of the decline of literature is the proliferation of other modes of entertainment. With the development of film, TV, video games and the Internet, the place of literature as a leisure activity and as a part of intellectual life has been constantly shrinking. We are told that young people don't read books anymore.[2] Does it mean that the place of literature in university curricula should be proportional to its importance in the lives of students, i.e. minimal? Or should literature be taught as a dead language that allows a glimpse into the intellectual life of former generations, as Latin used to be taught? My suspicion is that literature is still very much a living language, as we can see from the interest generated by writing programs, and by the popularity of book clubs and public readings of literary works. Literature has lost its hegemonic position within culture, which means that it can no longer be imposed on students as something that everybody should know; but I believe that it can acquire new life by being viewed as a member of a complex media landscape, and by being studied from a comparative point of view – a point of view that not only relates the literatures of different languages, but also compares the expressive power of different media. What we need to do to revive literature is to subject it to an operation that the Russian formalists called estrangement or defamiliarization. There is no reason literature could not convey a sense of pleasure and wonderment, once we no longer take its value for granted, no longer force-feed the great authors to students, and focus on its distinctive power of expression, compared to other media.

In this article I'd like to grab one of the so-called enemies of literature by the horns and try to tame it, by showing that it does not threaten to annihilate literature as we have known it for many generations, but on the

---

1   I find it symptomatic of the current disregard for the artistic nature of literature that courses in literary theory, at least in the US, usually consist of a review of ideological approaches, such as Marxism, psychoanalysis, feminism, deconstruction, and postcolonialism, but ignore the key technical concepts of literature such as genre, narrative, fictionality, rhetoric, and the various types of tropes.

2   In *The Shallows: What the Internet is Doing to Our Brains*, Nicholas Carr bemoans the decline of the deep concentration required by book reading, and mentions in support of his argument this remark by the distinguished scholar of digital culture N. Katherine Hayles: "I can't get my student to read whole books anymore" (2010, 9).

contrary, invites us to rethink its nature by offering a different experience of language. This perceived enemy, as my title indicates, is digital technology. The computer is responsible for applications that have seriously diminished the time people spend reading literary works, but it has also produced intriguing new forms of textuality. My guiding question will be: what has the computer done for the word? Since literature is the language-based art, this question really amounts to "what has the computer done for literature?".

When we think of computers, most of us associate them with number crunching, but this wide-spread stereotype has been seriously challenged by the developments of the past thirty years. In 1981, Theodore Nelson, who is best known for being the "father of hypertext", described the computer as a "literary machine". In 1995, as hypertext fiction was emerging as a new literary genre, Jacques Leslie challenged the traditional conception of the computer: "Ambiguity machines. Precision, Hah! Computers are better at poetry than they are at math". In 2002, N. Katherine Hayles celebrated the computer as a "writing machine" in a book by the same title, and more recently she declared that "literature in the twenty-first century is computational" (Hayles 2008, 43) – referring not only to the emergence of electronic texts that can only be experienced through the computer, but also to the fact that most print texts are composed and produced as books on a computer.

From a technological point of view, these claims are supported by the affinity of the computer for language, an affinity that becomes evident when compared to the computer's ability to process images. Words are made of discrete symbols, the letters of the alphabet, and these symbols are efficiently encoded in binary form. The ASCII code uses a string of 7 bits, easily held in the 8 bits of a computer memory byte (with one spare bit used to verify accurate transmission) to encode alphanumeric symbols. This scheme makes it possible to represent 128 different graphemes – far more than needed for the letters, digits and punctuation marks of Western writing systems. A text, consequently, can be held in a reasonably limited amount of memory. Because every symbol used by language is distinguished by a unique bit pattern (homonyms excluded), it is easy to search a digitized text for the occurrence of a certain word or string of words. The discrete nature of linguistic signs also enables the computer to understand language, at least to some extent, and to generate syntactically correct and meaningful sentences. Weather forecast systems, for instance, consist of text generated on the fly by a computer and spoken by a synthesized voice.

Images by contrast are difficult to encode and process because they are not composed of discrete elements. The computer divides them into pixels – dots of visual information on the screen – and encodes every pixel separately, unless some compression algorithm is used (but compression diminishes the overall visual quality of the image).[3] Matthew G. Kirschenbaum (2005, 139) observes that the word "image" can be encoded in 5 bytes using the ASCII code, but when saved as an image using a twelve-point Courier font, and encoded as a bitmap, it requires 192 bytes of memory. A bit-map, moreover, is very difficult to search for representational content. Computers can perform fantastic feats of image manipulation, as every Photoshop user, video game player, and movie aficionado knows full well, but they are only beginning to be able to tell whether a certain face expresses sadness or happiness or to point out all the cats in a series of pictures – a task that a three year old child performs effortlessly.

Yet for all their computational inferiority, images have steadily gained ground over pure text in digital culture, thanks to larger amounts of storage and increased processor speed. In 1995, the year of Leslie's declaration, one of the major forms of online entertainment was participating in a MOO or MUD, a text-based environment in which users create virtual personae and build an environment by posting verbal descriptions; now MOOS and MUDS have been supplanted by visually rendered MMORPGS (*World of Warcraft, EverQuest, Second Life*), and the construction of avatars and objects relies on the limited repertory of features provided by the building tools of the system, rather than on the almost infinite vocabulary that language supplies to the imagination. In 1995, most literary hypertexts were composed with the Storyspace program, an authoring tool that privileged text and imposed a layout on the screen that imitated the printed page; nowadays the few hypertexts that are still written are produced with multimedia tools, such as Flash or Director, and they blend text, sound and image. Meanwhile, two of the most gifted writers among hypertext authors, Michael Joyce and Shelley Jackson, have reverted to writing print fiction. The predominance of the visual aspect of language, or its frequent blending with music and images in the collection of digital texts recently put together by ELO (an acronym that

---

3   An alternative to representing images as bit-maps is to store them as vector graphics, this is to say, as a mathematical formula whose variables can receive different values, generating different versions of the basic shape. This mode of encoding saves space and allows dynamic manipulation, but it only works for combinations of geometric shapes. A cartoon figure could be rendered as vector graphics, but an impressionist painting could not.

stands for Electronic *Literature* Organization) confirm what Robert Coover called in 1999 "the passing of the golden age" for literary hypertext: "Even the word, the very stuff of literature, and indeed of all human thought, is under assault, giving ground daily to image-surfing, hypermedia, the linked icon. Indeed, the word itself is increasingly reduced to icon or caption".

THE SPECTACULARIZATION OF LANGUAGE

If digital art threatens the word, it is not through the invasion of text by images, a productive co-habitation susceptible of endless artistic variations that we observe in print as well, but through the downgrading of language into pure spectacle. Text as spectacle is text that either cannot be read, or that the user is not inspired to read. It is the hallucinating urban landscape of animated signs of Tokyo or Las Vegas, especially for the visitor who cannot read the characters; it is the strings of code that race down the screen in the opening scenes of the film *The Matrix;* and it is the stunning visual patterns of symbols that continually undulate, ripple, explode, or implode into other patterns but offer no readable content in Giselle Beiguelman's *Code Movie 1*, a work included in the ELO anthology.

Screen shot from Giselle Beiguelman's *Code Movie 1*

The spectacularization of the word is particularly frequent in digital installations, a form of art intended for relatively short visits. Since installations must maintain a steady throughput, for fear of creating a bottleneck in the exhibit, they cannot afford to let the visitor become immersed in reading. Many installation artists pursue the dream of a total language in which sound, shape, color, animation, spoken voice, and written text respond to the movements of the user's body. In this language, as Bill Seaman puts it, "the word is not valued in a hierarchy over other media elements or processes" (2004, 231) – it is just one signifying element among many others. But text is often the loser in this semiotic cornucopia. A case in point is Camille Utterback's and Romy Archituv's *Text Rain*:

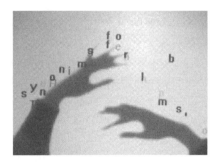

Snapshot from Camille Utterback's and Romy Archituv's *Text Rain*

In *Text Rain*…the interface of video camera and tracking software allows a viewer's entire body to engage with the text. In the *Text Rain* installation viewers see a mirrored black-and-white video of themselves on a large projection screen. Colored letters in the projection fall down on them from above, like rain or snow. The characters can be caught, lifted, and then fall again. If a person accumulates enough letters along their outstretched arms, or any other dark object, they can sometimes "catch" an entire word, or even a phrase. The letters are not random, but lines of a poem by Evan Zimroth (1993) about bodies and language (Utterback 2004, 221).

The installation can be interpreted as a dramatization and literalization of the themes of the poem, which alludes to the participation of bodies in a conversation that degenerates into "just talk", but the interactor is too busy trying to catch letters to pay attention to the words – nor indeed does the fragmentation of the text into individual falling letters make reading possible. As Roberto Simanowski observes in "Double Coding", "The letters have left language behind and turned into visual objects as part of a sculpture". It is only through what Simanowski calls a "double coding" stretching over two media that the textual component of the installation can be restored as meaningful text. The player must first read the poem in print form to be able to understand what the digital work is trying to say by using this poem rather than another. Left by itself, the installation is just mere letters.

For all their artistic merit, works like *Code Movie 1* and *Text Rain* do not promote the kind of semantic processing that supports the idea of the computer as a literary machine. But the relations between word and image are much more complex than the contrast of reading *versus* watching would suggest. We can distinguish three degrees of textual visibility, linked by a continuum of intermediary forms:

(1) Language as pure spectacle – no attention is paid to the meaning of words.

(2) Visible language: meaning results from an interplay between the graphic appearance of words and their semantic value. (This idea of visibility can be extended to other sensory dimensions, such as tactility and audibility).

(3) Invisible language: the reader extracts meaning from the text without paying attention to its appearance, besides identifying letters.

Here I take visibility in a literal sense, and I do not regard state 3 as necessarily incompatible with an aesthetic approach to language. We are, for instance, fully capable of appreciating the style of Proust without noticing the font or the layout of the book. Zone 1, which can be considered to lie outside literature, is illustrated by the texts discussed above, though the double coding of *Text Rain* places it further away from the pure spectacle end of the continuum than Beiguelman's *Code Movie 1*. Zone 2 covers most of poetry, with concrete, lettrist and l*a*n*g*u*a*g*e poetry situated closer to the visible pole than lyric poetry. It is also in 2 that I place graphically sophisticated postmodern narratives, such as *House of Leaves* by Mark Danielewski. Zone 3 is occupied by standard print novels, as well as by non-artistic, strictly informational texts. In the print medium, both zone 3 and zone 2 are richly represented, though the former is much more heavily populated than the latter; in the electronic medium, literary activity has increasingly shifted from zone 3 to zones 2 and 1, as the graphic capabilities of the computer have improved. Symptomatic of this trend is the fact that in the ELO anthology, the purely textual zone is mostly represented by older texts.[4] Why is it that language must fight for survival, and share the spotlight with other modes of signification in the so-called "digital literature"? To answer this question, I

---

4   For instance *Twelve Blue* by Michael Joyce (1996/97), *The Jew's Daughter* by Judd Morrissey (2000), and *Internet Text*, a project begun by Alan Sondheim in 1994. Two works of interactive fiction by Emily Short (*Galatea*, 2000 and *Savoir-Faire*, 2002) are also text-only, but this is a characteristic of the genre as a whole.

MEDIALITY

propose to sketch a technological typology of texts, and to adjust my answers to its individual categories.

A TECHNOLOGICAL TYPOLOGY OF TEXTS

If digital literature is to be more than the binary encoding of the kind of text that can be experienced in print form, it should take advantage of the distinctive properties of digital media. The most important of these properties are procedural nature (= code-driven operation), interactivity, multi-media capabilities, networking and what I call volatility of inscription: the possibility of changing the display by changing the value of memory cells. Truly digital texts should exploit more than one of these features, because code-driven operation applies to any text shown on a screen, for instance to this chapter as it is being written with a word processor, and multi-media effects do not require a digital platform, as we know from drama, the opera, film and TV.

The procedural nature of the computer can affect literary texts in at least three ways: how the text is generated, how it is structured for reading, and how it is presented. Generation is either human or computational;[5] reading structure is either linear (the default procedure) or "database", which means that the reader probes segments of text in a relatively free order, rather than parsing it systematically; presentation is either indifferent or sensitive to digital technology. If we cross-classify these three oppositions, we obtain the table shown on figure 3.

---

5   In this dichotomy I regard production through a word processor as human. Though there are certainly differences between writing by hand or with a typewriter and writing with a computer, these differences are too dependent on the individual writer, and too difficult to capture systematically to be regarded as inherent features of electronic writing attributable to the agency of the computer.

	Human generated linear text	Human generated database text	Computer generated text
Print presentation	1	3	5
Computer presentation	2	4	6

A technological taxonomy of texts

Category 1: Naturally generated linear texts for print

Neither produced by algorithms nor performed by the computer, the texts of standard oral and print literature are the prime examples of the first category. On this level, the computer's contribution to the text is a matter of thematization and imitation. Digital technology gives authors something new to think about, as the prophetic visions of cyberspace, computer networks, virtual worlds, nanotechnology and ubiquitous computing in William Gibson's and Neal Stephenson's science fiction novels demonstrate, and it gives literature a new post-alphabetic vernacular inspired by computer languages, such as this extract of a text of "code poetry" by the Australian digital artist Mez. Though it is diffused through the Web, it can be easily printed, because – in contrast to most of the works of its author – it makes no use of the properties specific to the medium:

```
($define! force-promise
clammered
($if (not?
glamouring
object
(handle-promise-result x)))
hammered
($define! handle-promise-result
amber
($gene (x y)
chambered
```

```
((not? (promise? y))
(iambic.pent((up))a)meter
(set-(h)eart(h)! (var x) y);
(set-earth! (var x) ()); delete y)
```

Category 2: Naturally generated linear texts presented on the computer screen
Any text of category 1 can be transposed to category 2, or vice-versa, as
the Mez poem demonstrates. But is it still the same text? Katherine Hayles
has argued that "the materiality of the medium" (or is it its physicality?)[6]
affects the nature of the text so dramatically that it severs the lines of identity between the print text and the electronic version. "Recreating a text in
another medium is so significant a change that it is analogous to translating
from one language to another" (2005, 109). The degree of identity between
medially transposed versions differs however according to the interpretation
of medium. If we give the term a semiotic interpretation, the medium of
literature is language, or perhaps written language, just as the medium of
painting is the image and the medium of music is sound; but if we give it
a technological interpretation, then the media of literature are the various
supports and modes of writing: the manuscript, the codex book, and the
computer. Transposing a text from one semiotic medium to another, for
instance a novel into a film or a story into a musical composition involves a
far more radical transformation than translating it into a foreign language,
since signs must be turned into other types of signs, but creating a digital
version of a print novel maintains the linguistic substance of the text, and
unlike language translation it is more accurate when performed automatically. A digital text consists of the same words (or more precisely, of tokens
of the same types of signs) as its print counterpart, but it is affected by the
computer in both obvious and subtle ways.

The obvious ways are the operations that can be performed on the text,
such as word searches, or changing the size of characters. Harder to capture,
but in a way more significant (for it cannot be avoided, while the operations

---

6   For Hayles, the "materiality of the medium" must not be confused with its "physical-
    ity". Materiality is an "emergent property" which does not exists "independently of
    a text's content", and is a "matter of interpretation and critical debate" (2005, 104).
    Hayles does not elaborate on the relations between materiality and physicality, a
    property which seems to be a given, but I would like to suggest that, in her view,
    materiality is the individual ways in which a work deals with, exploits or reflects
    upon its physical substance.

mentioned above are optional), is the cognitive impact of the computer on the reading experience. When we stare on a screen at the words of a digitized print text, we are not aware of the layers of hidden code that transform binary data stored in memory into a visible display readable by humans. It will take category 6 to bring these layers to mind. With a digitized text, the impact of the computer on reading lies in our sensory apprehension of the display, and not in its technological production; this sensory relation, furthermore, treats all texts alike and does not affect their individual meanings. If I may speak from my own experience, the kind of interface most commonly offered by computers – a rigid screen operated by a combination of keyboard and mouse – is not conducive to the kind of sustained attention that we devote to the lengthy texts of print-based literature. In a detailed phenomenological study of the experience of reading hypertext fiction, Anne Mangen (Mangen 2006, 243-49) points out many features of the standard GUI (graphic user interface) of digital texts that interfere with the pleasure of reading. The most significant of these features, in my view, is the disturbance of the haptic relation that we entertain with a text when we hold a book in our hands. The screen image is intangible, while the computer is experienced as very tangible. The overbearing physical presence of the computer distracts the user from the semantic dimension of the signs on the screen. Whether this difficulty in concentrating while reading from a screen is due to the enduring habits created by the book or whether there is something inherent in the interface that gets in the way of the semantic processing of language is a question that will not be definitely answered until a new generation that grew up with computers becomes the main consumers of digital texts. Unless, of course, a new display technology (Amazon's Kindle? Apple's iPad?) is developed that takes care of the present problems.

Category 3: Naturally generated database texts for print
The texts of this category are the non-digital examples of what Espen Aarseth calls "ergodic literature". The trademark of ergodic literature is that it requires "non-trivial efforts" to allow the reader to traverse the text (Aarseth 1997, 1). These works are organized as a database of human-created fragments of text, out of which a variety of readings can be created by following a certain protocol. With a story structured as a tree, the protocol consists of choosing one branch out of many options at every decision point; with a text printed on a deck of cards, like Marc Saporta's *Composition No 1*, the protocol tells the reader to shuffle the deck in order to create a "narrative" sequence (I put

narrative in scare quotes because narrativity, as a logical and temporal ordering of events, is incompatible with random ordering); with a design such as
Raymond Queneau's *Cent mille milliards de poèmes*, which consists of 12 sonnets cut into strips at every line and bound together at the spine, new poems
are created by leafing through the book and combining the fragments. These
reading protocols can be compared to the search function that enables users
of informational databases to retrieve information; in both cases, the text
parsed by the user during a traversal or a consulting session is only a portion
of the total information gathered in the archive.[7]

Category 4: Naturally generated database texts performed on the computer
The digital equivalent of the protocol-driven database texts of category 4
is hypertext, a genre which has become almost synonymous with digital
literature. As Robert Coover indeed writes: "And I continue to feel that, for
all the wondrous and provocative invasions of text by sound and image, all
the intimate layering of them and irresistible fusions, still, the most radical
and distinctive literary contribution of the computer has been the multilin-
ear hypertextual webwork of text spaces, or, as one might say, the intimate
layering and fusion of imagined spatiality and temporality".

Hypertext depends on the computer for its reading protocol – clicking
on so-called hyperlinks to make a new screen of text appear – but in the vast
majority of cases, its underlying database is human-generated and static: the
author writes all the fragments of text, specifies all the links, and the only
dynamic (i.e. run-time) creation lies in the variable sequence produced by
the reader's choices.[8] In contrast to the texts of category 4, the author does
not design an original reading strategy: what defines hypertext is a mode of
operation implemented by the system, and all the texts of the genre follow
the same protocol. The major difference between individual texts, beside
their content, lies in the shape of the underlying network of links and nodes:
this network may or may not contain loops, it can be more or less densely

---

7 The concept of database, which has been popularized by Lev Manovich (2001),
   tends to be applied to all digital texts. I believe this is an overuse: of my 6 categories,
   only 3 and 4, and some texts of 6, rely on a database, a concept that should not be
   confused with input data. According to the *Oxford American Dictionary*, a database
   is "a structured set of data held in a computer, esp. one that is accessible in various
   ways".
8 It is not technically impossible for the database to modify itself under user input,
   but in this case, the text belongs to category 6.

connected; and it may look like a tree, a wheel, a sea-anemone, or a tangled web, the favorite structure of literary applications.

In the informational domain, hypertext has been a huge success: who hasn't experienced the addictive pleasure of surfing from Web site to Web site, or across Wikipedia entries, gathering instant knowledge about whatever topic comes to mind? But literary fiction and informational writing are different language games. What makes surfing the Web so enjoyable is that the interlinked elements are for the most part textually self-sufficient, and the linking logic transparent, allowing the user to make informed choices; but in literary applications, linking operates intratextually rather than intertextually, and the names of the links tend to be opaque teasers that take the reader to unknown destinations.

Ever since the first hypertext fictions hit the market in the early nineties, the genre has generated lively controversies. Its advocates argue that it offers an alternative to the traditional modes of thinking of Western culture: an alternative whose values are, in the words of Eduardo Kac (quoted by Simanowski 2007, 45), fluidity, non-linearity, discontinuity, dynamism, and of course interactivity. All these ideas can be subsumed by the metaphor of emergent complexity (Strange however that fluidity and discontinuity should contribute to the same aesthetics: the flow must be made of pebbles rather than of liquid!). By fragmenting the text into a collection of recombinant fragments, by organizing them into non-hierarchical networks – the rhizome which grows freely in all directions is preferred to the tree, – and by putting the reader in charge of the sequence of the fragments, hypertext has been said to privilege multiple interpretations over authoritarian discourse, analogical jumps over linear logical reasoning, attention to the local over totalizing apprehension, flânerie open to serendipitous discoveries over goal-oriented navigation, and, in a bold claim of its early proponents that is no longer taken very seriously, to turn readers into authors.

The critics of the device wonder what kind of content truly benefits from these features. Lev Manovich (2001, 225) has claimed somewhat hyperbolically that database and narrative are "mortal enemies", because narrative is based on a linear logico-temporal sequence of events, while database refuses to order its elements. I have argued elsewhere (Ryan 2006, 144) that the relatively free order of hypertext is incompatible with the narrative effects of suspense, curiosity and surprise, all of which require a strong control by the author of the temporal disclosure of information. Far from creating a smooth flow, the jumps from lexia to lexia inhibit immersion in the story (if there is a story) and turn the text into a jigsaw puzzle. According to

Anne Mangen (2006, 170-78), the link-node structure of hypertext leads to an obsessive need to click that prevents devoting deep attention to the text on the screen. As a result, readers and critics engage either in a "myopic" reading focused on individual chunks of text, or on a "meta-reading" that interprets the text allegorically or "theoretically". This could explain why close readings of hypertexts concerned with their global meaning are relatively rare,[9] compared, on the meta side, to discussions of the genre as a whole dealing with its underlying ideology, its alleged effect on the reader, and how it differs from print textuality, or, on the myopic side, compared to extremely detailed techno-philological studies of how individual texts perform under different operating systems. Most recently, Michel Chaouli (2005, 608) has suggested that the more effort readers devote to the physical construction of the text through point and click interactivity, the less attention will be left for its semantic construction and aesthetic evaluation. This would explain why hypertext fiction, despite its seductive aesthetics (who would not prefer, at least in principle, dynamic to static meaning, fluidity to solidity, complexity to simplicity and agency to passivity?) has not become the dominant literary presence that its early advocates prophesized.

Category 5: Computer generated texts for print

Here the text is produced by an automated procedure specified by an algorithm, but the output of this algorithm can be presented in print. An algorithm is not a static formula that guides the writing of the text, as are freely adopted constraints such as writing a poem with a certain metric and rhyme pattern, or a novel without using a certain letter (such as Georges Perec's *La Disparition*); it is rather a dynamic procedure that creates a text through a series of precisely defined operations. In algorithmic writing, the creativity of the author resides in designing the procedure by which the words are selected and the text is produced. Whereas the language of a text composed according to a formal pattern is fully controlled by the author, at least on the level of the signifiers, the language of a text produced by an algorithm should create surprise for the designer of the system.

The authors of text-generating algorithms have a choice of two philosophies: either randomize the output, or seek semantic coherence. The first philosophy is inspired by the "mad-lib" party game, in which blindly chosen words are inserted into templates, producing syntactically correct but semantically incoherent output. The aesthetic appeal of these texts resides in the

---

9   Two exceptions to this trend are Ciccoricco 2007 and Bell 2010.

"exquisite cadaver" effect cultivated by Surrealism: unexpected encounters of meanings that shake the reader out of her thinking habits and challenge the imagination to construct a new, surreal world, based on connections between ideas that never get a chance to meet in the discourse of everyday reality. An example of the aleatory mode of generation is *The Policeman's Beard is Half Constructed*, a book supposedly "written" in the early eighties by a computer program named Racter (1984). (Actually, Racter is not entirely responsible for the text, because the human programmer selected the best outputs from many runs of the program). Here is an excerpt:

> A hot and torrid bloom which
> Fans with flames and begs to be
> Redeemed by forces black and strong
> Will now oppose my naked will
> And force me into regions of despair
> (1984, no page number)

Reading such texts initially challenges the imagination to construct meaning by pretending that they are the expression of a human mind (as the philosopher H.P. Grice observed, meaning is intentional), but when one realizes that the "author" is a machine, the text loses any kind of emotional or existential dimension. Most readers will quickly tire of poring over Racter's creations. "What message can a text have without a sender?" asks Roberto Simanovski of machine-generated texts ("Holopoetry", 57).

For the true hacker, the interest of aleatory text production does not lie in the output – whose poetic charm is highly dependent on the luck of the draw – but in the originality of the generative algorithm. To remain ahead in the fast-paced game of experimentalism, digital artists must find ever-new ways to produce nonsense and quasi-sense, adapted to the most recent technological developments. The Google search engine has for instance been requisitioned by practitioners of Flarf poetry (a movement dedicated to the exploitation of "the inappropriate") to collect random words and collate them into poems.

The alternative to making use of aleatory processes is the attempt to create meaningful texts through artificial intelligence techniques, such as placing semantic constraints on the insertion of lexical elements into syntactic templates. Whereas programs designed by the engineers of randomness result in an undifferentiated soup of verbal dysfunctionality, AI algorithms can attain various degrees of semantic coherence. But no text-generating program has yet succeeded in giving readers the kind of pleasure that one derives from even mediocre naturally produced literary works, except perhaps in the domain of haikus (a genre easily generated by computers, because it uses a very strict and very short formal template, and gives free rein to the reader's imagination). The achievements of the best of story-generating programs cast serious doubts on the predictions of Ray Kurzweil, a respected computer scientist turned futurologist who claims that by the year 2029, many of the leading authors will be machines (1999, 223). Progress in this area has been so slow since the seventies that AI would have to perform a quantum leap forward sometime in the next twenty years for Kurzweil's prediction to be fulfilled. Consider this except from a narrative created by Scott Turner's MINSTREL program:

> The Vengeful Princess
> Once upon a time there was a lady of the Court named Jennifer. Jennifer loved a knight named Grunfeld. Grunfeld loved Jennifer.
>
> Jennifer wanted revenge on a lady of the court named Darlene because she had the berries which she picked in the woods and Jennifer wanted to have the berries. Jennifer wanted to scare Darlene. Jennifer wanted a dragon to move towards Darlene so that Darlene believed it would eat her. Jennifer wanted to appear to be a dragon so that a dragon would move toward Darlene. Jennifer drank a magic potion. Jennifer transformed into a dragon. A dragon moved toward Darlene. A dragon was near Darlene (Turner 1994, 9).

The story is not as conventional as this unpromising beginning suggests: in a climactic episode that combines a sudden turn with an Aristotelian *anagnorisis* (recognition), Grunfeld, wanting to impress the king, slays a dragon, who turns out to be Jennifer, and the program slyly draws the moral: "Deception is a weapon difficult to aim". But even if we regard this text as a plot outline to be "post-processed" (i.e. rewritten) by a human author, it makes a reader aware of the complexity of the task at hand and capable of reverse-engineering the underlying algorithm to evaluate the achievement of "The Vengeful Princess". For the common reader, as Espen Aarseth observed (1997, 139), computer-generated stories are much more enjoyable when a glitch in the program creates a theater of the absurd.

Category 6: Texts generated and presented by computer
Of all my categories, 6 is the site of the most intense, vibrant and diversified activity; but it is also the one in which language is most likely to lose

its hegemony to other modes of signification. Its genres include digitized installation art, video games, online worlds, interactive fiction, interactive drama, and coded poetry (not to be confused with code poetry: while the former is performed by an invisible code, the latter makes code visible and presents it as an artistic object).[10] The vast majority of the more recent texts of the ELO anthology belong to this category.

The difference between categories 5 and 6 lies in the relations between generation and presentation. In 5, texts are generated and stored in a file, which can be later outputted either in print or on the screen. In 6, by contrast, generation and presentation are simultaneous and indistinguishable, because presentation exploits properties specific to the medium, especially interactivity and volatile inscription. When a text's development depends on interaction, it must present something to the user every time it needs input, and generation proceeds as a dialogue between user and computer in the real time of the user's encounter with the text. Similarly, when a text relies on volatility, every change on the screen must be controlled by a separate instruction, and the text must be displayed, or rather played, moment by moment *through*, rather than *after* the execution of the program. The inseparability of generation and presentation means that in contrast to the texts of category 5, the texts of category 6 cannot be taken out of the computer.

The distinction between categories 4 and 6 is much fuzzier, and many texts are located on the borderline between these two types. In both cases a program works on man-made input data and turns this data into a visible display (no program ever creates something out of nothing), but in the case of hypertext the data is pre-structured according to a certain pattern (this is why I call it a database), while in category 6, input data is a collection of building materials which can be stored in a variety of ways. Moreover, the program that handles the hypertextual database is a standardized writing/reading tool, such as the Storyspace software, while in category 6 the text is produced by custom-made code, and it is judged

---

10 The common denominator of all code poetry is that it bears a certain relation to computer languages, but this relation is highly variable: some code poems are computer produced, while others are written by humans; some are meant to be executed by the machine and to perform some definable task, while others combine standard alphanumeric symbols with exotic symbols borrowed from computer programming, creating a pseudo-code that makes no sense to the machine, but arguably speaks to the posthuman subjectivity that is being shaped by digital technology. Many of these graphic hybrids of code and human language could just as well be printed on paper as shown on a computer screen. When this is the case, they belong to category 1.

MEDIALITY

much more on the originality of the generative ideas than on the quality of the writing. The favorite authoring tools are Flash and Director, both of which include their own programming language. Another way to capture the difference between 4 and 6 is through what Chris Crawford calls "process intensity". This scalar criterion concerns the ratio of input data to computer code: in 4 a large body of data is submitted to a simple operation, the "fetch and display the content of a certain memory address" triggered by the hyperlink, while in 6 the input data undergoes operations of far greater complexity and diversity, especially since these operations differ from work to work.

Whereas the generative codes of category 5 consist mainly of invisible symbol manipulation that take place inside the computer, category 6 adds to this vocabulary several visible, output-centered operations. The most important is animation. With Flash and Director, words can be treated as images, this is to say, as bit-maps or as vector graphics, and it is easy to put them in motion, to deform them, to change their color, to make them fade in and out, to explode them into letters, to make these letters gather into other words or to disperse them into nonsense. Another prominent feature is replacement. In the hypertexts of category 4 replacement operates on the level of the whole screen, but with the greater coding sophistication of category 6 it can affect other levels, such as groups of sentences rather than whole pages, or individual letters within words. The palimpsest structure of Flash and Director allows yet another effect, the layering of different images. The working space of the program consists of superposed graphic overlays which can be made transparent or opaque during the run of the program, hiding each other or, on the contrary, revealing what lies below by being temporarily blocked from the display. All of these effects can be either automatic or user-triggered; in the latter case, they can be either the result of a deliberate action of clicking on a visible button or the unpredictable side-effect of a cursor movement, such as mousing over a hidden hot spot.

DYSFUNCTIONAL LANGUAGE

How can the fundamentally visual effects of category 6 affect meaning when they operate on words? It would take an individual examination of the works that use them to do justice to the variety of their particular adaptations, but the most dominant trend is one that is shared by Web art in general (or, arguably, by all avant-garde art): a fascination with the dysfunctional. Why this fascination? Because it is only in moments of malfunctioning, of rupture, of interference that we become aware of the codes and processes (technological, linguistic, cultural and cognitive) that regulate our social and mental life. Dysfunctionality is intimately related to self-referentiality, the leading concern of postmodern art.

Within language-based works, dysfunctionality aims at the reading process – or rather, at the reading process made familiar by print. Animation can be used to make words appear and disappear too fast for the user to be able to read them, as in *Chemical Landscape* by Edward Falco: the texts that accompany each of eight landscapes created by manipulating chemicals in a dark room fade out so quickly – like the image of an undeveloped film exposed to light – that all the reader can do is grab individual words, or at best fragments of sentences, jumping across the text rather than parsing it left to right and top to bottom. Repeat visits to the same landscape enable readers to capture different parts of the text, and eventually to process it completely, but the individual grabs never gel into a coherent story because of the difficulty of remembering the bounty of the previous visits. Replacement provides another way to frustrate the cognitive processes that allow the global understanding of text. In Judd Morrissey's *The Jew's Daughter*, mousing over a visually marked word causes a few lines within the page to be transformed into a different text. The new passage is not visually marked, and it fits syntactically so well within the old text, that it takes extreme concentration, or even photographic memory, for the reader to detect what is old and what is new – a concentration that detracts attention from the meaning of the text. (Alternatively, the reader can just read the new page without trying to locate the changes). The dynamic, internal self-modification of the page prevents any kind of temporal development on the level of content, and consequently hinders a narrative reading. There is indeed no reason to assume that the events and mental representations related on page 3 follow those of page 2, since the two pages overlap in their content. In both of these examples, the unusual interface brings attention to the reading process by de-automatizing the scanning of the text by the eye.

For those who think of language as a means of communication complex meanings through well-formed sentences and coherent texts, yet another form of verbal dysfunctionality typical of category 6 is the simulation of cognitively impaired speech. The incoherence of the text of Stuart Moulthrop's *Reagan Library* hints at a brain suffering from Alzheimer's disease, while the progressive invasion of the input text of Noah Wardrip-

Fruin's and Brion Moss' *The Impermanence Agent* by foreign elements randomly selected from the user's hard drive suggests the memory loss of Nana, the grandmother of the narrator. The prominence of impaired language in digital texts is easily explained by the relative ease of generating nonsense through erasures and aleatory procedures, compared to the difficulty of building logically well-formed discourse.[11]

One step further in the semantic disintegration of language is the decomposition of signifying units into their non-signifying minimal components. The founder of the Lettrist movement in poetry, Isidore Isou, claimed that the focus of poetry has shifted from the paragraph in Romanticism, to the word in Symbolism, and finally to the letter, starting with Mallarmé and continuing through Dadaism and Surrealism.[12] Lettrism, the culmination of this trend, is well represented in the ELO anthology, especially through the work of John Cayley, its best-known practitioner. In many of his works (for instance *Translation* in the ELO collection), Cayley experiments with an algorithm that morphs words into other words and languages into other languages by operating substitutions on the level of their individual letters. This mechanism limits reading to the occasional recognition of lexically well-formed combinations, or to guessing what the next existing word will be, as letters fill in blanks in a process reminiscent of the game Wheel of Fortune. The reader observes a continuous oscillation between sense and non-sense, waiting, sometimes successfully, sometimes in vain, for the aleatory mechanisms of the generative code to create sentential meaning, but unable to register all the intermediary stages between readable words, either because the letters roll too fast to be individually noticed, or because it is impossible to pay close attention to more than one of the multiple replacement processes that take place simultaneously on the screen. In Brian Kim Stefan's *The Dreamlife of Letters* similarly, but through different means, the user witnesses what Alan Liu (2004, 8-9) would call the creative destruction of textual meaning.

---

11 Evidence of this difficulty is the MINSTREL program mentioned above, which uses 27000 lines of code [program + tools] to generate a mere dozen well-formed stories.

12 See selections from the Lettrist Manifestos on Isidore Isou's home page: http://www.thing.net/~grist/l&d/lettrist/isou-m.htm

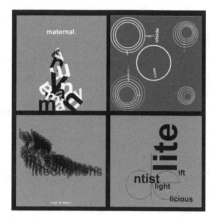

Screen shots from Brian Kim Stefans' *The Dreamlife of Letters*

The author took an unconventional creative essay (itself very fragmented in its syntax) by the poet and feminist theorist Rachel Blau du Plessis, selected individual words, presented them in alphabetic order, and made these words dance on the screen in a non-interactive visual show that highlights their common leading letter. As language dissolves into its elementary particles, it becomes a spectacle to watch instead of a text to read.

RETURN TO FUNCTIONALITY

Despite these trends, however, it would be premature to conclude that visuality and dysfunctionality are the only hopes for language to survive as art on the computer screen. Within category 6, there are at least two genres that depend crucially on readability. The first, Interactive Fiction (hence IF), is the only form of electronic literature since the early days of hypertext to abstain from any kind of association with images.[13] By detailing the multiple facets of IF, the playfully hyperbolic title of an article by Nick Montfort suggests why the genre has been able to attract readers through language and programming alone: "Interactive fiction as 'Story,' 'Game,' 'Storygame,' 'Novel,' 'World,' 'Puzzle,' 'Problem,' and 'Riddle'". In the article, Montfort succinctly defines IF as: "A program that simulates a world, understands natural language from an interactor, and provides a textual reply based on events in this

---

13 There are actually commercial types of IF that rely on cinematic animations, such as the later releases of the Zork adventures, but I am talking here of the more literary form practiced by such author as Robert Pinsky, Emily Short, Andrew Plotkin, Adam Cadre, and Nick Montfort.

MEDIALITY

world" (2004, 316). The user of IF plays the role of a character who wanders through an imaginary space, usually trying to solve a mystery. The engine that operates IF not only displays text that describes a fictional world and narrates events, it also builds a dynamic model of this world through a code that the user never gets to see. The system's responses to the user's input are based on this model: for instance, if the user types "drink the liquid", and the liquid has been coded to be a magic potion, the system may reply "you shrink to the size of an ant and you fall into the glass". It takes an extreme attention to the meaning of words, and an ability to synthesize the system's responses into a mental model of the topography and temporal development of the fictional world to be able find the answer to the puzzle, or, if there is no puzzle, to follow the story that unfolds in this world. The survival of IF in the age of the invasion of digital media by the image is due to its potential for a successful combination of verbal artistry and literary experimentation with the ludic activities of problem-solving and role-playing.

The other genre that relies crucially on the proper working of the semantics and pragmatics of language is interactive drama, a literary form still in the developing stages whose sole working example, at the time of this writing, is *Façade* (2005) by Michael Mateas and Andrew Stern. Interactive drama is a dialogue system with a built-in plot and a visual environment. The user plays the role of a character in the plot, interacting through language with system-controlled characters who respond with pre-recorded spoken lines. Since there is no real-time language generation, but rather, a matching by the system of the user's input with the best-fitting fragment of stored dialogue, the characters of *Façade* are often unable to respond coherently or promptly to the conversation of the interactor. But this relative and unintentional dysfunctionality is cleverly justified by the thematics of the work. *Façade* tells the story of a seemingly successful couple, Grace and Trip, who invite a guest for an evening. In the course of the conversation with the visitor it becomes clear that the marriage of Grace and Trip is fractured by deep resentments, and that their happiness is a mere façade. As the initially polite conversation with the guest degenerates into a bitter argument of the spouses over the state of their marriage, the frequent failure of AI to process the user's input can be attributed to the self-centeredness of Grace and Trip. Here the occasional dysfunctionality of the system is integrated as a mental feature of the characters into a logically consistent narrative.

Is it possible for a work to combine the strengths of print with the effects made possible by the distinctive properties of digital media? One way to solve this problem is through what Simanowski calls double coding: building the work on the complementarity of traditional and electronic textuality. The most common form of bi-mediality is to subject a digitized print text to a processing of category 6, making the original text available to the user. This is the case with *Text Rain* and *The Dreamlife of Letters*, discussed above. Both of these works create an implicit hierarchy between the two media by using a print text written by another author as input to their own digital performance.[14] Another type of bi-mediality is found in code poetry when the text can be both read as a print poem that addresses a human reader and executed as a program. This double interpellation is illustrated by Eric Andreychek's "Perl Port of Jabberwocky", a text which provides an amusing parody of Lewis Carroll's nonsense poem "Jabberwocky", and launches three dysfunctional processes – processes that do not do anything useful but do not harm the system – when executed as code (Ryan 2006, 220).

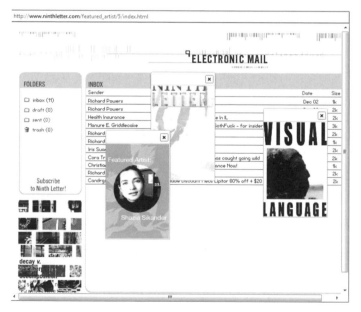

Screen shot from Richard Powers' They Come in a Steady Stream Now

14 By contrast, John Cayley's *Translation* is intertextual more than bi-medial, even though it uses sentences by Proust and Walter Benjamin, because it decontextualizes these sentences and does not provide access to the originals: the reader only sees the input texts as transformed by Cayley's code.

The implications of bi-mediality for the reading experience are power-fully demonstrated by Richard Powers e-mail story "They Come in a Steady Stream Now".

The work satirizes the proliferation of spam through a web-based story that simulates the interface of a standard e-mail program. Of the 17 messages that arrive one by one in the fake mailbox during the run of the program, ten are spam and seven "legitimate". The junk mail runs the familiar gamut of pornography, drug offers, and investment opportunities. In addition to the junk mail, the mail program is plagued by pop-up ads, which readers must close one by one before opening a new message. In contrast to the humor of the junk mail, the seven legitimate letters, addressed to the reader by a narrator named Richard Powers, contain a melancholic meditation on aging triggered by the junk mail's incessant hawking of drugs that promise to reverse the damage of time. In the last of the seven letters we read: "PLEASE REGISTER. The content you requested is available only to registered members. Registration is FREE and offers great benefits". The readers who dare to follow these instructions, mindless of the risk of viruses, by giving their e-mail address are rewarded with a message from Richard Powers in their own mailbox.[15] In it they find a link to a PDF file which can be downloaded and printed. This file contains the text of the previous six simulated mails, together with a very Proustian conclusion in which the present absorbs the past and the past becomes present, allowing the narrator to relive an episode of his childhood. By including all the previously read installments, the final delivery contrasts the reading experiences of the digital and print versions. In the e-mail simulation, the text comes to the reader as a collection of fragments that create distraction through their many windows, through frequent interruptions, and through the obsessive need to click. The printable text gives rise to an entirely new reading experience: now we can hold the entire text in our hands, enjoying a haptic relation with it which is absent from reading on a screen, we can read it without interruption, and we do not have to worry about competing windows. All these features, by freeing our attention from the interface and from the material conditions of reading, enable us to pay greater attention to the semantics of the text and to the poetic quality of language. (It also helps, of course, that we are re-reading rather than reading for the first time). The originality of Powers'

---

15 At least this was the case in 2005; since then the work has been reformatted, and I have been unable recently [2009] to coax it into sending me the e-mail.

achievement lies in the complementarity of the comic experience of the screen version and of the lyrical experience of the print version. In its play with two media, the text manages to combine the power of print literature to induce emotions with the cleverness of conception and innovative presentation that we have come to expect of digital art.

NETWORKING

My discussion so far has mentioned all but one of the distinctive properties listed at the beginning of this article. This missing property, networking, is the one that has had the deepest influence on the use of language. To borrow Henry Jenkins' term (Jenkins 2006, 2-3), computer networks have made culture participatory. They have inspired countless people to share their thoughts, their artistic creations, the story of their lives through blogs, personal web sites, or public online meeting spaces. They have given birth to an industry of fan fiction, by allowing people to upload their own versions of the cult narratives of popular media, or to create original stories out of video games by adding their own text or sound track to images captured though game-cameras, also known as machinima. They have made possible a wholly new genre of entertainment, the online world (and its ancestors the MOOs and MUDs), a genre that takes advantage, to the highest degree, of all the properties of the medium: procedural nature by relying on a coded world model, multi-media by allowing players to communicate through text and now voice in a visual environment, interactivity through avatar-creating, role-playing, building objects, or performing quests within the fictional world, and volatility of inscription, through a constant updating of the world by players and designers – an updating that turns these worlds into living environments. It is true that by facilitating the exchange of any type of self-expression and artistic project, networking has promoted images, video and music as much as, or perhaps more than language. But language remains the most important means of personal communication on the Web, as it is in non-digital life. Thanks to networked media, writing is no longer "a spectator sport played by professionals", as Michel Chaouli observes, "it involves player participants content to be amateurs", because they are motivated by the pure pleasure of writing, playing, creating personas, engaging in dialogue with each other, and publicly performing, rather than by the ambition to become authors. As Chaouli concludes, "chances are [that this activity] will not produce great literature, but it will probably be a lot more fun" (2005, 617). More fun, presumably, than those types of digital texts that maintain the distinction between author and reader – a distinction that cannot be entirely erased by interactivity.

CONCLUSION

Let me now turn to the question of what the computer means for the future of literature. I do not mean to discuss the fact that in the future books may be replaced by electronic reading machines: it is still for a large part books, still traditional literature that people read on these machines. The point of my question is whether the literature of the future will be the truly digital kind, the kind that takes advantages of the properties of digital media. The texts of the ELO collection certainly represent an avant-garde and experimental movement within textual art.[16] But this does not mean that they represent the future of literature, because avant-gardes and experiments can be dead-end branches on the tree of literary evolution as much as they can be productive innovations. Literary evolution is not a coach pulled by the horses of experimental forms, no more than it is a load pushed from behind by the forms of popular culture; it is much more a swarm of ideas that move back and forth between the front and the back, the avant-garde inspired by popular forms, and popular forms adopting ideas that were once avant-garde. The complexity of these exchanges makes it very difficult, if not impossible, to predict where the swarm is heading.

The great strength of digital media is to have created hybrid forms of expression that challenge the distinctions between traditional art forms. Most digital texts become much more attractive if we think of them as a new form of art than if we regard them as literature, because literature relies on the semantic dimension of language, while most digital texts use language primarily as a material substance. In digital texts words become visible, audible or even tangible entities, and they convey meanings through their

---

16 As the anonymous referee of this chapter observes, the techniques used by electronic texts bear an obvious resemblance to those used by the avant-garde of print literature. The cognitive challenge issued by these techniques brings support to Culler's claim that reading literature is an "unnatural" activity requiring a specialized competence. This competence becomes technological in the case of digital texts: with the works of the ELO collection, users must not only learn how to read the texts (reading is taken here in a broad sense of appreciating), they must also learn how to *operate* them. This is no small challenge, given the variety of the interfaces represented in the collection. Yet it is essential to the survival of literature as a whole that it not limits itself to works that require a specialized competence.

sensory properties much more than through their lexical and contextual significance. In the most extreme cases of dysfunctionality, they even speak to us through the loss of their sense. But every gain comes at a loss, and the gains of digital texts in the sensory domain are not substantial enough compared to the losses of the semantic domain to reduce traditional literature to a marginal role.

I am not a neuroscientist, and I am not claiming expertise in the mapping of the brain, but it seems to me that traditional literature, especially of the narrative kind, stimulates many different areas of the brain, belonging to both the right and the left hemisphere. This means that it recruits our logical as well as our emotional faculties. Digital texts by contrast are more narrowly focused on operations that popular science associates with the right hemisphere, such as symbol manipulations, formal transformations and spatial thinking. This may be why digital culture has been associated with the emergence of a new type of subjectivity called the posthuman or the cyborg, a subjectivity supposedly produced by the co-evolution of machine intelligence and human cognition.[17]

The strength of digital texts lies in the originality of text-producing algorithms. They will speak to you if you regard words as objects with which to invent new games, and if you expect language to perform a new dance choreographed by code to a music that the computer alone can play – the music of its special affordances. But if you value literature's power to express the drama of human experience, to propose a vision of life, to tell spellbinding stories, to articulate complex ideas and to exercise emotional power, then print-based texts will never be made obsolete by their digital rivals.[18]

REFERENCES

Aarseth, Espen. 1997. *Cybertext. Perspectives on Ergodic Literature*. Baltimore: Johns Hopkins University Press.
Andreychek, Eric. PERL port of Jabberwocky. http://c2.com/cgi/wiki?PerlPoetry.
Beiguelman, Giselle. 2004. *Code Movie*. http://collection.eliterature.org/1/works/beiguelman__code_movie_1.html.

17 The notion of cyborg was proposed by Donna Haraway (1991) and the concept of posthuman popularized by N. Katherine Hayles (1999), though there have been earlier uses of the term.
18 A preliminary, shorter version of this article appeared in *Genre* XLI, vol. 3-4, 2008, 33-58, under the title "What Has the Computer Done for the Word". Text reproduced by permission.

Bell, Alice. 2010. *The Possible Worlds of Hypertext Fiction*. London: Routledge.

Boyd, Brian. 2009. *On the Origin of Stories: Evolution, Cognition and Fiction*. Cambridge, Mass: Belknap Press.

Carr, Nicholas. 2010. *The Shallows: What the Internet is Doing to Our Brains*. New York: Norton.

Cayley, John. 2004. *Translation*. http://collection.eliterature.org/1/works/cayley__translation.html.

Chaouli, Michel. 2005. How Interactive Can Fiction Be. *Critical Inquiry* 31: 599-617.

Ciccoricco, David. 2007. *Reading Network Fiction*. Tuscaloosa: University of Alabama Press.

Coover, Robert. 1999. *Literary Hypertext: The Passing of the Golden Age*. www.nickm.com/vox/golden_age.html.

Crawford, Chris. 1987. Process Intensity. *Journal of Computer Game Design* 15. http://www.erasmatazz.com/library/JCGD_Volume_1/Process_Intensity.html.

Culler, Jonathan. 1975. *Structuralist Poetics*. Ithaca: Cornell University Press.

Dutton, Denis. 2009. *The Art Instinct*. New York: Bloomsbury Press.

Falco, Edward. 2006. *Chemical Landscapes*. http://collection.eliterature.org/1/works/falco__chemical_landscapes_digital_tales.html.

Flarf Poetry. Wikipedia entry. http://en.wikipedia.org/wiki/Flarf_poetry.

Haraway, Donna. 1991. *Simians, Cyborgs, and Women: The Reinvention of Nature*. London: Routledge.

Hayles, N. Katherine. 1999. *How We Became Posthuman: Virtual Bodies in Cybernetics, Literature and Informatics*. Chicago: University of Chicago Press.

— 2002. *Writing Machines*. Cambridge, Mass: MIT Press.

— 2005. *My Mother Was a Computer: Digital Subjects and Literary Texts*. Chicago: University of Chicago Press.

— 2008. *Electronic Literature: New Horizons for the Literary*. Notre Dame, Ind.: University of Notre Dame Press.

— Nick Montfort, Scott Rettberg, and Stephanie Strickland, eds. *Electronic Literature Collection*, vol 1. http://collection.eliterature.org/1/.

Isidore Isou home page. http://www.thing.net/~grist/lnd/lettrist/isou.htm.

Jenkins, Henry. 2006. *Convergence Culture: Where Old and New Media Collide*. New York: NYU Press.

Kirschenbaum, Matthew G. 2005. The Words as Image in an Age of Digital Reproduction. In *Eloquent Images,* eds. Mary E. Hocks and Michelle R. Kendrić, 137-56. Cambridge, Mass: MIT Press.

Kurzweil, Ray. 1999. *The Age of Spiritual Machines*. New York: Viking.

Lettrist Home Page. http://www.thing.net/~grist/l&d/lettrist/lettrist.htm.

Leslie, Jacques. 1995. Ambiguity Machines. *EJournal* 5.2. http://www.hanover.edu/philos/ejournal/archive/ej-5-2.txt.

Liu, Alan. 2004. *The Laws of Cool. Knowledge Work and the Culture of Information*. Chicago: University of Chicago Press.

Mangen, Anne. 2006. *New Narrative Pleasures? A Cognitive-Phenomenological Study of the Experience of Reading Digital Narrative Fictions*. PhD dissertation, Norwegian University of Science and Technology, Trondheim, Norway.

Manovich, Lev. 2001. *The Language of New Media*. Cambridge, Mass.: MIT Press.

Mateas, Michael and Andrew Stern. 2005. *Façade*. Downloadable from: http://interactivestory.net/download.

Mez (Mary Anne Breeze). (n.d.). Except from http://netwurker.livejournal.com/.

Montfort, Nick. 2004. Interactive Fiction as 'Story', 'Game', 'Storygame', 'Novel', 'World', 'Literature', 'Puzzle', 'Problem', 'Riddle', and 'Machine'. In *First Person: New Media as Story, Performance, and Game*, eds. Noah Waldrip-Fruin and Pat Harrigan, 310-17. Cambridge, Mass: MIT Press.

Morrissey, Judd. 2000. *The Jew's Daughter*. http://collection.eliterature.org/1/works/morrissey__the_jews_daughter.html.

Moulthrop, Stuart. 1999. *Reagan Library*. http://collection.eliterature.org/1/works/moulthrop__reagan_library.html.

Nelson, Theodore. 1981. *Literary Machines*. Swarthmore, Pa: Mindful Press.

Powers, Richard, with Jenifer Gunji, Joseph Squier, Jessica Mullen, Lauren Hoopes, Chad Kellenberger and Val Lohmann. 2004. They come in a steady stream now. http://www.ninthletter.com/featured_artist/artist/5.

Pratt, Mary Louise. 1977. *Toward a Speech Act Theory of Literary Discourse*. Bloomington: Indiana University Press.

Racter [Bill Chamberlain]. 1984. *The Policeman's Beard is Half Constructed: A Bizarre and Fantastic Journey Into the Mind of a Machine*. New York: Warner Books.

Ryan, Marie-Laure. 2006. *Avatars of Story*. Minneapolis: University of Minnesota Press.

Seaman, Bill. Interactive Text and Recomppbinant Poetics – Media-Element Field Explorations. In *First Person: New Media as Story, Performance, and Game*, eds. Noah Waldrip-Fruin and Pat Harrigan, 227-34. Cambridge, Mass: MIT Press.

Simanowski, Roberto. 2007. Holopoetry, Biopoetry and Digital Literature. In *The Aesthetics of Net Literature: Writing, Reading and Playing in Programmable Media*, eds. Peter Gendolla and Jörgen Schäfer, 43-66. Piscataway, N.J: Transcript Publishers.

— 2007. *Double Coding*. Paper presented at the conference "Remediating Literature", Utrecht, Netherlands.

Stefans, Brian Kim. 2000. *The Dream Life of Letters*. http://collection.eliterature.org/1/works/stefans__the_dreamlife_of_letters.html.

Turner, Scott R. 1994. *The Creative Process: A Computer Model of Storytelling and Creativity*. Hillsdale, N.J: Lawrence Erlbaum.

Utterback, Camille. 2004. Unusual Positions--Embodied Interaction with Symbolic Spaces. In *First Person: New Media as Story, Performance, and Game*, eds. Noah Waldrip-Fruin and Pat Harrigan, 218-26. Cambridge, Mass: MIT Press.

Utterback, Camille and Romy Arhitruv. 1999. *Text Rain*. Installation. Description at: http://www.camilleutterback.com/textrain.html.

Wardrip-Fruin, Noah and Pat Harrigan, eds. 2004. *First Person: New Media as Story, Performance, and Game*, Cambridge, Mass: MIT Press.

Wardrip-Fruin, Noah and Brion Moss, with a.c. chapman and Duane Whitehurst. 2002. *The Impermanence Agent*. Project and Context. *CyberText Yearbook*, eds. Markku Eskelinen and Raine Koskimaa, 13-58. University of Jyväskylä: Publications of the Research Centre for Contemporary Culture.

A DEFENCE OF (THE STUDY OF) LITERATURE

OR: WHY (THE STUDY OF) LITERATURE CANNOT BE REPLACED BY CULTURAL STUDIES AND FILM (STUDIES)

Werner Wolf

LITERATURE AND THE STUDY OF LITERATURE – INCREASINGLY OUTMODED ACTIVITIES?

"Why study literature?" – the key question of the present volume – could quickly be answered: literature ought to be studied because as a discourse with its own history and devices it is a human cultural activity complex enough to merit scholarly analysis; in short, if one still agrees with Alexander Pope that "[t]he proper study of Mankind is Man" (*Essay on Man* II.2), literature must be part of such "proper study". However, this answer may sound rather unsatisfactory, and the issue at hand merits more in-depth analysis. Perhaps the question 'why study literature?' is formulated in a potentially misleading way. Are we really asking why literature should be studied *at all*? If literature were just one minor manifestation of mankind's cultural activities, a handful of scholars would arguably be enough to deal with it, and literary studies could be reduced to a tiny, exotic discipline, one of those for which an enlightened Austrian politician some years ago coined the memorable phrase "Orchideenfach" – 'orchid discipline'. Yet this is not what literary scholars actually have in mind when putting the question 'why study literature?' self-reflexively to themselves as in the present volume. Rather, the real question would be something like 'why should the study and the teaching of literature occupy a prominent position in the educational system at schools and universities?'.

The general drift of a possible answer to this reformulated question from a literary scholar like myself is clear enough and would go in the following direction: 'Since reading literature is full of benefits for the individual as well as for society at large it is a particularly worthwhile object of study that merits a privileged place in education, research and society'. But there's the rub, for this positive view of literature is no longer a generally held conviction in our Western world. Rather, it would appear that the attitude that prevails nowadays is closer to the opinion voiced by one of Ian McEwan's recent fictional characters, namely neurosurgeon Henry Perowne in *Saturday* (2005), an enthusiastic representative of the (bio-)sciences, who dismisses reading literature as a waste of time spent on "sophisticated fairy stories" and wonders with reference to fiction in particular: "The times are strange enough. Why make things up?" (McEwan 2006 [2005], 66 f.).

Indeed, it is a truth universally, if by some sadly, acknowledged that literature is a cultural activity that has lost considerable ground in Western culture over the past few decades – perhaps not so much on the side of production, but certainly as far as its reception and its status in education are concerned. Not long ago, in the wake of the dominance of 19th-century bourgeois norms and attitudes, literature used to be regarded as one of the key expressions of national cultures and was firmly anchored in all stages of education. In primary and secondary education, this even included learning certain literary texts, most notably poems, by heart, and at university level literature used to be *the* dominant subject of studies in philological departments.

Yet all of this is now relegated to a by-gone age (cf. Delbanco 1999). Indeed, in our increasingly pluralistic societies, in which bourgeois attitudes have long ceased to be dominant, literature has lost much of its former centrality, and the study of the 'hard' natural sciences ranks much higher in social evaluation than the study of literature as one of the 'soft' humanities disciplines. In addition to the decline of bourgeois attitudes and the rise in status of the natural sciences, another reason for this development is certainly the emergence of new media. In fact, TV-transmitted films, computer games and internet surfing seem to have by far superseded the reception of literature as spare-time activities, in particular with the younger generation and thus the new media and 'media literacy' begin to appear more worthy of scholarly and educational attention. The public awareness of literature has declined in proportion. In connection with this, literature is no longer as present in the Western educational system as it used to be. This does not only apply to primary and secondary education but also to the study of literature in academia, on which I will concentrate in the following. To a certain extent the fate of David Lurie, hero of J.M. Coetzee's Booker-prize winning novel *Disgrace* (1999), is here symptomatic:

> Once a professor of modern languages [i.e., in the context of South Africa, of English literature], he has been, since Classics and Modern Languages were closed down as part of the great rationalization, adjunct professor of commu-

nications. Like all rationalized personnel, he is allowed to offer one special-field course a year, irrespective of enrolment, because that is good for morale. This year he is offering a course in the Romantic poets (Coetzee 2000 [1999], 3).

University teachers and students of literature are by profession sensitive to these new trends, since they are affected by them most directly. Accordingly, academic reactions to the new situation observable in literary departments can be regarded as particularly symptomatic of the decline in the importance of literary studies: an increasing number of originally literary scholars appear to be leaving the sinking ship and concentrating on other subjects. Film studies could be critically cited in this context as well as the recently emerging field of intermediality studies, in which I myself happen to be active. Even though many scholars (including myself) invariably take literature and literary theory as a point of departure, intermediality studies is, to a certain extent, in itself a departure from literary studies. And last but not least, the very fact that a volume such as the present one is dedicated to the question 'why study literature?' can be interpreted as an indication of the loss of the formerly self-explanatory status of our activities.[1] For some time now literary studies have appeared to no longer go without saying: a volume edited in 1996, which was apologetically entitled *Why Literature Matters* (Ahrens and Volkmann, eds.) and included an essay by Wolfgang Iser of the same title (1996), eloquently testifies to this fact. From a cultural-historical point of view, one could even point out that reflections on, and justifications of, a particular field tend to be motivated by the feeling that the objects in this field are about to become extinct.

If one were a pessimist, one could thus be tempted to agree that the dystopian vision of an (almost) literature-free society which Ray Bradbury described more than half a century ago in his novel *Fahrenheit 451* (1954) is fast approaching its realization in today's Western culture. One may even be inclined to say that this is happening without the political pressure eventually exerted in Bradbury's dystopian world – although even there the original development began without government intervention in a hedonistic, technology-oriented mass society (cf. 61). As for the academic

---

1   Moreover, the present book belongs to a whole series of volumes dedicated to the 'defence' or at least discussion of the functions of literature, all of which have appeared over the last few decades (cf. for example Henrich and Iser, eds. 1983; Ahrens and Volkmann, eds. 1996; Miller 2002; Gymnich and Nünning, eds. 2005; *New Literary History* 38.1, 2007; Felski 2008; and Jusdanis 2010).

study of literature, a prophecy Thomas Love Peacock formulated in *The Four Ages of Poetry* in 1820 (a text which triggered P.B. Shelley's *A Defence of Poetry* [1821]), seems to have weirdly come true as well: "[…] the progress of useful art and science […] will continue more and more to withdraw attention from frivolous and unconducive to solid and conducive studies; […] therefore the poetical audience will not only continually diminish in […] its number […], but will also sink lower and lower in the comparison of intellectual acquirement […]" (Peacock 1820/1891, 61). Even if one does not wholly subscribe to such pessimism, a new "Defence of 'Poetry'" (and of its academic study) seems to be the agenda of the day for anyone still interested in literature and wishing to allot it more than the status of a 'cultural orchid'. Such a 'defence' is the purpose of the present contribution, though on a much more moderate and less polemical scale than is the case in Shelley's famous essay.

A defence seems to presuppose an attack. For Shelley's "Defence", it was indeed Peacock's utilitarian hostility towards 'poetry' as voiced in a particular polemical publication, *The Four Ages of Poetry*. Today, it is, however, less a discernible attack or a particular publication which threatens literature and its study but rather a general cultural and media-historical trend. However, in the educational and academic context in focus at present, in particular university departments of philology, there are two areas competing with literature that must be mentioned: these are, first, Cultural Studies, in which literature is at best one among many 'signifying practices', and second, film studies, in which, apart from borrowings from literary theory, literature only figures where original literary texts have become filmicized or literature is part of the represented world. Thus, the question 'why study literature?', in these contexts, can be reformulated as 'why study literature rather than engage in Cultural or Film Studies?'.

In the following, I will bear these competing areas in mind, but would like to begin my defence with a survey of what the study of literature today typically means. I will then discuss some of the generally acknowledged functions of literature[2] which are often used as arguments in answering the question of why literature matters – for the importance of a subject

---

2 Of course, 'function' here means the 'external functions' as specified by Fricke (1997) in opposition to (text) internal functions. Moreover, I here also refer to Sommer's description of 'function' as "Wirkungspotential" ('effect potential', Sommer 2000, 328) without implying that individual functions can empirically be ascertained in each case.

matter is an indispensable basis for the claim that its study should occupy a conspicuous place. While most of these functions are indeed not covered by what is currently investigated in Cultural Studies I will show that even so, many of them can also be related to film. This will bring me to my main point, namely the question: are there sufficient benefits and a functional profile that are more or less exclusive to literature, to such an extent that they could support the claim that it should not only be read by the public at large but also studied on a major scale as part of the educational system and in academia in particular?

'LITERATURE' IN TODAY'S ACADEMIC STUDIES

When one wants to defend literature as a cultural medium and an object of academic research and teaching, one should begin by discussing what literature is in the first place. As we all know, this is an extremely difficult question to answer. 'Literature', seen from a diachronic point of view, is a relatively recent phenomenon[3] (and the same holds true of literary studies). And even when considered from a synchronic perspective focussing on today's view it is well known that most if not all individual qualities of literature can also be attributed to other discourses. Bearing this in mind Todorov, back in 1973, thus ventured to ask: "Could it be [...] that literature does not exist?" (2007 [1973], 12). However, this scepticism is perhaps throwing the baby out with the bathwater. Definition problems are after all common in the humanities and often rest on an inappropriate approach towards the concepts under discussion and on fuzzy notions in particular. Yet most notions of this 'fuzzy type' can be described by means of prototype semantics. This is true both of what literature is and of what functions it typically fulfils.[4] In either case, as we will see, one can obtain a profile of qualities and functions that is typical of literature rather than of any other discourse.

---

3   According to the *Oxford English Dictionary* 'Literature', defined as "Literary productions as a whole; the body of writings produced in a particular country or period, or in the world in general [...] also in a more restricted sense, applied to writing which has a claim to consideration on the ground of beauty of form or emotional effect", dates from 1812 (vol. 8, 1029).

4   For a prototypical approach to literature on the basis of a Wittgensteinian "family resemblance" cf. Hagberg 2007, 164, although he unduly limits his discussion to only one functional feature of literature, namely providing "aesthetic experience of [a] relational kind" (168).

As for the question of defining literature, I cannot go into detail here but will have to restrict myself to mentioning the typical qualities of literature as read and taught at our universities today.

Everyone involved in the teaching of academic introductory courses is familiar with the fact that the kind of literature taught – and perhaps made explicit – in such introductions may be characterized as follows: It is a public verbal medium which uses predominantly print in order to transmit fictional worlds of a high aesthetic quality. This description rests on six criteria:

1. the public use of the medium in question,
2. its verbal nature,
3. its written form of transmission,
4. the fictionality of its content,
5. the representationality, and
6. the aesthetic quality of the texts at hand.

At a closer look, however, the application of each of these criteria seems curiously one-sided and more true of what literature used to be in literary departments than what it is today. After all, there is an increasing awareness that private letters, for example, can become literature, too (1). It is, moreover (2), a topos in performance and intermediality studies that drama as a plurimedial form uses more than just verbal language. As far as the written form of transmission (3) is concerned, it is arguably an exaggeration and not yet applicable to our academic practice to claim with Katherine Hayles that "[l]iterature, in the twenty-first century is computational" (Hayles 2007, 99), yet literature is no longer transmitted exclusively through print media – and actually never was; one may also think of oral literature, on which Walter Ong conducted a renowned research project (cf. 2002 [1982]) and which has increasingly been studied ever since. Concerning the criterion 'fictionality' (4) one must admit that non-fictional texts are by now also studied as literature (since the 1950s there has even been a novelistic genre, the 'non-fiction novel', which sports this fact in its name). And as for representationality (5), it does not apply to texts that have also customarily been read in literature courses such as the predominantly argumentative essays which are to be found in Addison's and Steele's *Spectator*. Last but not least, the aesthetic quality of literature (6) – 'aesthetic' being in itself a historical notion dating from the 18th century – is no longer always a criterion either, for instance when studying popular genres such as Gothic fiction, detective fiction or pop lyrics.

Indeed, over the past few decades, as 'literature' as an academic subject has been considerably modernized (for better or, sometimes, for worse), it has expanded and gone beyond the aforementioned criteria, in fact so much so that the very idea of reading lists containing set, 'classic' texts has frequently been considered as no longer tenable. Some of these developments were already under way in the 1980s, as becomes clear from a comment made by Bob Busby, chairman of the 'Syllabus Review Committee' in David Lodge's satirical campus novel, *Nice Work* (1988):

> It's no use hankering after the good old days, which were actually the boring old days [...] The subject has expanded vastly [...] Now we have linguistics, media studies, American Literature, Commonwealth Literature, literary theory, women's studies, not to mention about a hundred new British writers worth taking seriously [...] (Lodge 1989 [1988], 351).

The topicality of the literature courses emphasized by Lodge's chairman may, on the other hand, in itself be taken as an argument in a defence of today's literary studies as actually no longer exclusively oriented towards an outmoded canon but rather as an academic pursuit in which contemporary authors, the New Literatures in English and fashionable subjects such as race, class and gender loom large.

Yet, in spite of this expansion – some may say, decentering – of what literature used to be, the old centre is still important and dear to many scholars, even though it may by now include postmodern classics such as – in English literature, which I teach – John Fowles' *The French Lieutenant's Woman* (1969) and perhaps Ian McEwan's *Atonement* (2001). In fact, the margins have broadened and the borders have become fuzzier than ever, but the center is still recognizable. For, arguably, a test among philological departments and beyond would reveal that very few people would in fact deny that authors such as Cervantes, Dante, Dostoyevsky, Goethe, Ibsen, Molière, and Shakespeare still represent, in our mental maps, what we conceive of as typical 'literature', literature as it continues to be taught in most philological departments. So, admittedly, the description of the characteristic features of literature given above needs to be relativized but is certainly not obsolete. Consequently, we should at least *also* if not predominantly have this kind of literature in mind when trying to answer the question 'why study literature?'.

MAJOR GENERAL FUNCTIONS OF LITERATURE, AND WHY LITERARY STUDIES CANNOT BE REPLACED BY CULTURAL STUDIES

Literature as a representational art is a culturally evolved activity that fulfils a plethora of functions and provides substantial evolutionary advantages for us as social and meaning-seeking animals, as Brian Boyd has recently argued with reference to narrative in particular (2009).[5] These functions can occur individually or in combination with each other and sometimes overlap. Obviously, a defence of literature as well as of the relevance of literary studies must focus on these functions. However, they have been discussed and variously emphasized by so many authors that individual summaries are hardly possible.[6] Instead, I would like to give a mere survey of literature's most important and generally acknowledged functions or groups of functions. They all hinge on some of the typical features of literature adduced above: besides literature's aesthetic quality these are in particular the features of fictionality and representationality.[7] These features converge in the typical quality of literature to provide a discourse through which fictional possible worlds (which may well be impossible according to everyday standards) are constructed that can be imaginatively experienced and can directly or indirectly represent relevant aspects of reality.

The first group of functions refers to the various possibilities of literature to contribute to our understanding of ourselves and the world and to sharpen

---

5　Boyd's monograph, although flawed by his obvious lack of acquaintance with recent narratology (which he nevertheless severely criticizes; cf. 2009, 384-392) as well as his off-hand dismissal of all religious stories as untrue (cf. 199-206), presents an intriguing evolutionary account of the human fascination with narratives and fictional narratives in particular. He offers one of the most detailed discussions of the various functions served by (narrative) representations and considers these functions to be based on the fact that we are social, curiosity-driven animals which are highly interested in understanding others as well as ourselves, possess an inborn capacity for representation and pretend play, are capable of empathy even with reference to representations owing to our mirror neurons, have a faculty for metarepresentation (the predisposition towards forming a 'theory of mind' about other humans), and moreover tend towards agential causal explanations.

6　Among the manifold publications in the field I would like to mention Henrich and Iser, eds. 1983; Jauß 1977, in particular 25-36; Miller 1990; Ahrens and Volkmann, eds. 1996; Fluck 1997; Gymnich and Nünning, eds. 2005; as well as the contributions to the recent volume of *New Literary History* dedicated to the question "What is literature now?" (vol. 38.1/2007), see also above, note 2.

7　Cf. Todorov 2007, 29: "The aim of literature is to represent human existence [...]".

our cognitive tools for these purposes. These are the *cognitive functions* of literature. Owing to their representational nature, literary works can, for instance, serve as cultural and historical documents of reality, of ways of life, of mentalities, in short of what Iser (in part critically) called "literature as evidence" (1996, 13). Creating evidence of reality may concern the fore-seeable future but mostly refers to the present, including topical themes and occurrences, and the past. This latter aspect highlights the frequently mentioned and indeed paramount function of literature as an agency of cultural memory, which must also be mentioned in this context.

Documenting facts, experience and knowledge about the past and present and storing them are, however, not the only aspects of the cognitive functions of literature. Interpreting the world on a macro- as well as on a micro-scale in order to make us understand it (better) (Todorov 2007, 17) also belongs to this category – and it is at least as important. On a macro-scale this interpretive sub-function can be encountered in the fact that literary works, through the presentation of possible worlds, regularly construct miniature models of (aspects of) reality. This model-building is essential to our understanding, for it permits us to cope with an otherwise bewildering chaos of possible facets of reality by means of selection and complexity reduction[8] (Lotman 1973 [1970], 22; Warning 1983 [1979], 205). Literary miniature models are especially efficient as interpretive tools when they are dynamic: in other words, when they are narratives. For narrative, while being by no means[9] the only macro-frame of literature[9], is arguably not only "the most powerful [...] of ways to assert the basic ideology of [a] culture" (cf. Miller 1990, 72), but generally the most important means by which humans train themselves for social interaction (Boyd 2009, 192), make sense of their existence in time and cope with their awareness of the contingency of life, the constant flux of positive and negative aspects of experience and the transitoriness of their own existence. Consequently, McEwan's character Henry Perowne is, of course, wrong when as part of his aforementioned dismissal of fiction he also objects to the statement "people can't 'live' without stories" (68). He is even clearly shown to be wrong when immediately after he has uttered this McEwan ironically makes him think of his own experiences in terms of a "story" (69).

---

8   However, the effects of this process are still complex enough to render high com-plexity one of the distinctive traits of literary texts, as will be argued below.
9   Argument and description also play a powerful role both in lyrical poetry and in other main forms of literature.

Another important facet of the cognitive macro-scale functions of literature is what Iser, in one of his earlier publications (1975, cf. also 1984, 303), termed 'the balancing function', i.e. the tendency of literature to highlight the lacunae left by existing, and in particular dominant, systems of meaning and thus to contribute to a more complete understanding of certain aspects of reality.[10]

The interpretation of reality provided by literature is also discernible on a micro-scale, in particular with reference to individual concepts, which we constantly use in order to come to terms with reality. Literature has been called a training ground for our faculty to cope cognitively with reality (see Stierle 1975, 366, 385[11]), since it furnishes us with concepts of all kinds and illustrates their meaning – and all of this in texts that tend to be of high complexity and thus present formative challenges to our cognitive faculties. In addition, literature also cognitively functions as an "inter-discourse" or a meta-discourse which can enter into a dialogue with all other human discourses, including literature itself: it can mirror or mimic these discourses, criticize them and generally reflect on them on a meta-level (Nünning 1995 II, 124, 251).

Interpretation as furthered by literature is, however, not merely a cognitive activity focused on abstract concepts; other discourses can do this as well or even better (e.g. philosophy). In the case of literature, interpretation typically goes along with mental representations of possible worlds as imagined realms of readerly experience. Providing this mental dimension is what I would like to call the *experiential and imagination-activating function* of literature. This crucial function also has several facets. One of them could be described as providing us with 'applied knowledge'. The aforementioned model-building function of literature is also shared by the natural sciences, yet the nature of the models differs considerably. Although scientific models, like all models, serve the function of complexity reduction, they mostly remain in the sphere of abstraction and must be 'read', as it were, from the

---

10 Later on Iser reformulated this function and stressed the fact that literature can act as a "perturbing noise" in society (Iser 1996, 16), opening spaces of freedom not occupied by dominant discourses and drawing attention to marginalized ways of looking at and understanding the world. Iser's old balancing function can be re-encountered in Dubreuil's reflections (2007), although he does not seem to be aware of the affiliation, when he claims that "literature enacts theory's cracks" (67) and "gives […] ways of understanding the defects of disciplinary thought" (66).

11 Cf. also Boyd 2009, 130, 190, 192, and Stierle 1983, 181: "Die Fiktion schafft gleichsam Inbegriffe von Schemata der Erfahrung".

outside. Literary world models provide experiential models which, so to speak, one can enter and look at from the inside through imagination and by becoming immersed in them (Ryan 2001), aesthetically illuded (Wolf 1993) or even enchanted (Felski 2008). Already Shelley, in his "Defence of Poetry", attributed this function to literature when he said: "We want the creative faculty to imagine that which we know [...]: our calculations have outrun conception; we have eaten more than we can digest" (1962 [1821], 249). Indeed, putting concepts into imaginable practice and illustrating them with particular cases rather than dealing with them in the abstract and general manner of argumentation is a main feature of literature – be these concepts ethical ones such as justice and love, scientific ones such as entropy and causality or of any other kind. What is more, this putting into practice, since it merely happens in imaginary possible worlds in which we only participate mentally, has the advantage of allowing us harmless experience in "secure situations" (Boyd 2009, 191), exempt from negative consequences which could accompany real life experience and experimentation.

However, literary imagination can become a testing or exploratory ground not only for "that which we know" but also for that which we have not yet thought of,[12] as well as for what we do not know enough about and either have not yet put into practice or dare not put into practice, hoping that it will never occur in reality in the first place. Fantasy literature, science fiction, utopias and dystopias typically fulfil such testing and exploratory functions, and something similar can be said about literature generally enabling us to assume imaginatively the point of view of other people and beings (Todorov 2007, 28). As an extra bonus, literature can develop new or alternative models of reality, thus providing explorations and experience of Otherness in an 'off-line', non-committal way. One may subsume these functions under the rubric of the (world-)*constructive function* of literature as a 'worldmaking' discourse (cf. Goodman 1978) or the potential of literature to elicit "thought experiments" (Boyd 2009, 194) by transcending the here and now.

In addition – and still as a part of this constructive function –, literature, as Todorov recently said, can typically "expand [...] our universe" (2007, 17). It does so by forming a locus of human self-questioning (cf. Delbanco

---

12 To the extent that literature tends to elicit a high degree of imaginative immersion (aesthetic illusion) and can devise and explore worlds never thought of in other discourses, including natural history and science, the literary function of 'experience in action' surpasses the experience provided by non-literary factual texts.

1999, 35) and by providing imaginative experiential explorations of that which is rationally "inscrutable" (Iser 1990, 953), in other words of that about which we will never know anything for sure.[13] According to Wolfgang Iser's literary anthropology (cf. 1984, 1989, 1990), such explorations of what he calls "das Entzogene" (cf. 1984, 305; 'that which is rationally hidden to us') are a vital function of literature and concern 'eternal' themes such as love, our identity and the identity of others, death and how to make sense of the contingency and negativity of life (actually issues which show a remarkable continuity in relevance and in which literature borders on religion). To use Iser's words, literature thus "allows us to conceive what knowledge and [real life] experience cannot penetrate" (1996, 20)[14] and, one may add, what the natural sciences cannot fully penetrate either.

Identity is not only one of the 'inscrutable' phenomena that literature 'enacts' but also a phenomenon created or at least stabilized by literature. In fact, *the contribution to identity formation* also features among the commonly mentioned basic functions of literature. This function extends to both individual and collective identity. As far as individual identity is concerned, it is in the nature of literature to offer us not only representations of facets of what we may think of as our own identity, but also representations of Otherness.[15] An important means of contributing to individual identity is also the invitation many literary works proffer to their recipients to take part in imaginary roleplay and to occupy points of view other than the ones we hold in our everyday lives. This is achieved by virtue of the aforementioned experiential and illusionist dimension of literature, provided it elicits a special form of aesthetic illusion, namely at least partial identification and empathy with fictional characters (cf. Jauß 1977, 227-258).

As for collective identity, the contribution of literature in this respect is frequently based on the aforementioned cognitive function of literature as cultural memory. A presupposition of literature working in this way is the condition that individual texts become acknowledged objects of a community's discourse (in the past, literary studies had an important share in furthering this discursivation). The collective unit of identity for which literature can serve as a stabilizing factor may range from a nation and a

---

13 Cf. also Cochran 2007, 129: "literature's confrontation with the incommensurable".

14 Cf. also Miller 1990, 74: "What cannot be expressed logically [...] we then tell stories about".

15 Cf. Hagberg 2007, 169: "[...] literature [...] is [...] a tool employed for the relational construction of selfhood".

particular class to a group of intellectuals and literary scholars to whom literature also provides part of their identity. With an eye to this contribution to collective identity literature – and the 'classic texts' in particular – can also be said to serve a *social function*,[16] which is stressed by Boyd (2009) from his evolutionary perspective since literature promotes "within-group social cohesion" (199) and alongside its other social benefits for the recipients also provides social status for the story-teller (cf. ibid., 167-169).

Yet another bundle of functions may be subsumed under the term *guiding functions*. These include, but are not restricted to, moral instruction (the Horatian function of *prodesse*). It has been stressed by various authors (e.g. Ahrens and Volkmann, eds. 1992; Gymnich, Nünning eds. 2005; Fludernik 2008) that the guiding function of literature can be particularly strong in matters ethical,[17] but ethics is only one field among many in which literature can provide guidance and orientation. As is well known, literature or 'poetry' can act as "criticism of life" (Arnold 1903 [1880], 5), or in Lotman's terms (1973, 186 ff.), it can work as part of a critical 'aesthetics of opposition' (which may also be linked to the aforementioned Iserian 'balancing function' of literature). In addition to criticism of an existing reality and systems of meaning literature can also support institutions, systems of meaning and so forth and thus sport what Lotman called an 'aesthetics of identity' (Lotman 1973, 186 ff.). The various forms of guidance, philosophical, religious, political, social, ethical and otherwise, and the general potential of literature to give or create meaning in spite of the human awareness or fear of contingency, suffering, death and other negativities, all converge in what in poststructural times has repeatedly – and perhaps overly – been stressed, namely the 'construction of reality'. As we have seen, literature can indeed contribute to such 'construction' in various ways, although not all of reality need therefore be regarded as a construct.

Some of the functions mentioned so far become particularly important for literature to the extent that other institutions or fields of experience do not or no longer fulfil them. In such cases literature assumes what may be

---

16 Cf. Stierle 1975, 385. Obviously, this function is endangered where the importance of generally acknowledged 'classics' fades and gives way to such vast and divergent areas of texts that a common ground which would still allow a dialogue among non-specialists can no longer exist. This is arguably the – problematic – situation in much of today's literary studies.

17 Todorov 2007, 27 even attributes to literature the potential to "give us [...] a new capacity for compassion"; this, of course, is linked with the aforementioned function of literature to provide us with views and perceptions different from our own.

termed a *compensatory function* (cf. Jauß 1977, 25-32). Thus literature can take over ethical instruction where traditional institutions such as schools and churches are felt no longer to carry out this task in a satisfactory or accepted way. The compensations which literature can offer may, however, go substantially beyond this particular case and range from the compensations for deficits perceived in public institutions and systems of meaning to the compensation for personal lacks in the fields of emotional experience, adventure, sociability and so forth. The latter aspect can be related to what literature has often been blamed for doing, namely providing an escape from reality; however, one should acknowledge the fact that escape is not per se always negative or reprehensible.

Finally, it should not be forgotten that one of literature's main functions besides instruction has traditionally been pleasure of various kinds (the Horatian *delectare)*, including indulging in mental games and the manifold possibilities between the Barthesian poles of consumerist *plaisir du texte* and (de)constructive *jouissance* (see Barthes 1973). As a rule, this *entertainment and ludic function* is linked to other functions, notably the experiential and imagination-activating as well as the compensatory functions, and has indeed often been excused by its being subservient to more 'serious' purposes. Yet one should not underrate the pleasure triggered by literature's entertainment function. It can range from the simple interest in the novelty of 'novels' to providing spaces of playful, a-rational and non-utilitarian freedom; it may emerge when literature meets what Iser called the human wish to fictionalize ("Fiktionsbedürfnis" [cf. Iser 1984, 301]) or when it allows exciting immersions into interesting possible worlds and thus triggers a strong, usually emotion-centred aesthetic illusion in the recipients. Among the enjoyments provided by literature one must also, and perhaps above all, count aesthetic pleasure: the satisfaction experienced when reading accomplished, well-wrought verbal art, the ecstasy which can sometimes be felt when one has the chance of appreciating exquisite beauty.

The list of possible functions served by literature which I have just given in my survey is long and certainly not yet complete. It alone may seem sufficient to give a positive answer to the question 'why does it make sense to *read* literature?'. But the question in focus in the present volume, 'why *study* literature?', is not exactly the same thing. Yet this latter question can also only be answered in a positive way – and this is what I am striving at – when the object of the study under discussion is meaningful and worth being investigated. It may be that not all of the aforementioned functions of literature are felt in today's academic studies, yet one can take it for granted that they inform literary studies to a large extent. At any rate, the plethora of functions served by literature, and notably the crucial role literature in a broad sense plays for humans as storytelling animals that ask for meaning, indeed supports the meaningfulness and relevance of literary studies.

Yet, in principle, the same list of functions could also be used for the justification of Cultural Studies if one regarded literature as a central cultural activity. However, in today's Cultural Studies as practised in many departments of English and in particular American studies, literature is no longer accorded such centrality. Rather, under the auspices of Cultural Studies, it has sunk to one signifying practice, one form of representation and one social institution among many.[18] More often than not literature is used in Cultural Studies with respect to one of the cognitive functions only, namely as 'evidence' of something else, in particular of how contemporary social reality is shaped or 'constructed', a question which is often combined with a strong and usually critical emphasis on class, race and gender.[19]

As a consequence, the mostly non-literary objects of Cultural Studies can compete with literature in some but by no means all of the areas mentioned, and the same is true of the respective disciplines. Thus the cultural objects studied under 'cultural' auspices can, for instance, share with literature parts of the aforementioned cognitive functions (e.g. the record keeping function, mostly with reference to short-term cultural memory), the function of stabilizing collective identity as well as private identity through the confrontation with Otherness, and moreover they can participate in the guiding function and in some of the compensatory functions. Yet since the focus of Cultural Studies is neither on representations as triggers of experience and immersion, nor on the mechanisms used by artefacts to activate the imagination, nor on the means of exciting aesthetic pleasure, important literary functions and objects of literary studies tend to escape Cultural Studies. This is particularly discernible with respect to aesthetic functions since aesthetic aspects of artefacts tend to be irrelevant in this context (this is why "close

---

18 In a particularly radical essay on intermediality or rather 'heteromediality', an essay which is explicitly informed by "British Cultural Studies", Jörgen Bruhn, for instance, has recently argued in favour of both "dethron[ing] and demystify[ing] the privileged literary work" and "tear[ing] down the purist idea of 'pure' or 'absolute' music" as basis of intermedial comparison (2010, 231, 233).

19 For a programmatic propagation of Cultural Studies of this type see Grossberg/ Nelson/Treichler, eds. 1992.

readings [...] are [...] not required" any longer [Nelson, Treichler, Grossberg 1992, 3]). There are further aspects that are important for literary studies but less so for a Cultural Studies perspective. This applies to the functions triggered by immersion or aesthetic illusion, such as the stabilization of personal identity and the imaginative expansion of our world-knowledge; it also applies to the interpretive and sense-making functions of literature, notably the effects achieved by means of narratives[20] and generally by textual investigations of the 'inscrutable'.

However, let me make it clear that I do not want to deny Cultural Studies its status as an important field of research and academic training. What I want to say is simply that Cultural Studies focuses in part on other phenomena than literary studies, and therefore literary studies cannot simply be subsumed under, or transformed into, cultural studies (cf. Wolf 1999), as Anthony Easthope once proposed (1991).

QUALITIES AND FUNCTIONS SPECIFIC TO LITERATURE, OR WHAT MIGHT HAPPEN IF *FAHRENHEIT 451* BECAME REALITY?

Even though the foregoing reflections may have made it clear why one should study literature and not relegate it to a sub-branch of Cultural Studies, one major problem has as yet to be dealt with. Most of the functions adduced above as a means of 'justifying literature' and with it literary studies can also be fulfilled by film and could thus also serve to promote film studies – not least because film is also a representational art transmitting stories and thus miniature models of reality. Does this then mean that it would be possible to exchange literary studies for film studies – with no substantial losses incurred and with the benefit of meeting a trend and demand in today's culture? Obviously, if one wants to defend literature in this medial context, one must ask from a media-comparative or 'transmedial' point of view: are there any medial qualities and resulting functions that are specific to literature and that can be used as arguments in answer to the question 'why study literature and not just films?'. In what follows, I will argue that indeed there are such specificities both with respect to degree and kind. All of them rely on the fact that literature is mainly a

---

20 It is revealing in this context that the term 'narrative' as used in Cultural Studies does not necessarily mean a narrative representation as exemplified by novels and plays but a cultural topos such as the myth of the frontier in the history of the westward expansion of Western civilization in the USA.

verbal art and in this differs from all other representational media, which at best use language as one but not as the main medium.

As far as qualities and functions are concerned that are *specific to literature in degree* one may say that there is no other medium in which a similarly high degree of *conceptual complexity* can be achieved in the information transmitted. All media using verbal text share the potential of complexity inherent in language only to the extent that they rely on language. As for pictures, whether static as in painting or dynamic as in film, they can also convey complex information. Yet this information largely also rests on concepts, and these concepts, as a rule, remain in an implicit state as long as they are not linked with, or expressed by, language. In addition, if one concedes that the quantity of information can have an impact on complexity and that this quantity is in turn related to the average reception time required for the deciphering of the information, one must admit that no other medium can compete, in this respect, with a long novel such as Joyce's *Ulysses*; arguably, the degree of complexity in such a novel is higher than in films whose viewing time rarely exceeds one and a half to two hours. Yet literary complexity need not necessarily be linked to quantity of information expressed in textual length or size, as the example of *Ulysses* may induce one to think. Rather, it may also be an effect of suggestive condensation as is typical of poetry in particular (consider the density of meaning of an extremely short poem such as Ezra Pound's "In a Station of the Metro": "The apparition of these faces in the crowd;/Petals on a wet, black bough" [quoted from Ferguson, Salter, and Stallworthy, eds. 2005, 1297]).

If literature indeed possesses a tendency towards a high degree of complexity, some of the functions mentioned in the previous section appear to be specific to literature by degree. One may especially mention, among the cognitive functions, the extent to which literature's complexity allows it to document aspects of reality in detail and exercises or challenges our conceptual expertise, and moreover the degree to which it provides experience and activates the imagination; one may also point out the role of complexity for the construction of multi-faceted, detailed possible worlds and, among the pleasure-inducing functions, the field of aesthetic pleasure, which can also be considerably enhanced by a high degree of complexity.

Moreover, the particular nature of literature as a verbal representational art gives it a specific *inter- and metadiscursive potential*. The fact that, as mentioned above, literature can enter into a dialogue with all other human discourses, mirror them, criticize them and generally reflect on them on a meta-level is actually a faculty in which literature also excels in degree compared with film. Film can, of course, also imitate other discourses, arts and media or comment on them metareferentially, yet where verbal discourses are concerned the best way to do this is, again, through verbal discourse. This is where film is limited since, as the American term for film, 'movie', indicates, it is a medium that predominantly relies on dynamic pictures rather than on language. While the potential of metareference is certainly not alien to film and has indeed increasingly been exploited over the past few decades in this as well as in other media (see Wolf, ed. 2009), filmic self-reflexivity has arguably not reached the depth and extent of self-scrutiny which literature has unfolded over the ages – from Pseudo-Homer's parody of the *Odyssee* in *Batrachomymomachia* (*The Battle between the Frogs and the Mice*) to McEwan's *Saturday*.

The third field in which literature excels in degree is *the extent of the knowledge and experience stored*. In fact one may affirm without exaggeration that literature is the representational medium which possesses the maximum range and historical depth when it comes to specific messages in their original form. The emphasis here is on 'specific messages' or information and on 'original form'. Specific information refers to the fact that literature, owing to its verbal nature, can transmit messages more precisely and in a more detailed way than any other medium, as far as thought and speech representation is concerned. Admittedly, film also uses words but to a lesser extent than literature, which is a much more intensely verbal art (although the visual aspect of course also plays a role in drama). One field where the limitations of film with reference to the representation of language are traditionally said to be especially discernible are the well-known problems film has with the rendering of thoughts, problems which, for example, novels do not have.[21]

Now one could argue that even though film (like all other media beyond literature) may lack specificity as far as the representation of human thought is concerned and generally cannot give language the privileged status that it has in literature, film can nevertheless in principle deal with the same range of human realities as literature. This, however, is perhaps true from

---

21 Drama, in principle, also has difficulties in rendering characters' thoughts but has overcome them through age-old and generally accepted conventions, in particular asides and soliloquies. Film has, of course, also developed devices in this respect but remains much more focused on the (visual) surface of storyworlds than on characters' thoughts.

MEDIALITY

the point of view of synchronic reality, but certainly not from a historical, diachronic perspective. Both literature and film can deal with the past in an unlimited way – as far as the level of the represented is concerned. Yet concerning the level of representation, the substantially different extent of the history of both media becomes obvious. While recorded literature goes back in written form nearly five millennia (considering the earliest Sumerian texts), film hardly has more than a century of media history. This is not a trivial difference, for as we as literary and medial scholars know best, medium is not a mere neutral channel or "hollow pipe" (Ryan 2005, 289) through which information is conveyed. Rather, medial form matters essentially, and it therefore makes a noticeable difference whether information, a representation, or a story is transmitted in its original verbal form, or translated into another language. The difference becomes even more substantial when the translation or transposition is from one medium into another, e.g. from literature to film. Although the *Odyssee* in film may be recognizably similar in content aspects to the *Odyssee* as a verbal epic, both medial versions are obviously not the same thing, differing vastly in poetic, evocative power, subtlety of connotations and so forth.

It is, however, true that literature is certainly not the representational art or medium that can boast the longest history in mankind. Literary scholars must yield the first rank here to painting, in particular petroglyphs. Thus the "carliest creation of art on rock surfaces in Australia" is estimated by art historian Andrew Sayers to go back as far as "somewhere between 30,000 and 50,000 years ago [...] which makes Australia's rock art the oldest continuous art tradition in the world" (Sayers 2001, 13). However, scholars are notoriously uncertain about the exact meaning of the figures discernible on rockart sites, and if they want to go beyond speculation are more or less forced to infer uncertain meaning from later and contemporary stages in Aboriginal art. All of this uncertainty derives, of course, from the lack of verbal records and shows that among all arts and media literature possesses indeed the greatest historical depth with respect to representations that can be read with some accuracy. It is therefore through literature that we can best enter into an at least imaginary dialogue with humans of many different cultures and of ages long before our own. Bearing this in mind one can even claim that one of the aspects of literature which makes it "cultural capital" (Culler 1997, 41) is the fact that it is mankind's largest and deepest cultural memory or, as I have said elsewhere "the greatest store room of human knowledge [wisdom] and experience through the ages" (Wolf 1999, 168). If this is true, it gives special weight to all the functions of literature adduced above, even though many of them are shared by film, and makes literature a special tool "to better understand the world and ourselves" (Todorov 2007, 31).

Besides the two features mentioned in which literature excels in degree, there are some areas in which it is *unique in kind*. As has been repeatedly stressed, literature is the only representational medium that can exclusively rely on language.[22] This has crucial consequences: the language-centred quality of literature enables it to combine abstract ideas with concrete possible worlds in an unparalleled way so that recipients are offered an intellectual and imaginative experience that is not only informative, imagination-activating, world-constructive, identity-forming, guiding, compensatory with respect to various deficiencies, and pleasurable, but above all, *contributive to our making sense of our existence*, and in a unique way at that. It is unique because language is humankind's privileged means of sense-making, but also because the concepts stored in language are an excellent means of evoking memories, representing experience and stimulating thought as well as the imagination. At first sight, one may think that rendering experience in the multimedial way film does is most efficient, as this medium combines language with sound and images. However, to the extent that our awareness of reality relies predominantly on concepts, the imitation, construction or evocation of (a seeming) reality in its acoustic and visual appearance first requires an at least subconscious translation into verbal concepts before one can understand the representation. The verbal, conceptual nature of literature allows it to short-cut this process by immediately presenting the recipients with the respective concepts. This is why 'mere words', notably in poetry, can have such an evocative effect, can trigger emotions as well as reflections, and can appeal even to non-sophisticated recipients as if they were confronted with a condensed and hugely intensified form of reality. The poetry recitals in *Fahrenheit 451* and *Saturday* – which incidentally both refer to Arnold's classic "Dover Beach" – are impressive metareferential illustrations of this specifically literary potential.

However, providing intense, and in particular emotional experience should not be overstressed, since aesthetic complexity, for those who

---

22 This is, of course, not to say that represented drama as a plurimedial artefact does not also rely on other media or channels of communication; yet even in drama, the script can in most cases evoke the corresponding performance better than a film script.

become aware of it, always also acts as an antidote here. Aesthetic over-structuring can be perceived as a covertly metareferential signal marking the artefact status of the respective literary work. Over and above the palpable fact that one is reading a novel or poem or that one is present at a theatrical performance, literary complexity is thus apt to prevent recipients from losing their cognitive distance and becoming entangled in the delusion of a complete immersion into the represented worlds. This is also why in dystopian worlds such as *Brave New World* or *Fahrenheit 451* film appears to be privileged as a mass medium that favours such non-rational near-completeness of immersion, and this is also the reason why in the worlds constructed by these novels literature is suppressed, for it does not so easily allow full immersion and complete evasion. However, the potential to put the metareferential 'brakes' on immersion is at best a quality where literature excels in degree; yet literature is again unique in the concreteness and complexity of the metareferential reflections it is able to elicit. For over and above the option of triggering metareferentiality by implicit showing, it is again the verbal nature of literature which allows it to exploit explicit metareferentiality in the mode of telling in a way unparalleled by other media (as, for instance, postmodernist fiction may illustrate).[23]

Finally, the specificity of literature as a verbal art can also be seen in the fact that at least certain aspects of most works and most aspects of some works – poems as well as, in particular, 'experimental texts' – are virtually *immune to intermedial transposition*, for in them the general medial principle according to which it does not only matter what is being uttered but also how it is uttered is particularly discernible. A good example is Steve Coogan's 2005 film *A Cock and Bull Story,* in my opinion a failed attempt at filmicizing Laurence Sterne's highly experimental novel *Tristram Shandy.* Admittedly, in this film the metatextual self-reflexivity of Sterne's novel has been transposed into metafilmic self-reflexivity. Yet the specific literary metareferentiality and general quality of Sterne's text, both as far as the simulated orality and the foregrounding of the materiality of the written medium are concerned, have apparently proved immune to intermedial transposition. Indeed, how could one ever transpose the typographical devices used by Sterne into film or, to come back to lyric poetry, a sonnet

---

23 It is therefore no coincidence that the theory of metareferentiality (mostly using the term 'metafiction') has predominantly been developed within literary studies (for the transmedial nature of metareference and the position of literature and literary studies in it see Wolf, ed. 2009, and Wolf 2009, 3-6 in particular).

by Shakespeare with its metrical and semantic intricacies or even shaped poetry like George Herbert's "Easter Wings"?[24]

Ex negativo, the medial specificities of literature could also be summarized by the question: what would happen if Ray Bradbury's dystopian world as depicted in *Fahrenheit 451* really came true and society relied more or less exclusively on film and TV (or computer-generated Virtual Realities for that matter)? For a start, the individual, private reception of texts largely escaping the control of governments and other institutions would be substantially jeopardized and with this the formation and *support of individuality* at large. Written literature, as it has been read over the past few centuries, both through its form of transmission and its contents, is in fact better able to support individualism than any other medium. As for the form of transmission of literature which is currently most typical, namely print, it allows readers to enjoy uncontrolled reception at an individual pace and a freedom from sophisticated technical support unparalleled by any other medium. As far as the various contents of literature are concerned, they can always have a covertly subversive, non-conformist tinge, since literature forms a vast storehouse of texts from many different cultures and cannot be controlled by virtually any institution. It is true that films and the internet have also acquired dimensions that more or less escape, for example, government control, and that on the other hand attempts at imposing censorship on literature existed in the past and still exist. Yet, arguably, the relative independence of the reception of printed texts from all mechanical devices and the possibility of reading them in nearly any place is an undeniable advantage which only printed literature has – and which can be used for emancipatory purposes. In Bradbury's novel even the dependence on the printed medium is minimized in the 'hobo camp' society of intellectual outsiders who still love literature, since here individuals learn texts by heart in order to ensure the continuity of cultural memory independently of the hazards of textual materiality. They thus try to preserve the contents as well as the individual forms of the literary storehouse of world-knowledge and wisdom for a future society, a society less hedonistically and technologically oriented than the one depicted as dominant in *Fahrenheit 451*. At any rate,

---

24 In order to prevent misunderstandings I hasten to add that I do not claim here that literature is the medium which most resists intermedial transposition; I merely use resistance to such transposition as evidence of the fact that literature possesses some specific qualities that are unique to it; with reference to other qualities something similar could, of course, be said of other media as well.

a world without literature that relies in particular on electronic media – as prefigured to a certain extent in Bradbury's novel – would be in greater danger of succumbing to control; and in such a world it would be easier to produce and reproduce streamlined personalities, while suppressing Otherness and nonconformism.

It would also be a society in which the *cognitive functions* of the media could be *reduced* to streamlined information on, and interpretations of, reality, if information is not bracketed off altogether in favour of propaganda or cheap entertainment. Such potential impoverishment could also affect cultural memory and the confrontation with Otherness. This in turn could result in the loss of an important potential for emancipation which literature possesses as a result of all the innumerable alternatives stored in its rich mega-library. These alternatives can activate critical individual thought and tend to support hedonistic consumerist passivity and uniformity less than film (like) media – as illustrated *ex negativo* in *Fahrenheit 451*.

As far as the experiential function of literature is concerned, a world without literature relying exclusively on film or film-like virtual reality-creating media could easily be in danger of intensifying experientiality to the point of creating illusions that become *delusions* by forcing recipients to totally immerse themselves in the represented worlds, thus depriving them more or less of the possibility of taking a rationally distanced point of view. Another dystopia could here also be invoked, namely Aldous Huxley's *Brave New World* (1931). In this world, 'feelies', which uncannily anticipate perfect Virtual Realities, play a role parallel to the happiness-inducing drug 'soma', while the reading of Shakespeare becomes a subversive activity, not only because of the non-conformist world and norms Shakespeare's texts stage in comparison to the dystopian reality but also because literature fosters an imagination which is almost by definition transgressive since it frequently goes beyond the known and the apparently possible.

Even if dystopian perspectives of a world without literature as depicted in *Brave New World* and *Fahrenheit 451* may seem exaggerated, the tendencies they adumbrate may still create sufficiently bleak outlooks to persuade anyone that a world *with* literature is highly preferable to one where literature has been forgotten or has become so marginalized that only a tiny group of insignificant specialists are dealing with it any longer. Today, such a situation no longer seems so remote. Already in our world the 'pictorial turn' announced by J.W. Mitchell in 1995 (cf. 1995, 11 ff.) can be felt to be increasingly gaining momentum, creating a society ever more reliant on pictures and visual (or indeed multi-sensory) input rather than on verbal information. As a consequence, some critics fear that substantial human faculties linked to the reading of complex and long texts are less cultivated than before. Pictures, in particular those produced by the mass media, are more overwhelming than texts, seem treacherously easy to understand and do not invite individual imagination and reflection as much as complex representational texts do, while at the same time being much more ambiguous than verbal artefacts. Pictures, in particular when bombarding the viewers at an increasing speed (as appears from the history of filmic frames and the genre of the video clip) may indeed, as is often said, deprive recipients of the chance to develop the faculty of creating and observing long-term coherence and maintaining critical distance in favour of a rapid scanning of highly immersive visual information of which coherence and translatability into rational discourse and reflection is no longer expected. The current complaints about the substantially decreasing faculty of students to write logically coherent and theme-centred essays of some length and depth may illustrate the point and show what is already happening to a generation which has been exposed to visual and computer transmitted information to a hitherto unknown degree, while at the same time the willingness and ability to focus on reading in particular long and complex literary texts seems to be decreasing even among students of philological departments.

CONCLUSION: LITERATURE AS AN IRREPLACEABLE MEDIUM AND LITERARY STUDIES AS AN EQUALLY IRREPLACEABLE RESEARCH AND EDUCATIONAL INSTITUTION?

To conclude: the dystopian and culture-pessimistic scenario which I have just drawn may be exaggerated, and it may convincingly show the benefits of literature to the converted only, to whom such preaching is unnecessary anyway. Nevertheless, I trust that the arguments outlined in this essay will justify the conclusion that literature is in fact an irreplaceable medium (as irreplaceable as, for example film is, albeit in other ways) and that consequently the same irreplaceability may apply to literary studies (as well as to film studies and other disciplines, including, of course, the natural sciences).

As we have seen, most of the individual functions which literature fulfils can also be served by other means and media, yet not all of them to the same extent, and certainly there is no other medium that can combine all of these functions and create the uniquely rich profile provided by literature. Literature or 'poetry' is an old medium, yet it has never been the only medium of representation, the visual medium having existed alongside it throughout all of its history. In more recent times ever more representational media – and with film a particularly powerful and influential medium – have emerged, and this has no doubt reduced the relative importance of literature to an increasingly discernible extent. Yet, as media history teaches us, the emergence of new media hardly replaces old media but rather leads to a reconfiguration of a more diversified medial landscape. In this landscape literature will continue to occupy a conspicuous position, for as a verbal art (and not only in the narrow sense which has been in use since the 18th century) it is such a unique cultural achievement of mankind that a world without it would be almost inconceivable – and it would certainly be substantially impoverished.

While literature in a broad sense seems in fact to be irreplaceable, literary studies at first sight appear to be a different matter – hence the question mark at the end of the title of this section. Literary studies, in particular studies centred on national literatures, date back to the 19th century and are thus a relatively recent phenomenon. We all know that academic subjects and educational structures are constantly evolving so that a given state of affairs is always transitory. However, we also know that the differentiation of subjects and disciplines in our societies seems to go in the direction of ever more specialization rather than in the reverse direction, and it is moreover clear that the institutionalization of the research and teaching of discourses contributes to the preservation of cultural memory and cultural techniques. Literature in itself is in principle independent of its study – it has emerged without it, and in spite of certain interrelations between study and practice, has to a large extent and for most of its history existed in a separate realm: the realm of imaginative creation, which is different from the realm of rational academic discourse. In this context one may recall a warning which the great Shakespeare scholar Wolfgang Clemen once gave to 'the literary scholar who attempts to comprehend artworks with scholarly methods [and] attempts to approach by rational means what is essentially irrational'.[25] Literary studies, even when not downright nuisible to literature, as has been claimed with an eye to (post-) modernist practices in literary departments (cf. Delbanco 1999), certainly have their limits when it comes to promoting their object literature. Yet

---

25 "[...] der Literaturwissenschaftler versucht, ein Gebilde der Kunst mit wissenschaftlichen Methoden zu erfassen, einem in seinem Kern irrationalen Phänomen mit rationalen Mitteln nahezukommen" (Clemen 1983, 18).

this does not mean that these studies, if conducted in a sensible way, are not a highly valuable means of providing frameworks for the preservation (and sometimes also re-discovery) of literary texts as well as for providing keys to the understanding of literature without which much would remain obscure. Literary studies are also an important means of preserving awareness and knowledge of older texts in particular – thereby contributing to cultural memory – and they are, or ought to be, instruments that help to select what merits being kept in the active, working memory of a culture and what can be permitted to recede into more remote and passive areas of the cultural storehouse.

All of this renders it at least probable that literary studies in one form or another will continue to exist. Whether this will happen in the present institutional or departmental framework (as the study of English as opposed to French, German, or South African literature, etc.) is a different matter. Yet given the cultural importance and in many respects uniqueness of literature as a human discourse, and an intellectual, emotional and imaginative resource, literary studies should continue to play a role in education on all levels in some form.[26] It is the prime task of literary educators – and one of society at large – to guarantee that the ability not merely to read literature but also to appreciate it and its cultural contexts, conventions, devices and other conditions of understanding it is handed down to future generations. If everything else fails, this should suffice for answering the question why one should continue to study literature – not as an orchid discipline but on a large scale. Thus the actual question is not whether literary studies are irreplaceable – of course, they could be replaced or even vanish altogether – but whether in our present cultural framework we would consider replacing or abolishing them a good idea. When put in this way I hope that it will not only be literary scholars selfishly intent on preserving their own discipline along with their posts and chairs who will argue that, given the present organization of our culture, literary studies ought *not* to be abolished nor be replaced by other studies – neither on

---

26 After what has been said, Todorov's seemingly old-fashioned trust in literature may no longer appear so outmoded, when he asks rhetorically: "What better introduction to the understanding of human behavior and passions than an immersion in the works of great writers who have been working on that task for thousands of years? And, at the same time, what better preparation for the many professions that deal with the relations among people, with the behavior of individuals and groups?" (2007, 31).

the level of secondary and tertiary education nor on the level of university research, but rather it should coexist with other disciplines including film and cultural studies as well as, of course, the natural sciences. Literary studies deals with only one perspective on reality among many, but it is one which enriches our worldview in a particular way. I therefore trust that those who may be tempted to answer the question 'why study literature?' cynically with 'why indeed?' will not be those who will direct our cultural future. The obvious question to be raised in the wake of 'why study literature?' would be 'what kind of literary studies should be pursued?' – but answering this question would be quite a different story.[27]

One final point should be emphasized here: in the long run literary studies will only be able to justify its existence if it remains distinguishable from other disciplines, in particular from Cultural Studies. One of the most obvious ways of ensuring this is for literary scholars (to continue) to focus on verbal texts as aesthetic constructs of a particular quality requiring a particular approach (cf. Mahler 2010); this focus will often include but also go beyond a culturalist approach in which literature is merely or exclusively regarded as evidence of some cultural facets and developments for which other discourses can provide evidence as well.[28]

REFERENCES

Ahrens, Rüdiger and Laurenz Volkmann, eds. 1996. *Why Literature Matters.* Anglistische Forschungen 241. Heidelberg: Winter.

Arnold, Matthew. 1903 [1880]. The Study of Poetry. In Matthew Arnold. *Essays in Criticism: Second Series*, 1-55. London: Macmillan.

Austen, Jane. 1972 [1813]. *Pride and Prejudice*, ed. Tony Tanner. Harmondsworth: Penguin.

Barthes, Roland. 1973. *Le Plaisir du texte.* Collection Tel Quel. Paris: Seuil.

Boyd, Brian. 2009. *On the Origin of Stories: Evolution, Cognition, and Fiction.* Cambridge, London: Belknap Press of Harvard University Press.

Bradbury, Ray. 1954 [1953]. *Fahrenheit 451.* Frogmore: Panther.

---

27 Something similar could be said about the study of literature in comparison to the study of the natural sciences, to which I have occasionally alluded; this issue would in fact also merit more attention, but would have exceeded the frame of the present essay.

28 I would like to thank Nicholas Scott for a proof reading of, and critical thoughts concerning, the present paper as well as Jutta Klobasek-Ladler for expert help with the editorial side of the manuscript.

Bruhn, Jörgen. 2010. Heteromediality. In *Media Borders, Multimodality and Intermediality*, ed. Lars Elleström, 225-236. Houndmills, Basingstoke: Palgrave Macmillan.

Clemen, Wolfgang. 1983. Der Leser und die Grenzen der Literaturwissenschaft. In *Interpretationen zur Englischen Literatur. Studien zur Englischen Literatur 2*, eds. Dieter Mehl and Wolfgang Weiß, 17-27. Münster, Hamburg: Lit.

Cochran, Terry. 2007. The Knowing of Literature. *New Literary History* 38.1: 127-143.

Coetzee, J.M. 2000 [1999]. *Disgrace*. London: Vintage.

Culler, Jonathan. 1997. *Literary Theory: A Very Short Introduction*. Oxford, New York: Oxford University Press.

Delbanco, Andrew. 1999. The Decline and Fall of Literature. *The New York Review of Books*, November 4: 32-38.

Dubreuil, Laurent. 2007. What Is Literature's Now? *New Literary History* 38.1: 43-70.

Easthope, Anthony. 1991. *Literary into Cultural Studies*. London/New York, NY: Routledge.

Felski, Rita. 2008. *Uses of Literature*. Malden/Oxford: Blackwell.

Ferguson, Margaret, Mary Jo Salter and Jon Stallworthy, eds. 2005. *The Norton Anthology of Poetry*. Fifth edition. New York: Norton.

Fluck, Winfried. 1997. *Das kulturelle Imaginäre. Eine Funktionsgeschichte des amerikanischen Romans 1790-1900*. Suhrkamp-Taschenbuch Wissenschaft 1279. Frankfurt a. M.: Suhrkamp.

Fludernik, Monika. 2008. Ethik des Strafens – Literarische Perspektiven. In *Bausteine zu einer Ethik des Strafens: Philosophische, juristische und literaturwissenschaftliche Perspektiven*, eds. Hans-Helmuth Gander, Monika Fludernik and Hans-Jörg Albrecht, 213-231. Würzburg: Ergon.

Fricke, Harald. 1997. Funktion. In *Reallexion der deutschen Literaturwissenschaft. Neubearbeitung des Reallexikons der deutschen Literaturgeschichte*, ed. Klaus Weimar, 643-646. Vol. 1. A-G. Berlin: de Gruyter.

Goodman, Nelson. 1978. *Ways of Worldmaking*. Indianapolis: Hackett.

Grossberg, Lawrence, Cary Nelson and Paula A. Treichler, eds. 1992. *Cultural Studies*. London, New York: Routledge.

Gymnich Marion and Ansgar Nünning, eds. 2005. *Funktionen von Literatur: Theoretische Grundlagen und Modellinterpretationen*. Studien zur Englischen Literatur- und Kulturwissenschaft 16. Trier: Wissenschaftlicher Verlag Trier.

Hagberg, Garry L. 2007. Imagined Identities: Autobiography at One Remove. *New Literary History* 38.1: 163-181.

Hayles, N. Katherine. 2007. Intermediation: The Pursuit of a Vision. *New Literary History* 38.1: 99-125.

Henrich, Dieter and Wolfgang Iser, eds. 1983. *Funktionen des Fiktiven*. Poetik und Hermeneutik 10. Munich: Fink.

Iser, Wolfgang. 1975. Die Wirklichkeit der Fiktion. Elemente eines funktionsgeschichtlichen Textmodells der Literatur. In *Rezeptionsästhetik: Theorie und Praxis*, ed. Rainer Warning, 277-324. UTB 303. Munich: Fink.

– 1984. Anglistik. Eine Universitätsdisziplin ohne Forschungsparadigma?. *Poetica* 16: 276-306.

- 1989. *Prospecting: From Reader Response to Literary Anthropology*. Baltimore: Johns Hopkins University Press.
- 1990. Fictionalizing: The Anthropological Dimension of Literary Fictions. *New Literary History* 21.4: 939-955.
- 1996. Why Literature Matters. In Ahrens and Volkmann, eds. 1996: 13-22.

Jauß, Hans Robert. 1977. *Ästhetische Erfahrung und literarische Hermeneutik I*. UTB 692. Munich: Fink.

Jusdanis, Gregory. 2010. *Fiction Agonistes: In Defence of Literature*. London: Eurospan.

Lodge, David. 1989 [1988]. *Nice Work*. Harmondsworth: Penguin.

Lotman, Jurij M. 1973 [1970]. *Struktura chudožestvennogo teksta*. Moscow. *Die Struktur des künstlerischen Textes*, ed. Rainer Grübel. Frankfurt a.M.: Suhrkamp.
- 1972. *Vorlesungen zu einer strukturalen Poetik*, ed. K. Eimermacher. Munich: Fink.

McEwan, Ian. 2006 [2005]. *Saturday*. London: Vintage.

Mahler, Andreas. 2010. Performing Arts: 'New Aestheticism' and the Media. *Arbeiten aus Anglistik und Amerikanistik* 35.1: 101-120.

Miller, J. Hillis. 1990. Narrative. In *Critical Terms for Literary Study*, eds. Frank Lentricchia and Thomas McLaughlin, 66-79. London/Chicago: University of Chicago Press.
- 2002. *On Literature. Thinking in Action*. London, New York: Routledge.

Mitchell, W.J. Thomas. 1995. *Picture Theory: Essays on Verbal and Visual Representation*. Chicago, London: University of Chicago Press.

Nünning, Ansgar. 1995. *Von historischer Fiktion zu historiographischer Metafiktion*. Literatur – Imagination – Realität. 11. Trier: Wissenschaftlicher Verlag Trier. 2 vols.

Ong, Walter. 2002 [1982]. *Orality and Literacy: The Technologizing of the Word*. New York: Routledge.

The Oxford English Dictionary. 1989. J.A. Simpson and E.S.C. Weiner, eds. 2nd edition. Oxford: Clarendon.

Peacock, Thomas Love. 1891 [1820]. The Four Ages of Poetry. In P.B. Shelley. *A Defence of Poetry*, ed. Albert S. Cook. Boston.

Pope, Alexander. 1963 [1733-34]. *An Essay on Man*. In Alexander Pope. *The Poems: A one-volume edition of the Twickenham text*, ed. John Butt, 501-547. London: Methuen.

Ryan, Marie-Laure. 2001. Narrative and Virtual Reality: Immersion and Interactivity in Literature and Electronic Media. Baltimore/London: Johns Hopkins.
- 2005. Media and Narrative. In *The Routledge Encyclopedia of Narrative Theory*, eds. David Herman, Manfred Jahn and Marie-Laure Ryan, 288-292. London: Routledge.

Sayers, Andrew. 2001. *Australian Art*. Oxford History of Art. Oxford: Oxford University Press.

Shakespeare, William. 1997. *The Norton Shakespeare*, ed. Stephen Greenblatt. New York: Norton.

Shelley, P.B. 1962 [1821]. A Defence of Poetry. In *English Critical Texts: 16th to 20th Century*, eds. D.J. Enright and Ernst de Chickera, 225-255. London: Oxford University Press.

Sommer, Roy. 2000. Funktionsgeschichten: Überlegungen zur Verwendung des Funktionsbegriffs in der Literaturwissenschaft und Anregungen zu seiner terminologischen Differenzierung. *Literaturwissenschaftliches Jahrbuch* 41: 319-341.

Stierle, Karlheinz. 1975. Was heißt Rezeption bei fiktionalen Texten? *Poetica* 7: 345-387.

– 1983. Die Fiktion als Vorstellung, als Werk und als Schema. Eine Problemskizze, ed. Henrich and Iser, 173-182.

Todorov, Tzvetan. 2007 [1973]. The Notion of Literature. *New Literary History* 18. Rpt., transl. by Lynn Moss/Bruno Braunrot. *New Literary History* 38.1: 1-12.

– 2007. What Is Literature For? *New Literary History* 38.1: 13-32.

Warning, Rainer. 1983 [1979]. Pour une pragmatique du discours fictionnel. *Poétique* 39: 321-337. Der inszenierte Diskurs. Bemerkungen zur pragmatischen Relation der Fiktion, eds. Henrich and Iser 1983: 183-206.

Wolf, Werner. 1993. *Ästetische Illusion und Illusionsdurchbrechung in der Erzählkunst: Theorie und Geschichte mit Schwerpunkt auf englischem illusionsstörenden Erzählen*. Tübringen: Niemeyer.

– 1999. Literary and, or, into cultural studies or vice versa? Reflections on two discursive fields and their missing link in English Studies. In *Crossing Borders: Interdisciplinary Intercultural Interaction*, eds. Bernhard Kettemann and Georg Marko, 161-176. Tübingen: Narr.

– 2009. Metareference across media: The concept, its transmedial potentials and problems, main forms and functions. Wolf, ed. 2009: 1-85.

– ed. 2009 in collaboration with Katharina Bantleon and Jeff Thoss. *Metareference across Media: Theory and Case Studies – Dedicated to Walter Bernhart on the Occasion of his Retirement*. Studies in Intermediality 4. Amsterdam, New York: Rodopi.

MEDIALITY AND LITERATURE

LITERATURE VERSUS LITERATURE

Morten Kyndrup

The Modern history of the development of the interrelationship between individual medialities and levels of inter- or trans-mediality is very complex. There are many reasons for this. One of them is the fact that a fair number of standard explanations, the *idees reçus* of this story, on closer examination turn out to be more or less ideologically biased and often even substantially counterfactual. This holds true all the way down to the very term "medium", which presupposes the idea of "something" being mediated, and which thereby seems to ignore the materiality of mediality itself on a very basic level – as if this materiality were detachable from the engendering of "meaning".[1]

As a consequence, literature's specific and somewhat peculiar position among medialities and art forms can by no means be described in few words. However, it is possible to highlight a couple of key events which have had and continue to have a significant influence on the formation of this specific position. One of these would be modernity's inclusion of what had hitherto been conceived of as the arts (in the plural), into one "Art as such" divided into art forms. This conceptual change was fully realized during the eighteenth century and from then on it has made sense to conceive of the art forms as vehicles which in different ways express the "same"; hence the collective singular "art". This "same" might take the shape of a principle (Batteux 1746), or may become the backdrop for directly discussing the art forms comparatively (Lessing 1766). The singular art forms thus became and have remained different roads to or expressions of the "same", that is, art as such, including and emphasizing art's increasing autonomy, its elevated aura, its exposure of a privileged ("aesthetic") experience. This process tied

---

1 This is one of the reasons why we make use of the term "mediality" and not just "medium" in this context. Where substantial impacts of media's material constitution are concerned, see in general the work of Friedrich Kittler, for instance (Kittler 1995).

the art forms together in a historically new way, which in turn rapidly gave rise to a complex and often subtle division of labour among them. Each art form now became simultaneously understood in terms of its distinct "difference" and as a part of the same "same".

Another key event was Romanticism's elevation of literature to a distinctively privileged position amongst the art forms starting in the beginning of the nineteenth century. Not only did literature become the indisputably highest ranking art form; it was assigned this position with explicit reference to its cognitive potential, being the art form which – in Hegel's words – had liberated itself from the surface and the sensuous ("das äusserlich-sinnliche"). In other words, literature is here defined as the art form capable of reproducing the truth about the essence of things most purely, uninfected by the superficial temptations of the senses (Hegel 1986, 123).

This privileging of poetry has had institutional consequences up to our own time. First of all, literature became the central *Bildungsdisziplin* in the school system, which ensured literature had an important role in the paradigm of philology, both in its mother tongue appearances and in the ones dealing with foreign languages. Furthermore literature's epistemic privilege as compared to other art forms places it considerably closer to aesthetics (in the latter's sense of "philosophy of art"). An illustrative example could be the chair of aesthetics at Copenhagen University, which was for long periods automatically given to poets.[2] We still see the result of this today as a clear feature of the landscape of the humanities at the universities: in Denmark, for instance, we have a quantitatively overwhelming dominance of literary scholars. We have strong and active literary departments both in the national language (Danish/Nordic) and in foreign languages, in addition to strong departments of comparative literature. This situation is more or less the same in all of the countries with which we normally compare ourselves.

THE CENTRIFUGALITY OF LITERARY STUDIES

Historically, the specific combination of the distinctive function of literary studies with this heavy dominance where quantity is concerned has had

---

2   A chair of Aesthetics was installed at University of Copenhagen already in 1788, and was occupied among others by the Danish "national poet" Adam Oehlenschläger from 1810. On the transformation of aesthetics through its "marriage" with Art from early Romanticism and on, see Kyndrup 2005 or more extensively (in Danish) my book on the aesthetic relation (Kyndrup 2008).

a peculiar impact on the main paths of development taken by these studies in the Western world. On the one hand, the overwhelming quantity of literary scholars has led to a constant centrifugal movement away from the discipline. Paul de Man once maliciously remarked that departments of literature had grown into "large organizations in the service of everything except their own subject matter", since the study of literature had become the art of applying disciplines such as psychology, politics, or history to the literary text (de Man 1986). However, this dynamic of centrifugality has also been fruitful in the sense that literary departments and literary scholars have become the founding fathers (and mothers) of an important series of theoretical and paradigmatic innovations and expansions which have proved important to the humanities since the mid 20th century. This applies to specific trends such as cultural studies, postcolonial studies, and gender (including feminist) studies. The same holds true for more general theoretical currents such as reception theory/aesthetics as well as specific innovations within the broader arts studies area (for example, the new art history and interarts studies). All of these currents have literary studies and/ or scholars amongst their distinctive preconditions.

On the other hand, and perhaps paradoxically, this same plenitude and inspirational pregnancy of literary studies has generally speaking led to surprisingly little focus on literature itself in the sense of attention to the mediality of literature and its specific capabilities. The trend of centrifugal emigration as such cannot account for this; rather, this emigration should itself be seen as one of the consequences of this lack of focus on literary mediality. The cause is above all to be sought in the very concept of literature which had led to the privileged status assigned it by Romanticism. Because literature has been attributed distinct capabilities with regard to truth content, an emphasis on the form/content dichotomy has arisen. Literature became and has remained the art form within which the artist as *homo significans* has been celebrated most unambiguously – to the extent that the fact of possessing outstanding writing skills is no longer considered a decisive precondition for becoming a great writer. What you have to express is far more important. The study of literature's mediality in itself – at the universities as well as in the school system – has for a long time been considered a kind of impertinent insult to the elevated status of literature, and so-called formalist studies of literature have throughout the discipline's history generally had a hard time finding resources and institutional support.

Attempts have been made over and over again, especially over the last fifty years, to have it out with the constitutionally low priority given to literature within literary studies. Paradoxically enough, however, many of these uprisings rapidly merged with the centrifugal current and were thus exported to neighbouring fields and the meta-disciplines (to which they brought unquestionable advantages). Furthermore these attempts have not really been able to alter the anatomy of literary studies in terms of their role in public cultural life. Here themes, convictions, and truths have remained at the centre of attention. Consequently, scholars whose work focuses on these levels of meaning are still most prominent in public life.

WHAT IS LITERATURE?

Thus concludes a rough sketch of the reasons for the specific position and institutional history of literature and literary studies. The question "Why study literature?" might of course be answered in brief: because literature exists and plays a significant role in the processes of engendering meaning in our society, both historically and currently. But as we have seen by now, an additional answer might be: because literature has actually been studied far too little, or at least has been studied too little as literature. Maybe we should start over again by asking "What *is* literature?". This question might then be considered along a series of transmedial parameters or phenomenal axes, which could also be used in relation to other medialities, thereby revealing their similarities and differences in relation to literature. Such a discussion might also contribute to answering the question about whether the distinctive institutional position of literature might have causes other than the historical factors mentioned above. And furthermore it might even help to clarify the issue of how intermediality as a research topic might be relevant and interesting.

In the following analysis, I shall – tentatively and anything but exhaustively – examine literature in relation to the following parameters: time, space (including beholder's position), sign system, fictionality and mode of speech.

TIME

Literature is a time-based – a sequence-based-medium. It engenders meaning in the course of time. Literary meaning can never be grasped in one moment; neither can it be recalled or reproduced in terms of one moment. Any real mental reconstruction of a work of literature will in one way or another have to repeat or include the specific sequential course of the work. It must take into consideration the proper course of time char-acteristic of that particular work of literature. Any work of literature we experience unfolds and inscribes its own "time" into our time, and does so in a specific, complex and crucial way (as described among others by Paul Ricœur (1985, esp. t. III, 329ff)): A work of literature is a loop in our time which, while it possesses its own time, is nonetheless still inscribable in our mortal time (the one with a past, a present and a future), which in turn is inserted into the universal flow of time. The time-loop installed by a work of literature may itself reveal a diversity of layered or embedded time levels (for instance, by referring to various fictitious spaces). But in any case, the literary work establishes its own time at the very level of its technical engendering of meaning sign by sign – and thus through its concrete perception by each specific receiver.

Literature shares this property of sequentiality with theatre, film, music and dance. The time loop of the fictive also characterizes film, while it is not a property of theatre (real time perception). Visual arts such as painting, sculpture, or architecture do not unfold over the course of time at all.

SPACE

Now to space and the receiver's position: Literature is not a performance art form like theatre or music; it is a non-performance art along with painting, sculpture and film. However, it differs from these art forms in that it does not share any real world space with its beholder. Painting and sculpture both include their beholder in the real space of the existence of a given work as do both film and the performing arts to varying degrees. But literature? If any written text could be seen as implicitly referring to an original oral speech act, one might talk about some kind of indirect sharing of space. However, this is not the case; written texts have long since become an independent medium. Reading a text aloud today automatically consigns the oral level to the function of representing the written text, i.e. as being ontologically secondary.

The perception of literature is exclusively individual (when read): litera-ture is normally experienced neither collectively nor simultaneously. This is a huge difference relative to both the performing arts (theatre, music, dance) and the visual arts, which may be experienced in shared spaces with other spectators. (This is also a natural option for film, obviously).

Literature does not engage several senses directly (indirectly of course it does, but this is another story). Most other medialities (with the exception of music) are obviously multi-sensuous. While a work of literature does unfold a kind of "space", it is a very special one which does not resemble any other known space. We will come back to that later.

SIGN SYSTEM

In relation to sign systems, it is useful to recall Nelson Goodman's distinction between autographic and allographic arts (or medialities) (Goodman 1972, 95ff). *Autographic* art forms are those in which the work of art is characterized by displaying traces of the artist's proper work at the level of appearance, i.e. at the level of the sign. Painting, sculpture and other visual arts are the fundamental examples. The performing arts may also be "autographic" with respect to the performer. *Allographic* art forms, on the other hand, are constituted by conventional signs that do not bear physical traces of the artist's work at the level of the sign. No copy of Defoe's *Robinson Crusoe* or of the musical score of Beethoven's Fifth Symphony or of the text to Beckett's play *Fin de Partie* can have more authenticity or reality than any other copy (providing that the copy in question is correctly copied). Defoe's handwritten manuscript is in no sense closer to being the authentic work of art than any other copy of the novel would be. Conversely, a reproduction of Picasso's *Les Demoiselles d'Avignon* has absolutely no value as an authentic artwork (and forging it would constitute a serious criminal act). In short, autographic artworks can be forged; allographic artworks cannot.

Literature is an allographic art form. Any writer would love copies of his work to be spread around the world. Furthermore, the sign system of literature is the same one we make use of in most of our everyday communication: verbal language. This means, firstly, that any trained language user – all are, at least within our native languages – connects every conventional signifier with its signified almost automatically, decoding the signs immediately. Secondly, this means that when any such "signified" belongs to a work of literature, thus forming part of this work's world – signifying through the world of the work – the signifier activates the recipient's archive of real-world signifieds at the same time. As a consequence, literature unavoidably produces a kind of double representational effect that reaches all the way down to the micro level of individual words. The work of literature is unable to escape directing its reader out of the world of the work, while of course it continually directs him into it as well. This is a very distinctive feature of literature (which is shared by other language-based art forms such as theatre). If we turn to another allographic art form such as (written) music, no such effect of double referentiality occurs. No single note "D" has any direct reference whatsoever to the real world; only through its dynamic effects within the work's specific framework is it capable of engendering musical "meaning".

FICTIONALITY

When it comes to mode and status of "fictionality", literature once again holds a distinct position. Literature creates pictures/representations in the shape of "worlds". But these worlds are described worlds: they have their own times, own spaces, sign systems, inhabitants, beholders – and even their own fictions (with their own times, own spaces, sign systems, inhabitants, etc.). These worlds may look exactly like the one we live in and call our "real world", but they may also differ, from a tiny twist to an all-encompassing displacement of rules, times and ways of behaving. At all events, any literary world appears to us as a world of its own, directing us at the same time into and out of the world we live in. No wonder, then, that the English word for prose literature is precisely "fiction". However much they resemble the world we live in, literary worlds are distinctively different, both logically and ontologically.

No other art form really resembles literature in this respect. In the case of music, there is no direct world reference at all. Film, on the other hand, while it clearly unfolds "worlds", actually (pretends to) depict what is "really" in front of the camera, staged or not (which has made theorists like Stanley Cavell[3] claim an ontologically distinct status for reality in film). Theatre often unfolds a fictitious world, but this world is there right in front of the beholder, in full scale, real time, flesh and blood. Visual arts may refer to or represent motives from the real world (or from history, non-existing worlds, etc.), but here as well the representing level is still "real" – i.e. the picture including its depicted motive is part of the reality of the beholder (as pinpointed in Magritte's *Ceci n'est pas une pipe*). In the case of literature, only the specific collections of conventional signs are "really" present. The fictitious spaces are as such spoken spaces.

---

3   (Cavell 1979). Cavell's point of view is highly disputable and has indeed been disputed.

"Spoken" in which sense – and what is a spoken world anyhow? In this connection it might be relevant to take a look at the phenomenon called *utterance* or *enunciation* (as elaborated by Émile Benveniste in his revision of Saussure and traditional structuralism) (Benveniste 1974). Apart from the "real" utterance taking place in the sense of a writer "talking" to a reader with his text, a piece of literature can be construed as if a "someone" is addressing another "someone" with "something" – all included or embedded in the text itself (i.e. as implied instances of author/narrator and beholder). This is called enounced enunciation, "uttered utterance" or "spoken" speaking/ beholding positions in the text. In the light of this approach it is easy to see how the "spokenness" of literature's fictional world creates the conditions for a specific variability of perspectives on this viewed world (thus changing this "world" itself, since its spokenness is our only access to it). That variability may apply to epistemic competence (what is known? by whom? why? who sees? who talks?), to distinctions of time and space by the points of view in action, and not least, to any kind of parabasis, i.e. narrative positions in some form of reflexive (meta)position relative to the narrated world (ironic, distanced, ignorant, etc.). Correspondingly, a variety of "modelled", embedded beholder's positions are depicted and available to the real beholder. Recent narratology has analysed these distinctions thoroughly, based on the groundwork by Wayne C. Booth (1983/1961) and Gérard Genette (1966-72). As concerns the question of epistemic competence, both deconstructionist criticism (for instance Weber 1987, Culler 1988) and reception theory (Iser 1993 or Eco 1990) have from different perspectives contributed decisively to our knowledge about literature too.

No doubt the artefacts of any other art form/mediality may in principle also be analysed as uttered or embedded utterances, enounced enunciations. Any communicative act "frozen" into an artefact possesses an implied sender and a model recipient – or rather a system of such instances. However, the way in which this takes place depends on the specific mediality in question. It is in any case much easier to understand literature like this. Again this is due to literature's foundation in the sign system of our daily communication, where our semiotic competence is relatively higher and works more automatically in its decoding activity. This competence extends to the built-in double referentiality mentioned above.

However, this ease of interpretation has, beyond a doubt contributed immensely to the traditional fallacies (the intentional, the referential, etc.) in the understanding of literature. We proceed as if literature's fictional worlds were actually real (and not just real in terms of fictions); as if the engendering of such fictional worlds were literature's one and only purpose and reason for existence; and as if such worlds could be born out of sheer replication of truths or ideas – in other words, as if the formal construction and impact of linguistic expression had no independent importance whatsoever with regard to the "meaning" produced. In any event, the fundamental features of literature as a medium which are often obscured by these forms of literary fallacy have contributed to the special role and position of literature among the art forms.

LITERATURE'S MEDIALITY

Now to sum up this brief sketch of some of the determining characteristics of literature as a medium – characteristics which define its "mediality". Literature is time-based. It inescapably positions itself in the course of "ordinary" time, and yet it unfolds its own time, capable of mounting this time into our time at any given moment we choose. In terms of space, literature's world is physically unconnected with that of its beholders. And yet it is capable of unfolding its own space, and of giving us access to that space, on specific conditions under its own authority. We perceive literature individually, each of us from our own specific position in time and space (which we ourselves, not the work of literature, decide). And yet we perceive the "same" artefact. This artefact is thus constitutionally unsharable – but nonetheless to share.

Since literature's act of communication is exclusively based on verbal language, the same sign system we use for everyday communication, it inevitably refers to our "real" world by "representing" parts of it. And yet it definitively points away from our world by unfolding a world or worlds of its own. Literature is thus deemed to be fictional" and unreal – but at the same time the reality of its fiction makes it an undistinguishable part of our real world as well. Fictions are not fictitious – fictions are real.

Literature addresses us explicitly, or rather addresses explicitly embedded, possible representatives of us within its own body. We cannot escape these distinctive representatives, and yet we are offered the possibility of conceiving of these representatives as possible variations of ourselves in relation to such factors as epistemic competence, temporal and spatial position, and mode of approach. This "addressed-ness" determines our access to the specific world unfolded by that distinct work of literature.

As I briefly indicated above, each of the other medialities will have its own specific properties when analyzed in terms of the same parameters. At some points different medialities may share properties, sometimes along the main axis of distinction between performing and non-performing arts, sometimes along that of allographic and autographic artefacts, sometimes along that of fiction-producing versus non-fiction-producing. But no other medium shares all of its properties in these respects with literature. The same set of questions asked of different medialities gives distinct sets of answers.

WHY STUDY INTERMEDIALITY?

Literature, in other words, is a distinct medium, the entire mediality of which is beyond question different from that of any other medium. Literary studies, however, have to a considerable extent failed to see and to understand literature's defining properties for what they are: distinctive and qualifying preconditions for the formation of distinctive meaning – both in general and in the case of individual literary artworks. Some of the reasons for this oversight have been hinted at above, both at the level of literature's institutional history, and in relation to the issue of the inherent properties of the medium. This assertion of a historical failure, of course, may be far too general, and may even seem unjustified, recent theoretical developments taken into consideration. The problem, as we have seen, is actually not that no highly qualified studies have been made respectively of the problems of time, of space, of fictionality, of sign-system status, of enunciation, of distribution of epistemic competence or of the phenomenology of reading/ readers in the case of literature. Still, the fact remains that despite the great and groundbreaking work that has been done in the field since the beginning of the last century, much literary study still proceeds as if literary worlds and real life were interconnected in a more or less unmediated way. And where the above literary studies of time, space, narration etc. are concerned, they have only rarely been brought together into analyzing the mediality of literature as such, in its status of including a specific set of parameters like the ones here examined, all of which might in turn be applied also to other media (but in different constellations).

All in all our knowledge of literature as a medium is therefore still far from adequate. This is my first conclusion, which immediately leads to a call for more work, for more studies of literature as literature.

My second conclusion has to do with the interrelationship between disciplinary studies of specific medialities such as literature, painting, and music, on the one hand, and interdisciplinary studies (interarts, comparative arts etc.) at a more general level of "mediality" on the other hand. Over the last twenty-five years the interest in the interdisciplinary level has been steadily growing. In general this has been a fine and fruitful process which has enhanced our understanding of the arts, although we have also encountered a certain number of exclusively empirical studies of medial transformations which lack any far-reaching theoretical perspective. A lot of interesting work has been done, work which has brought the understanding of mediality as such to a considerably higher level.

It is, however, important not to turn things upside down. The study of mediality in general and/or of intermediality presupposes the existence of studies of the distinct medialities as a "feed line". There has thus been a tendency in the disciplinary landscape to reduce the study of the individual medialities such as literature to precisely that: a feed line, a somewhat secondary subject. This, in my opinion, should never be the point of interdisciplinary or intermedial studies. While this kind of work is highly necessary and should be developed further (and fed by disciplinary studies), its primary goal must still be to qualify and clarify our knowledge of the specific medialities. In this case the question "Why study literature?" could be countered: "Why study intermediality?". And the answer to that should read: to increase our knowledge about individual media – in this case, literature. Literature *as* literature, let it be understood.

REFERENCES

Batteux, Charles. 1746 ("Abbé Batteux"). *Les beaux arts réduits à un même principe.*

Benveniste, Émile. 1974. La forme et le sens dans le langage, *Problèmes de linguistique générale II.* Paris: Gallimard.

Booth, Wayne C. 1983 [1961]. *The Rhetoric of Fiction.* 2nd Ed. Chicago: University of Chicago Press.

Cavell, Stanley. 1979. *The World Viewed. Reflections on the Ontology of Film.* Enlarged edition. Cambridge, Mass.: Harvard University Press.

Culler, Jonathan. 1988. *Framing the Sign. Criticism and its Institutions.* Oxford: Blackwell.

Eco, Umberto. 1990. *The Limits of Interpretation.* Bloomington: Indiana University Press.

Genette, Gérard. 1966-72. *Figures I-III.* Paris: Seuil.

Goodman, Nelson. 1972. *Problems and Projects.* Indianapolis: Bobbs-Merill.

Hegel, G.F.W. 1986 [1835-38]. *Vorlesungen zur Ästhetik I.* Frankfurt: Suhrkamp (stw 613).

Iser, Wolfgang. 1993. *The Fictive and the Imaginary. Charting Literary Anthropology.* Baltimore: Johns Hopkins University Press.

Kittler, Friedrich. 1995. *Aufschreibesysteme 1800/1900.* München: Fink.

Kyndrup, Morten. 2003. *Kunstværk og udsigelse* (*ACTS* 18). Aarhus: Aarhus Universitet.

Kyndrup, Morten. 2005. Art Theory Versus Aesthetics. The Story of a Marriage and its Decline and Fall. In *Perspectives on Aesthetics, Art and Culture*, eds. Claes Entzenberg and Simo Säätela, Sthm.: Thales.

Kyndrup, Morten. 2008. *Den æstetiske relation. Sanseoplevelsen mellem kunst, videnskab og filosofi*. København: Gyldendal.

Lessing, Gotthold Ephraim. 1766. *Laokoon oder Über die Grenzen der Malerei und Poesie.*

Man, Paul de. 1986. The Return to Philology. In *The Resistance to Theory*. Foreword by Wlad Godzich. Manchester: Manchester University Press.

Ricœur, Paul. 1985. *Temps et récit I-III*. Paris: Seuil essais.

Weber, Samuel. 1987. *Institution and Interpretation*. Afterword by Wlad Godzich. Minneapolis: University of Minnesota Press.

LOCALITY
AND
TEMPORALITY

SVEND ERIK LARSEN
Literature as Global Thinking

SUNE AUKEN
Not another Adult Movie:
Some Platitudes on Genericity and the Use of Literary Studies

BRIAN MCHALE
Models and Thought Experiments

ANNE-MARIE MAI
Literary Studies in Interaction

LITERATURE AS GLOBAL THINKING

Svend Erik Larsen

> "What was in this book?" Ralph asked, unhappily.
> "Mad things", Turner replied, "to blow the world up; anyhow, the world that
> you and me knows. Poems and things".
> (White 1988 [1957], 255)

WHY (STUDY) LITERATURE?

The umbrella question of this volume, *Why study literature?*, brings us to a fork in the road. In one direction we are led to the immediate answer: to educate professionals. There is a need for professionals in the field, working as critics in the media, as teachers on all levels of education where literature is part of the curriculum, as researchers in universities, research centers and large libraries, as librarians, as publishers and editors and as organizers in various cultural institutions. Here, the professionals of literary studies are doing more than just responding to various needs and wishes from students, readers and users in general. They are also responsible for shaping this readership and thus place literature as an active part of our cultural environment.

Relevant as such an answer may be, in its content and its consequences, the forked road also points in another and more troubling direction, somewhat hidden if we take the open question concerned with the study of literature as the only question that calls for our answer. To my mind we have, first and foremost, to address a more fundamental question: *why literature?* Why is literature so important that we study it and want to use our professionalism thus gained to promote literature in various ways? This has not always been the case. During centuries when the imitation paradigm reigned supreme in the literary world, literature was studied by those who wanted to know how to write it, guided by Horace's *ars poetica* in particular. In other cultures, like China, the established canon was also studied by those who wanted to compete for a high position in the imperial administration.

Hence, asking the question "Why literature?" in order to underpin the study of it through the institutionalized activities we know today in the westernized cultures, also implies more than an ontological question that can be left to philosophers of aesthetics. There is a necessary historical dimension to it: "Why literature – today?". Only if we can propose answers to this question will we be able to substantiate our answers to the first question on the study of literature, which then may be positive or negative, leading to changes or to the consolidation of the professions of literary studies and their cultural outreach.

This underlying question is the focus of my article. The brief version of my answer is: literature is a necessary model of global thinking. That is why it is worth studying it, enjoying it and disseminating knowledge about it today. The longer answer can be found on the following pages.

TEXTS WITHOUT BORDERS

Where should we start looking for a more detailed answer? An obvious place would be the well established cultures and institutions of canonized literatures, feeding on a long tradition of literary criticism. But here it would be difficult to distinguish between literature as a cultural necessity we have to reshape over and over again to keep a culture alive, and as just a cultural routine we could not suppress even if we wanted to. So, I prefer first to leave the cultural highway of the literary cultures and move to its fringes.

Here I meet the young German-English Frederick Sinnett who in 1849 traveled from England to Australia to work as an engineer. To the Europeans, Australia was impassable, more due to the climate and the landscape than to the aboriginals. The native people were not taken into consideration; at least they were not considered the rightful owners of the land.

Just like other places colonized by Europeans, most white Australians lived in a belt along the coasts. Some farmed a little ways inland, others became merchants, and still others were missionaries, adventurers, gold diggers, and former prisoners. This was not what a European would call civilization. The black population was not even counted. But young Sinnett abandoned engineering and became an enterprising journalist who set to work on cultural education in the outback.

Sinnett did not doubt that literature was a necessary and unavoidable part of this process. It should not be introduced only after the elementary material safeguards of a basic life have been established. It is there already as part of them. Sinnett wrote about this in 1856 under the title "The Fiction Fields of Australia":

Man can no more do without works of fiction than he can do without clothing, and, indeed, not so well; for, where climate is propitious, and manners simple, people often manage to loiter down the road of life without any of the "lendings" that Lear cast away from him; yet, nevertheless, with nothing between the blue heaven and their polished skins, they will gather in a circle round some dusky orator or vocalist, as his imagination bodies forth the forms of things unknown, to the entertainment and elevation of his hearers. To amend our first proposition, then, works of fiction being more necessary, and universally disseminated, than clothing, they still resemble clothing in this, that they take different shapes and fashions in different ages (Sinnett 2008, 1).

Here, in the Australian outback, is precisely where the basic cultural and personal necessity of narration manifests itself fully.

Sinnett wished above all to show the Europeans that the crude settlers who balanced on the edge of the known world had literature that could be evaluated according to the same standards as back in Europe. Even though it was not possible to identify an Australian Shakespeare, the region belonged to what was then regarded as European world culture. But Sinnett's text also demonstrates his own unconscious historical limitation. In his essay he refused to take into consideration the aboriginal people's way of thinking. But to be able to support the claim of literature's global importance, he had to refer to them nonetheless. Even the black natives cannot refrain from listening to a black story-teller, he notes in the above quotation. Literature transcends cultural borders.

And there is power behind the transcending words of literature. It is the strength of words that enables authors' works to continue out into the world across all boundary posts and to rearrange the borders of the known and the unknown on readers' inner maps along the way. The works determine cultural agendas even though the authors are imprisoned, voluntarily or involuntarily exiled, censored, or killed. Anne Frank could not go outside, but her diary could, and it continues to circulate out there. It assumes its unrivalled place across the narrow walls in her hiding place. The German Thomas Mann left Nazi Germany and went to the United Sates, but his works outdistanced other authors by several lengths on their German home ground and also earned a Nobel Prize. The same goes for the works of the Russian author Aleksander Solzhenitsyn, which became both Russian and global major works.

More and more authors like these are appearing. They come from one place, live willing or unwillingly in other places on the globe and perhaps move again, like the Afghani author Atiq Rahimi in Paris, the Iranian Azar

Nafisi in Baltimore, or the Chinese Xiaolu Guo in London. Their books are translated, become bestsellers and perhaps also films, even though they have not yet gained a foothold in their home countries, and even though many are less well-known where they live. But this will not continue. Authors from the Near and Far East, from former European colonies in Africa and other places, and from multicultural regions like the Caribbean are those who, in a globalized world, are already moving the borders in our heads and homes from a global perspective, just as the European authors did when Europe was the world.

Today literature not only cuts across the border between motherland and colonies. In modern globalization all the geographic and cultural borders that come into contact with one another are part of the cross-cutting movement of literature, but without a cultural fixed point. Russian-American Vladimir Nabokov became a global bestselling author with *Lolita* in 1955. In an interview in *Playboy* in January 1964, he explains how he himself cut across borders:

> I am an American writer, born in Russia and educated in England where I studied French literature, before spending fifteen years in Germany. I came to America in 1940 and decided to be an American citizen, and make America my home. [...] I propelled myself out of Russia so vigorously, with such indignant force, that I have been rolling on and on ever since (Nabokov 1973, 26-27).

To the question of why he always lives in furnished apartments, he answers that he does not want to become too rooted in his own things and places.

Things have changed in the hundred years since Sinnett's reflections at the edge of the Europeanized world. Nabokov, too, has a European linguistic and cultural background and uses it. All anyone can do is to use their background, regardless of where they come from. But in contrast to Sinnett, Nabokov does not just take it as it is; he consciously chooses how he wants to use it. He chooses to become an American citizen but he also chooses a fundamental and incessant movement out into the world. It is not rootlessness that he describes, but the notion that everywhere he is he experiences the boundary between the local and the global as *his*. It is what he works with linguistically and culturally in his works. The uneducated cultural worker Sinnett and the refined Nabokov lived with their own respective backgrounds in various phases of the long cultural process of globalization. But for both of them it is a matter of literature contributing to the formation of this process, so we can understand it as *ours* in the place where we are.

Today we pose both the question "Why study literature?" and its underlying question "Why literature?" in the cultural framework of globalization. But globalization has spread throughout so many parts of our lives that the word cannot be limited to certain disciplines or areas of life – economics, social sciences, politics, media, and communication. Its importance and effects are still open and waiting to be made concrete, understandable, and relevant in our everyday lives; just as was the case with industrialization and urbanization at the time of Balzac and Dickens.

It is this incomplete process in which literature actively participates. This is why literature is more deeply engaged in the globalized cultural processes than merely by delivering literary images and counter-images of the airports, development projects, and protest meetings of a globalized world. Of course, today literature throws about current global themes: rootless people, journeys from place to place, financial dramas, terrorist activities, the power of the media, and religious conflicts. And of course many texts are obviously critical towards the power games of globalization, the collapse of values, wars and poverty, and changes in communities. Literature fills the themes with tension and strong feelings that we cannot live without if we wish to be engaged in them.

But literature contains more than the themes of the day. Literature has always wandered past the boundaries between culture and language – with its translations, linguistic influences, media, motifs, genres, and symbols. It disrespectfully pretends that globalization has always existed. The cross-cutting cultural movements gathered speed at the same time that Gutenberg began printing books in 15th-century Europe. This is why literature has always gotten involved where new cultural understandings and meanings have arisen, and where traditions have been broken, and in the cultural innovations of the time. It gives the cross-cutting global movements some meanings that the themes do not deliver, concentrated as they are on our contemporary world. Literature brings culture's long tradition of transgression along with it into modern globalization, which then takes on new meanings and perspectives with a resounding echo of past experiences of border-crossings.

It would be naïve to pretend that power and money are not involved in the relationship between literature and globalization. Whether authors want it or not, literature is wrapped up in both. It is not only the battleground of ideas. The institutions that lubricate the links between works, society, and the public are rapidly changing: education systems, political campaigns, book trade shows, private and public distribution networks, subsidies for authors, copyrights, international prizes, and so on. We are talking about cultural power, a great deal of cultural power. Nor should we forget that market conditions contribute to decisions about what is written and read: concentrations of publishers, the relationship of books to major media conglomerates, film rights, copyrights, TV programmes, and so forth. We are talking about a lot of money here.

But the question "Why literature – today?" does not first of all lead to the question "Why produce or sell literature?", but rather "Why read literature?". At the center of it all is the sensual pleasure of being surprised by detail and the deep fascination in discovering the vision that opens up. This is how literature expands the abstract circuits of globalization with a historical dimension and with a concrete, individual experience. Both in the narrow, academic conceptions of globalization and in the trendy and superficial use of the concept the two dimensions are usually lacking. But without them we cannot relate to globalization as a concrete cultural process that we ourselves are a part of, and that we can be involved in shaping. Literature uses all its means to try to get us to understand the world in this perspective across its borders.

LANGUAGE IN A MEDIA LANDSCAPE

This is the perspective that is fostered by Nabokov and Sinnett. Even though Nabokov does not disturb us with his private torments, cutting across borders exacts a price from authors and publishers. Also for Sinnett; he left Europe with the beginnings of tuberculosis, had hard working conditions in his attempt to create a journalistic public and cultural self-awareness in a country that was mostly a European colony of convicts, and died already in 1860, not even 40 years old. But authors do not pay any bigger price than the others who transgress boundaries. Others who grapple with cultural, linguistic, and social boundaries in their education, their work and throughout their lives are not given anything for free either. As people, authors are not more interesting than other pattern breakers. They are all everyday globalists in a common cultural process. Authors are just better at telling about it.

Nabokov does not tell about his private life, but about the conditions that make him an author. When he says, "I am living in Switzerland for purely private reasons" (Nabokov 1973, 28), it is not a piece of information but a discreet "What business is it of yours?". There is thus good reason to focus on authors' writings instead of their persons. They can use language

LOCALITY AND TEMPORALITY

to make the sky fall down. They can write in such a way as to make their own and others' experiences become greater than their individual lives and the readers' individual horizons. This is not because literature is a distinct language. It is rather because literature uses the language we also use to order a beer, argue, encourage our children, lie about our debt, and put our feelings and understanding of reality into words. Language interacts with all the other media we use for these purposes. And of course literature does this too. Novels become films, and literature learns from film how to refine its use of viewpoints and narrative modes. Literature circulates in the global cultural landscape along with other media.

But media like pictures, gestures, sound, games and sports cannot manage without language. Sports can be directed by whistles and arm movements, but the rules for the course of the game are written down in language. And complaints about the referee are not dealt with by whistling at him or shaking a fist. These actions have the reverse effect and language will be necessary afterwards to settle things. Even silent body language requires language, so that I can become aware that it is something *my* body does. Film, TV, and digital images are full of language in what we see, but even more in what underlies their origins in screenplays, scripts, and contracts.

When we include our open and uncertain experiences of globalization in our language it is more than just a linguistic enterprise. We thereby enable ourselves to include them in the medium that most subtly forms our daily lives, their trivial tasks as well as their high points, and our reflections on life. Culture breathes through the lungs of language.

TRANSLATION

But cultures do not have the same language. Regardless of how universal the experiences and opinions are that language grabs hold of, they are always anchored in the place where the language functions. Images, sounds, and gestures reach across cultural boundaries without always noticing the boundaries. But when literature cuts across borders, we cannot avoid noticing the tension in the language between local understanding and global perspective, both in its meanings and in its vocabulary – for instance, technical words, other loanwords, common phrases, and small words. France has a declared policy of white-washing smuggled goods from other languages – but cannot prevent the cross-cutting practice of language. Language in use is never pure, nor is the literature that exploits language. Love of language and literature as purely national is an unconsummated love affair that has nothing to do with the real life that language and literature lead. This life is deeply promiscuous.

This is why translation is an important part of the work of literature, especially in a globalized context. Through translation we do not merely transfer statements and forms of expression more or less correctly from one language to another. Translation is a means of giving cultural differences an overall shape. We challenge and develop the very capacity of language to express meaning in all the languages involved in the translation, and in this way expand their cultural register on the home front. Translations of the Bible in 15th and 16th century Europe were of greater importance for a crosswise expansion of the capacity of the European languages as written and cultural languages than the developments that took place within the individual languages. The Greek and Latin Biblical texts used by the translators were themselves translations. Languages develop because they are used to speak about a world that is bigger than that of those who use the language, and they cannot avoid becoming intertwined when they meet across the limitations of the language users. The boundary between the local and the global goes right down the middle of language, and we express the boundary every time we speak.

This is why language also has open boundaries and is constantly moving them. Mixed languages later gain the status of national languages, and these languages will gradually be absorbed by others. This is how pidgin, Creole, Yiddish, and immigrant Danish in the Nørrebro district of Copenhagen have been formed. They emerge as special languages from a mixture of several languages that are not entirely mastered, but the mixtures work in practice. Since the languages are involved in creating necessary relations between various people in a particular place, sooner or later the languages influence one another and the main language of the place so much that the jargon and the main language both change. A common language grows forth that can be spoken on many levels and is itself gradually changing. This is how Afrikaans came into being in South Africa and Swahili in a belt through Central Africa. In the Mediterranean in the early European Middle Ages, people used a cocktail of early Italian closely related to Latin and Greek, Turkish, and Arabic as a practical common language for trade and communication across the local regions and the participant countries in the crusades. This messiness was called *lingua franca,* a term still used today for the various versions of globalized English.

Those who believe that English is the main language of globalization are therefore mistaken. First, English already consists of many kinds of English today. Just take a look at the computer's spelling program: British, American, Australian, and many other variants are represented. But secondly, these stable variants are in a minority. Global English, which can successfully be used for improvising at the meeting places of globalization, is broken English, a *lingua franca* just as messy as that of the Middle Ages. It is what we all master, but it can be confusing when a dozen different versions of broken English are used simultaneously. But then we improvise. As a rule, and still successfully, without referring to standard English grammar. This practical language of communication has been christened *Globish* by Jean-Paul Nerrière, a Frenchman and former IBM vice-president. He dryly notes that it works everywhere, but that people whose native language is one of the many kinds of English are handicapped.

GLOBAL LITERATURE?

This is the broad linguistic and cultural palette that literature works with when it uses language. The strength of language has always been that understanding is more important than formal correctness, even though guardians of language often maintain the opposite. This strength is the linguistic starting point of literature. Literature is not global because it takes place in airports or in some Nowhereland, nor because it deals with international terror networks or voyages in the Pacific.

This type of literature only comprises what we might call *global literature,* a more recent literary subdivision like Victorian literature, Danish modernism, magical realism from South America, or Southern literature from the U.S. It is a particular group of writings with a certain thematic and perhaps formal commonality residing in a delimited historical period close to our own times. Global literature is both exciting and relevant. However, the question "Why literature – today?" does not address a particular literary genre or sub-genre, but the more comprehensive problem of how we can use literature from various times and places actively to take into account the global and fractured cultural processes we are currently experiencing.

In the age of globalization, all places are communities to some people and at the same time foreign to others. All places have their particular traces of the same globalization process that we are also a part of where we live, and all places can be the starting point for understanding globalization. Literature does not use language as an external medium polished with rhymes, rhythms, and exciting events and people; rather, literature uses language to maintain that cultural processes are fundamentally linguistic processes, and that the meeting with the local and what lies beyond takes place in the most subtle way in language and by means of language.

Literature therefore only seems to distinguish itself from normal language. It uses imagery, invents odd persons and unreasonable events, changes fixed temporal and spatial patterns, and indeed goes beyond everything we can confirm in the physical world. The literary "imagination bodies forth the forms of things unknown", as Sinnett has stated in the quotation above. Literature does not, however, use other linguistic features besides the ones language already has when we, for example, fantasize about unattainable vacations and lottery winnings. It does have a greater self-consciousness about what it does with language than we do in everyday life. And it shows this directly in the material pleasure it takes in language. In literature, linguistic self-consciousness moves to the forefront, so language can acquire a central cultural function: to transgress the boundaries of what we expect, but in such a way that we notice that it happens in the same language that we use to organize the world we know.

LITERATURE AS AESTHETIC EXPERIENCE

This self-conscious use of language is the aesthetic side of literature. Often people regard aesthetics as shiny wrapping paper that has nothing to do with the contents. But all practical work must focus on its material to be effective. A mechanic must master his tools and know the durability and suitability of his materials. A bicycle repairer must know what a saddle feels like to the rider. The focus on and pleasure with the material does not lead away from the matter at hand, but to the core of the matter, also in literature.

Aesthetics is what makes a piece of writing something tangible that we can sense: the sound and the feel of the book, the layout, the rhythm of language repeated in our bodies, something specific that we can tell others about and find our way back to. With aesthetic self-consciousness the piece of writing becomes a distinctive thing among other things we can sense and grasp just as concretely as a tool or a sculpture. As language literature is at the heart of basic cultural processes at large so that literature and culture always engage interdependently in the changes of culture; as an aesthetic phenomenon it interferes with the aesthetical forms of other media and art forms so that the changes in literature and the use of literature take place in historically specific media landscape of interrelated media and art forms. With its double foundation in the interactive domains of language and aesthetics, literature is not eradicated by other media or art forms – far

LOCALITY AND TEMPORALITY

from it. But its role is changed in respect to the other media used in our culture. It is a cultural busybody with the capacity to mix with all other types of language use and with all other art forms. In contrast to much literary theory, aesthetic and linguistic autonomy is not the business of literature. It works as a jack-of-all-trades in the global culture workshop of language and aesthetics.

Therefore, the idea that aesthetics should be a diversion that art in particular is good at is a recent and narrow conception of aesthetics. The original meaning is concrete and is not about art in particular. The Greek word *aisthesis* means sensual experience pure and simple, as opposed to abstract thinking, *noesis*. Greek words with *–is* usually refer to an activity. So aesthetics concerns everything about the things around us, both natural and manmade things that we can experience with our senses.

Art came to play a special role among the things we ourselves produce. The hidden forms and principles that control the ways of nature became visible to our senses in art. Therefore, to the Greeks, their statues that have been imitated throughout European cultural history did not depict specific bodies. They made the ideal forms for the body visible and perceptible to us so that we could still have a concrete experience of its hidden dimensions, with our own senses. Not until later is art regarded as the most important aesthetic medium, and to some as even the only one, rather than merely one example of a concrete, individual sensual experience.

Today we must return to the original meaning of aesthetics. When literature consciously works on its aesthetic effects, there is only one aim. And it is not escapism. On the contrary: otherwise abstract and inaccessible conditions are made concrete, accessible, and relevant to the individual reader. Aesthetics builds a bridge between these two dimensions in our experience, the abstract and the concrete. This bridge building is the primary cultural function of literature. Aesthetic self-consciousness is what causes a piece of writing to look the individual reader right in the eye: "You who are reading now, you are the one I am addressing". The Polish-English author of the seven seas, Joseph Conrad, expresses this in a manifesto: "all art, therefore, appeals primarily to the senses, and the artistic aim when expressing itself in written words must also make its appeal through the senses, if its desire is to reach the secret spring of responsive emotions" (Conrad 1950, ix).

This is the center of literature's irresistible fascination it exercises on Digger, one of the main characters in the Australian-Libanese David Malouf's novel *The Great World* (1990). Digger describes reading in this light. As an adult he becomes a forced laborer as a Japanese prisoner of war in Malaysia during the Pacific War until 1945. His fellow soldier Mac is also interested in reading, and after he is beaten to death, Digger acquires his letters from Iris back home. He knows them by heart:

> The letters were just a few hundred words. But the words themselves were only part of it. Reading took time. That was the important thing. Constant folding and refolding had split the pages, and in the continuous damp up here the ink had run and was hard to read. Each time he took them out, especially if his hands were shaking and wet, he ran the risk of damaging them. But he liked the look of the unfolded pages, their weight – very light they were – on his palm. Even the stains were important. So was the colour of the ink, which differed from letter to letter, so that you could se, or guess, where Iris had put the pen down in mid-sentence to go off and do something. So what you were reading was not just the words (Malouf 1990, 145).

This concrete experience involving all his senses is what makes him keep reading, both when he imagines a bigger world somewhere else and when he feels the stationery. It is the here-and-now sensual experience that Digger has every time he reads the letters that opens up a larger world beyond the words. This is also what happens when we hear the words, feel the book, see the sentences black on white. The reading is both a repetition and a unique experience. No cola or popcorn is necessary, unlike at the movies or in front of the TV, where we do not have a direct sensual experience of the screen.

Literature is therefore not a cultural phenomenon with more or less aesthetic glitter that we can ignore, so we can make do with the common meaning and deeper meaning of the words. Literature is not a cultural phenomenon *because* it is an aesthetic phenomenon, for it is the aesthetic dimension that puts its linguistic complexity to work the individual reader's sensual experience of the text and world.

The medium of literature in this work is language. It is a medium we all share. This is why literature is also part of the shared resources of a culture, even though not everyone reads it and not everyone has an equally large vocabulary or mastery of language. The same goes for film. Even though not everyone goes to the movies or watches DVDs, film has an impact on our visual surroundings through advertisements, fashion, and the design of urban space. Literature also has an impact on the language everyone uses, readers of literature or not, when its effects further circulate outside literature. Expressions, images, idiomatic phrases, ideas and realizations that enter into our daily language without us thinking about it have developed on the extensive continents of literature. When literature expands the world, it is not just expanding some world or other or someone else's world, but *our* world. If language is the lungs of culture, literature is the deep breathing that ensures a regular supply of oxygen.

Although the question "Why literature – today?" directly points to the contemporary context of globalization, it does not exclude literature of the past, but includes all literature that serves as the basis for our understanding of this perspective. Literature is not first and foremost a text corpus in which global literature is one grouping; rather, it serves an active linguistic and cultural function with aesthetic effects. We can only understand its signification today by seeing it in respect to our globalized cultural conditions and in respect to other modes of expression and media that also help our concrete experiences with these conditions to cut across the world we know.

TO SEE THINGS FOR THE FIRST TIME

Forming the study of literature as an answer to the question "Why literature – today?" is somewhat different from what we used to do. The explosive opening of the borders of the world, the circulation of translations in a changing media landscape of multiple interconnected media has created new cross-cutting perspectives and made regional phenomena global, such as immigration, climate changes, environmental preservation, energy supply, and religious ideas. But new border barriers have been set up in places where a new regionalization has strengthened local awareness. In a broad sense, new cultural themes and challenges have been created and thus new frameworks have emerged for the way literature works far beyond what I can touch upon here.

When the boundaries of literature shift, traces are left not only in the new literature but also in older literature. Although the books already standing on the shelves have obviously not changed, their meaning to us changes because we have different cultural horizons when we read them. Globalization is not without history even though it pokes a hole in the familiar speech bubbles of local history about life in an open-air museum. It gets us to look for texts and conditions from the past other than those usually found at the top of the pile. Works we read inattentively before and others we have read in a different light have also helped build the open platform on which we are now teetering. Globalization was underway before we saw it clearly enough to give it the name. We must not, of course, invent the tradition we are grabbing at. That would be cultural counterfeit. But among the writings and material that cultural history has already placed around the cultural platform of the day, we should choose the elements we can use to make railings and fences so as to maintain the balance in our current uncertain situation.

We should therefore not merely study the new literature; we should also re-read existing literature. In the old European colonies, including the U.S. in particular the native literary traditions from both before and after colonization came out into the open. This rediscovery lent more coherence to history for the present inhabitants with mixed cultural roots. To this process also belongs an often agonizing realization that the colonies belonged to the native population before the colonial powers began helping themselves at the big colonial buffet. Under difficult negotiations and lawsuits, some of the indigenous populations are having their rights acknowledged and some of their land is being restored, now and then accompanied by apologies. The past cannot be restored, but history can be rewritten and transformed in practice today under global conditions. It is not an unqualified success, but without the stories and other artistic modes of expression that have kept the concealed tradition going and a cultural memory alive, nothing at all would happen.

Frederick Sinnett did not pay attention to the stories or rights of the indigenous people. In spite of open and curious eyes, he was still an arch-European on the edge of what he considered to be the world. However, the task is not only to dig up overlooked traditions. We must also reinterpret the obvious tradition we know, alter the shades of light and dark, pull something out of oblivion, push something else into the background, see new aspects of the writings that remain fully illuminated. We must restructure our own tradition so we can still see it as ours, also under the current conditions.

Of course, traditional texts have gained renewed life by cutting across cultural boundaries and barriers to the imagination, even though the aim of the literary history that sorted through them was first and foremost to enclose them in national and other local contexts. But literature swings outward before turning inward, and much of the early literature can get us to swing along with it. The same is true for the traditional literary concepts. They must also be reused and modified rather than replaced with shiny new ones. It would certainly be the easiest thing to do because then we do not need to take a closer look at how we usually read literature. Reading that does not invite both understanding contemporary literature and restructuring traditional texts and concepts is not reading under the conditions of globalization.

On the occasion of Mozart's 250th birthday in 2006, the Slovenian cultural theorist Slavoj Žižek pointed out the necessary risk we run when we look at tradition in a new light. We risk losing it:

> Every single modification contains a risk and should be judged according to its own internal standards. Only one thing is certain: the only possibility of remaining faithful to a classical work lies in exposing it to this risk. Those who avoid it, and stick to the original wording, choose the best way to betray the spirit of classicism (Žižek 2006, 339).

The study of literature is a way to taking precisely this risk. The Australian Nobel Prize winner Patrick White describes the process in an autobiographical essay from 1958:

> Writing which had meant the practice of an art by a polished mind in civilized surroundings, became a struggle to create completely fresh forms out of the rocks and sticks of words. I began to see things for the first time (White 1988, 16).

Literature can make us see what we know as though we were seeing it for the first time. It is our chance to make it *ours* again in a new way, and to see the unknown as something that can be expressed in *our* language for the first time.

Tradition is the way a present is put into a historical perspective, and that includes the present of globalization. Globalization is neither the temporary end station of the long, straight highway of history or some here-and-now economic operation without history. It is an opportunity to reinterpret parts of history so that it becomes a resource for us today.

THE TRANSLOCAL PERSPECTIVE

Literature, both old and new, has always been a model for global thinking that makes concrete the conflict between local experience and the world beyond the local. Under the shifting conditions of cultural history the contents of this model have changed, but it always functions so that we can use historical experiences with this kind of thinking under new conditions, such as those of modern globalization.

The national delimitation of literature is only a knot that briefly ties together all the cross-cultural threads that are the real lifelines of literature. The most important aim of literary history in a globalized world ought to be to show how local literature opens up, and always has opened up, towards the world outside the local area in order to be created at all, not how it forms a particular context within it. It was not the world outside Verona that killed Romeo and Juliet, but Verona's destructive inwardness. Literature helps us avoid paying what Amitav Ghosh, in *The Glass Palace* (2000), calls "the price of a monumental inwardness" (Ghosh 2000, 349).

If the reader now expects a definition of the perfect globalized work of literature, I can and will not deliver. Today world literature does not first of all indicate "quality" as Goethe had it when he used the term in the 1820s; instead it points to a cultural aesthetic function. World literature does not exclude certain kinds of literature or certain local and historical literatures, but includes all literature, from whatever locality and in whatever language, using it in a way that creates new contexts between historical periods, between texts and genres, and between local and transgressive phenomena.

No literature *is* simply world literature, but all literature in local languages *can become* it through the interpretations of the world that it invites when we as readers accept the invitation. This happens when literature cuts across cultural boundaries set by the place and time: literature is always locally anchored and transgressive at the same time, an idea already suggested by Georg Brandes in his essays "World Literature" (1899) and "On Reading" (1899). Texts become world literature by moving the world's boundary posts in the languages in which they are written rather than by being incorporated into a canon of world literature. All texts move these posts, but some do so better than others. Ibsen is not *more* theater than an amateur show performed by undergraduates; it is *better* theater. The good works are not more world literature than the others either; they are just better at being it.

Obviously, perfect art works that break open time and place do exist. We cannot forget them. They make us wonder, almost, perhaps, feel fear. They are new every time we encounter them as our knowledge, viewpoints, and entire life experience and cultural surroundings change. Some of us would probably have difficulty living without them, but we would certainly not be able to live if we only wanted to live side by side with perfection. Perfection does not say anything about the participation of language in the processes of culture. It is wonderful to stumble over as an exception, but in literature, as in the rest of life, perfection is useless as a fixed norm for practice. Many authors who we could not be without would fall through with a crash. The work of Balzac, Dickens, Tolstoj or Dante are often uneven, at times loose. Such writers were all in the middle of a cultural process they could not grasp, and they take us along with them. They write about the confusion of it rather than its clarification.

Globalization confronts literature and readers with new challenges determined by neither the literature nor the readers themselves. These challenges arise in the encounter between the demands and needs of a developing globalized cultural space and the resources that literature and language offer. In this encounter, new cultural conditions can call forth forgotten or unknown reserves in literature and tradition, and, conversely, with these resources literature can make us capable of shaping the cultural processes of globalization ourselves. Without us, in the place where we are, the processes do not take place at all.

Some purport that the local and the global have merged, so that now we are all *glocal*. This linguistic innovation is more clever than intelligent. The term casts a shadow over the fact that the relationship between the local and the global is fractured with shifting temporal and spatial boundaries. It requires circumspection and insight to get a context out of it. Literature is about this bumpy process rather than about a seamless glocal context. Literature is a mode of expression that we have at our disposal to make human experience be part of globalization.

In this situation there are two fundamental approaches to reading or studying literature. Like Harold Bloom, I pose the question, how and why should we read literature? However, in the foreword to the book *How to Read and Why?* (2000), his answer is different. The reader is the lonely wolf whose focus on himself increases through reading. Gradually, the reader is lifted above time and space to strengthen his sense of self *sub specia aeternitatis*. Reading unfolds like the growth of personal life. Maturity and the complete reading only come at the end, if not to say when it is too late. There is a silent assertion here that different life stages and experiences can be evaluated according to the same standards for maturity and its convergence with the age of retirement. I disagree. If I act like a retired man when I am 25, I am too mature. And if I act young with young people as a 70-year-old, I am immature. With or without literature there is no ideal maturity as a normative common denominator.

Bloom is of course right that both literary works and readers are unique phenomena that can wander across time and place, literature with its significations and us with our ideas. Like the reader, however, literature is also always anchored outside itself; it is historical. To look more deeply into one's own eyes without getting a greater sense of the world outside is a higher kind of blindness. Literature today makes us see globalization as a concrete experienced cultural process in its present and historical dimensions, constituting a relevant challenge to both literature and its readers. That is why we should study literature and risk loosing it when testing it in the modern world – we will regain it in a new perspective.

REFERENCES

Appadurai, Arjun. 1996. *Modernity at Large*. Minneapolis: University of Minnesota Press.

Apter, Emily. 2006. *The Translation Zone. A New Comparative Literature*. Princeton: Princeton University Press.

Arendt, Hannah. 1957. Karl Jaspers: Citizen of the World. In *The Philosophy of Karl Jaspers*, ed. P.A. Schilpp, 539-555. La Salle: Open Court Publ.

Beck, Ulrich. 1997. *Was ist Globalisierung?* Frankfurt a.M.: Suhrkamp.

– 2004. *Der kosmopolitische Blick*. Frankfurt a.M.: Suhrkamp.

Beck, Ulrich, Anthony Giddens and Scott Lash. 1994. *Reflexive Modernization*. Stanford: Stanford University Press.

Bloom, Harold. 2000. *How to Read and Why?* London: Fourth Estate.

Brandes, Georg. 1906 [1899]. *On Reading. An Essay*. New York: Duffield & Co.

– 2008 [1899]. World Literature. In *Mapping World Literature. International Canonization and Transnational Literatures,* ed. Mads Rosendahl Thomsen, 143-147. London: Continuum.

Conrad, Joseph. 1950 [1897]. Preface to *The Nigger of the "Narcissus"*, vii-xii. London: Dent and Sons.

Damrosch, David. 2003. *What is World Literature?* Princeton: Princeton University Press.

Ette, Ottmar. 2001. *Literatur in Bewegung. Raum und Dynamik grenzüberschreitenden Schreibens in Europa und Amerika*. Weilerswist: Velbrück Wissenschaft.

– 2005. *ZwischenWeltenSchreiben. Literaturen ohne festen Wohnsitz*. Berlin: Kadmos.

Ghosh, Amitav. 2000. *The Glass Palace*. New York: HarperCollins.

Glissant, Edouard. 1981. *Le discours antillais*. Paris: Le Seuil.

Larsen, Svend Erik. 2005. Self-Reference: Theory and Didactics between Language and Literature. *The Journal of Aesthetic Education* 39/1: 13-30.

– 2008. World Literature or Literature Around the World? In *World Literature World Culture*, eds. Karen-Margrethe Simonsen and Jakob Stougaard-Nielsen, 25-36. Aarhus: Aarhus University Press.

Lechner, Frank and John Boli, eds. 2004. *The Globalization Reader* (2. ed.). London: Routledge.

Lefevere, André. 1990. Translation: Its Genealogy in the West. In *Translation, History and Culture*, eds. Susan Bassnett and André Lefevere, 14-28. London: Pinter.

Lefevere, André and Susan Bassnett. 1998. Where are we in Translation Studies? In *Constructing, Cultures. Essays on Literary Translation*, eds. Susan Bassnett and André Lefevere, 14-28. Clevedon: Multilingual Matters.

Malouf, David. 1990. *The Great World*. London: Vintage.

Milner, Andrew. 2005. *Literature, Culture and Society* (2. ed.). London: Routledge.

Nabokov, Vladimir. 1973. *Strong Opinions*. New York: McGraw Hill.

Nerrière, Jean-Paul. 2005. *Parlez Globish! Don't Speak English*. Paris: Eyrolles.

Noyes, John K. 2006. Goethe on Cosmopolitanism and Colonialism: *Bildung* and the Dialectic of Critical Mobility. *Eighteenth-Century Studies* 39/4: 443-462.

O'Brien, Susie & Imre Szeman. 2001. The Globalization of Fiction/The Fiction of Globalization. *South Atlantic Quarterly* 100/3: 603-626.

Pratt, Mary Louise. 1992. *Imperial Eyes. Travel Writing and Transculturation*. London: Routledge.

Prendergast, Christopher, ed. 2004. *Debating World Literature*. London: Verso.

Saussy, Haun, ed. 2006. *Comparative Literature in an Age of Globalization*. Baltimore: Johns Hopkins University Press.

Sinnett, Frederick 2008 [1856]. *The Fiction Fields of Australia*. Milton Keynes: Dodo Press.

Tabbi, Joseph and Michael Wurtz, eds. 1997. *Reading Matters. Narratives in the New Media Ecology*. Ithaca: Cornell University Press.

Thomsen, Mads Rosendahl. 2008. *Mapping World Literature. International Canonization and Transnational Literatures*. London: Continuum.

Tomlinson, John. 1999. *Globalization and Culture*. London: Polity Press.

White, Patrick. 1989. The Prodigal Son. In *Patrick White Speaks,* ed. Christine Flynn and Paul Brennan, 13-17. Sydney: Primavera Press.

White, Patrick. 1988 [1957]. *Voss*. London: Vintage.

Žižek, Slavoj. 2006. Mozart as Kritiker postmoderner Ideologie. In *Mozart. Experiment Aufklärung im Wien des ausgehenden 18. Jahrhunderts*, ed. Herbert Lachmaier, 339-344. Wien: Hatje Canz.

NOT ANOTHER ADULT MOVIE:

SOME PLATITUDES ON GENERICITY AND THE USE OF LITERARY STUDIES

Sune Auken

A key question when discussing the reasons for literary studies is whether the study is an aim in itself or a means to achieve some other purpose. One of the fundamental discrepancies here seems to be that although literary studies as a means to an end is the easier argument to make, very few people actually engage seriously in literary studies for any other purpose other than their own need to understand and enjoy literature.

For a number of years now I have been bringing up the question "why study literature?" in all my freshman classes. Even before their first day at the university practically all of my students have been asked why they want to study literature, and precious few have had any particular luck answering it. Thus, they are often intimidated and frustrated by the question, and they spend a lot of time dodging it or mulling it over. But more than that, they *feel* the discrepancy just described. They feel awkward trying to defend the study of literature for its own sake, and thus they tend to resort to the second line of argument, but not entirely without feeling that they are somehow betraying themselves. And in one important sense they obviously are: they have one motive for studying literature, interest, but they indicate other reasons that are easier to defend socially. This situation calls for a response from us as teachers of literature. A major reason for the importance of this subject is that we fail our students, we fail our subject matter, and in an important sense we fail ourselves too if we are not able to give a meaningful answer to the question "why study literature?"[1] The crisis of legitimacy is read-

---

1   In the 20th century the *importance* of literature has been held as an equally central assumption in movements otherwise opposed. The "Great Books" tradition, towards which I admit having a profound weakness, presupposes an inherently edifying effect in the studying of literature – to the point where Eliot (1968) can make this claim about I. A. Richards: "Mr. Richards, like every serious critic of poetry, is a serious moralist as well" (Eliot 1968, 17). The importance of literature, if not the edifying effect, is

ily apparent in Fleming (2000), whose presentation of the two paradigms underlying literary studies, the "wisdom" paradigm and the "knowledge" paradigm, is lucid, but whose own solution to the crisis in the dominant knowledge paradigm is woefully inadequate.

It is essential to realize that the question itself is more interesting than threatening. The real threat lies in the questioner's presupposition, not in the question. It seems that the question in itself is frequently asked not from a desire to obtain a sensible answer, but from a desire to expose the study of literature as useless and the student as lazy or as an egotistical. So the presupposition is that the question has no meaningful answer; hence the scare effect on the students. However, when asked in an open-minded hermeneutical context,[2] the question is both fundamental and enlightening as it involves such issues as the nature of language, the nature of literature, the nature of humankind, the nature of society, etc. Also: as teachers of literature we really *want* to know why literature is worth studying and teaching, and, if anything, it is our experience as both readers and teachers that makes it really worth studying. Why else would most of us have intense experiences of meaning when teaching it, and why else would our students have similar experiences from learning it?[3]

The basic claim of this short and tentative article is that the concept of genre – difficult, slippery and manifold as it is – shows us that to study literature for its own sake actually by and of itself leads to knowledge readily relevant in a number of other contexts. The point is that not only do we avoid the choice between studying literature for literature's own sake and

---

confirmed in much criticism of literature. Abbreviated to the point of parody: Marxist criticism portrays literature as an important part of an oppressive superstructure. Feminist criticism portrays it as an important part of a patriarchal oppression. Queer theory establishes literature as an important part of a heteronormative oppression. And deconstructive criticism features it as an important expression of logocentric oppression. They all agree that it is exceedingly important, though usually for worse. For a more nuanced criticism of several of these positions see Bredella 1996.

2   Cf. Gadamer 1990, 368-384.

3   This intense experience of meaning C.S. Lewis, who is far less of a literary aristocrat than Eliot, holds to be the real literary experience that singles out real literary reading as a separate activity. After having described how the persons who read literature for status always adjust their opinions and their tastes "at exactly the right point", Lewis continues: "Yet, while this goes on downstairs, the only real literary experience in such a family may be occurring in a back bedroom where a small boy is reading *Treasure Island* under the bed-clothes by the light of an electric torch" (Lewis 1961, 8).

LOCALITY AND TEMPORALITY

studying it for some other purpose, we actually get better access to the things usually put forward as the "real" purpose of studying literature *by* studying it for its own sake.

The understanding of how genres – or perhaps rather, generic structures – work within literature is of far-reaching importance in the fields of literary history and literary theory. Long after the ambition to produce anything akin to a sound genre system has been abandoned, we continually refer to generic concepts. Indeed we seem unable to go anywhere in literary studies without these concepts. A few recent titles, chosen more or less randomly: *The Novel. An Anthology of Criticism and Theory, 1900-2000* (Hale 2006), *Novel Histories. The Fiction of Biblical Criticism* (Boer 1999), "Shall We Continue to Write Histories of Literature?" (Gumbrecht 2008), *Fiction on the Fringe. Novelistic Writing in the Post-Classical Age* (Karla 2009), *Narrative Negotiations. Information Structures in Literary Fiction* (Veel 2009) and *Music in Contemporary British Fiction. Listening to the Novel* (Smyth 2008). Even in this very short list, generic terms are prolific: "Anthology", "History of Literature", "Novel" and "Fiction" (both repeatedly), "Narrative", "Histories", "Criticism" and even "Music".

Within the study of genre, my personal interest has for a long time been drawn to the role that generic structures play in our interpretation of concrete works of literature. It is my conviction that even on the most basic level, our understanding depends on our ability to comprehend the complex and interwoven generic structures of which the work is composed.

The ability to recognize and interpret generic structures is not limited to our comprehension of literature, nor does it only take place in scholarly interpretation. Generic interpretation of literature is only a part – though a very important and illuminating part   of our wider competence in comprehending the culture or cultures to which we belong. And what frequently happens in scholarly interpretation is only – if "only" is the right word – a reflected and refined version of interpretative moves carried out by each of us on a daily basis. We continually make interpretations and decisions based on our culturally conditioned knowledge of the generic structures surrounding us. And if, for some reason, our knowledge of these structures is imperfect, faulty or incomplete interpretations may occur.

An example from everyday life: a few years back I was in a movie rental store in the otherwise pleasant company of my eldest son, who was by then four years old. Now, like other four-year-olds, he had rather fixed opinions about his needs and wants, and from the children's movie section he yelled across the store "Honestly, dad, not another adult movie!". I sometimes wonder how most kids manage to survive their childhood without getting strangled by their parents.

But I should have been proud, of course. My son was exhibiting a very high degree of generic competence, and only made a very slight mistake. He knew the overarching genre "movie"; he knew that within his culture a major possibility for getting access to a movie was in a rental store like this one. He also had the specific generic competence to know what *kind* of film he wanted his father to rent. He even displayed superior generic control in being able – by juxtaposition – to name the kind of film he did not care for. This gave him access to some sort of genre system based on rhetorical categories: there are movies made for children and movies made for adults. What he did was simply to assume the existence of generic – and communicable – categories based on this distinction. This led him to the category "adult movie", which he used in communicating his wishes across the store. From his point of view, the communication was a complete success, at least insofar as I, the object of his utterance, understood his opinion perfectly. But there was of course one slight glitch in my son's knowledge about the cultural situation into which he was speaking. Apparently, not really having a conscious concept of such matters, he was unaware that the generic term "adult movie" is a euphemistic term for "pornographic movie" – and thus caused his father some embarrassment in the movie rental store.

What is exemplified by this anecdote is that generic categories are always present in meaning-making, that our use of them is creative and that even slight juxtapositions of categories can have a huge impact on the interpretations possible in the situation – sometimes even to the point of parody. The situation also exemplifies the conventional power of genre. Even though the use of pornographic material is so widespread that most people in the rental store probably had first-hand experience of it, and even though nobody suspected me of exposing my son to pornography (I hope!), the situation was exceedingly awkward.

Another question central to the study of genre is active in the situation as well: the convergences across the demarcation line between fact and fiction. My son wanted a particular *kind* of fiction and so he used a generic term. However, the effect may have been a story worth telling, but it most certainly was not fiction. Now, much has been said about the demarcation line between fact and fiction.[4] I can merely add a few platitudes: within genre studies, especially when it comes to generic interpretation, there is a constant

4   Cf. Cohn 1999, Walsh 2007.

intertwining of the two spheres. Looking through the trash box of my e-mail account, I came across a letter sent by the "U.K National e-Lottery" with a genre given in the e-mail header reading "*Notification Letter*".[5] The letter itself reads:

Congratulations,

Your email won(71,500 British Pounds) on our online draw, 15th June, 2009.

To claim, kindly provide your: Full Name, Full Address, Telephone Number, Occupation, Sex, Age & Country of Residence via email.

Best wishes.
Mary Westley.

Online Co-ordinator

Read within the genre given in the paratext, this is a notification of a very big prize, which has apparently been won by the recipient of the e-mail, in this case me. There is, however, ample evidence to suggest that something is not quite right. There are a number of mistakes in the English of the letter and a strange looking typo ("won(71,500 British Pounds)"), all rather puzzling in a letter coming from something sounding as official and British as the "U.K National e-Lottery". It also seems highly unlikely that I can win a lottery I never bought a ticket for, and somewhat unusual that I appear to have won a big prize from an organization that does not even know my name. On top of these intratextual and rhetorical clues comes culturally conditioned generic knowledge: I have seen a number of similar e-mails offering me either diplomas from strange, hitherto unknown universities, willing sex-crazed girls, shady economic deals or a number of more or less attractive things, and I know these offers to be concealed scams to get at my money. So we are basically dealing with two different genres here, a "notification letter" and a "scam". The notification letter is fictional, the scam is real. However in order for the scam to be successful, it has to pose as another genre, and as soon as the reader recognizes the true genre of the letter, the intended effect is nullified. The "notification letter" only exists as a cover for the scam, but the scam is never apparent in the text, and it cannot

---

5   I pick up the thread here from a similar though shorter analysis in Frow 2006, 100.

show itself in the text without losing its intended effect. So the con trick can only succeed if it successfully poses as a member – and in this case an utterly fictional member – of another genre: the "Notification Letter" loses its intended effect as soon as it is recognized as fictional.

Turning to a different and much more complex example, we will find that the immediate recognition of the fictionality of what poses as factual is a precondition for the intended effect. Margaret Atwood's Booker Prize winning novel *The Blind Assassin* (2000) contains a number of newspaper clippings. One of these (apparently from *The Globe and Mail*, dated October 7, 1938) has the headline "Griffen Lauds Munich Accord". In this article, a Canadian industrialist named Richard Griffen is quoted from a speech entitled "Minding Our Own Business". According to the article, Griffin praised the British Prime Minister Neville Chamberlain for the Munich Accord. A central part of the article reads:

> In reply to questions about the status of Czecho-Slovakia under the Accord, he (Griffen. sa) stated that in his opinion the citizens of that country had been guaranteed sufficient safe-guards. A strong, healthy Germany, he claimed, was in the interest of the West, and of business in particular, and would serve to "keep Bolshevism at bay, and away from Bay Street". The next thing to be desired was a bilateral trade treaty, and he was assured that this was in progress. Attention could now be turned away from sabre-rattling to the provision of goods for the consumer, thus creating jobs and prosperity where they are most needed – "in our own backyard". The seven lean years, he stated, would now be followed by seven fat ones, and golden vistas could be seen stretching through the '40's.
>
> Mr. Griffen is rumoured to be in consultation with leading members of the Conservative Party, and to be eyeing the position of helmsman. His speech was roundly applauded.[6]

Anyone searching through the political history of Canada in the 1930s for a pre-eminent industrialist and ambitious politician by the name of Richard Griffen will search in vain – obviously. There is nothing unrealistic about a Canadian businessman saying something to a similar effect at the time, but this exact person never said it; in fact he never existed. This is not a great revelation, as reasonably cultured reader who has come this far in Atwood's masterpiece will be fully aware that Griffen is a fictional character, having encountered him in that capacity over several hundred pages. Moreover, the

---

6   Atwood 2000, 555f.

reader will be aware that the overall generic context of the newspaper article or newspaper clipping (a small, but significant paratextually determined generic difference) quoted is a piece of fiction: Atwood's novel. These generic inferences – made at first glance by virtually all readers preconditioned by Western literary culture – are nonetheless so strong that Atwood actually has to insert a footnote informing the reader that one of the clippings – though fictionalized, of course, by the generic context – has actually been taken from a genuine article and copied into *The Blind Assassin*. Without this footnote, one would automatically have regarded this clipping as an invention alongside all the others.

The generic competence that allows the reader to recognize the fictionality of the newspaper clipping is, however, only the first step in a complicated interpretative process. A further step is the recognition that, despite the fictional nature of the clipping, it also involves a number of factual generic codes connected to the genre of the newspaper article or newspaper clipping. The generic distinction between the two becomes increasingly relevant here as the newspaper article is a text appearing within the paratextual framework of the whole newspaper, alongside other – possibly equally important – articles, aimed at a geographically and temporally limited readership. In this form, the life span of the text is exceedingly short. It is meant to be read one day and forgotten, or at least replaced by other articles the next. By contrast, the newspaper clipping is an article that has been singled out and saved for perusal at a later – possibly very much later – point in time. In Atwood's novel this later point is represented both by the publication date of the novel and by an autobiographical manuscript by Griffen's aged widow, Iris Chase Griffen, written in 1998-1999, which makes up the main part of the novel. Thus, we are dealing with a classical case of an embedded genre – or in the terms of Bakhtin, a relationship between a primary and a secondary genre.[7]

One genre, the embedded or primary genre, does not appear on its own terms, but is mediated through or embedded in another genre whose total structure makes up the whole of the utterance – of which the embedded or primary genre is only a part. But still the embedded genre maintains a lot of its original properties. Indeed, those properties are usually why the embedded genre is there in the first place – and why the embedded genre is recognized at all. In this case the reader needs generic knowledge about real life newspapers to understand the fictive function of a clipping like this one, including understanding that because the fictive newspaper clippings

7   Bakhtin 2000.

draw on the credibility and objectiveness of the actual genre, the newspaper clippings give a credible and objective view of Richard Griffen which is not part of Iris' personal interpretation.

At least one more crossover between fact and fiction is at work in this text. Though the newspaper clipping is fictional and it appears in a work of fiction, viz. Atwood's novel, it presupposes that the reader has some actual knowledge of European history – at least The Munich Accord and Hitler's conquest of Czechoslovakia, and consequently the early history of World War II. It is also important to know that Richard Griffen may be fictional, but his views were shared by a number of important political and economic figures in Western Europe, Canada and the US, as is acknowledged by the last sentence in the quotation above, where Griffen's remarks are said to be "roundly applauded". If the reader knows that The Munich Accord was one of the great failures of the appeasement policy, that Hitler was a monster, that there was nothing whatsoever to be gained by a strong Germany under Nazirule, that the acceptance of the conquest of Czechoslovakia was a failed and callous policy, and that the seven years following 1938 were not seven fat years, but the years of the bloodiest war in history, he will have a striking characterization of Richard Griffen that confirms the hateful description given of him by his ex-wife. The picture drawn even takes on a certain apocalyptic aspect through the biblical imagery employed by Griffen in his reference to the seven lean and the seven fat years.

The intertwining of the two spheres, the factual and the fictive, is predominant in all kinds of literary discourses – though diverse, complex and contextually situated – but this example also illustrates, the distance between the genres actually used in everyday life and the literary application of these genres. As Cohn points out, fictional genres are not obliged to be in accordance with historical data – they can employ them, transform them and incorporate fictional as well as empirically true elements side by side.[8] This is frequently the case in the diary novel, the epistolary novel, the autobiographical novel and other similar forms – all fictive transformations of actually existing genres. These uses of genre are both a continuation and remodelling of the employed genre whenever it is contained within a fictive frame.

If we turn to the diary novel, the fictive character is no different from other diary writers in the sense that they are both describing – for private eyes only – their experiences, thoughts, emotions, etc. shortly after they took place. By virtue of the short time elapse, it is quite plausible that both

---

8   Cohn 1999, 15.

the fictive and the factual diary writer are capable of rendering lengthy observations, detailed descriptions of events, clothes, weather reports, etc., but this does not make the form any more "natural" or identical to the real life genre; even though the entries in the diary novel feign to be "for private eyes only", the novel as a whole is not thus intended, and this clearly affects the formalistic, rhetorical and thematical levels of the novel. For instance, one of the most common differences is that the diary entries will frequently exceed what a diary writer could have managed to put down on paper in the time the fictive frame allows for writing the entry – a case in point is Ishiguro (1996). Furthermore the entries in the diary novel often have a stylistic and rhetorical eloquence way beyond the real diary. However, the most striking difference is the focused thematic line in the diary novel in contrast to the actual diary; because the entries in the fictive diary make up a coherent story, there is nearly no room for remarks that do not add to either that story or the characterization of its characters. Even what seems to be a digression, such as the multiple catalogues in Fielding's *Bridget Jones's Diary* (1998) of her weight, calorie consumption, and number of drinks and cigarettes each day, serves a function in the larger narrative whole. They characterize Bridget's self-obsession and show what is primarily on her mind. Moreover, these catalogues are a means whereby she can gain some measure of self-control. Even though the novel has gone to great lengths to mime the actual diary, e.g. through abbreviations ("alcohol units 1 (v.g.), cigarettes 9 (v.g.) calories 1800 (g.)" (43)), the omission of the subject and rather short paragraphs with nearly no lengthy observations, the novel is a coherent story, which describes Bridget Jones' journey over exactly one year from a lonely, desperate "singleton" to a person able to "form functional relationship with responsible adult" (3). In short, *Bridget Jones's Diary* primarily uses incoherence as a feature from the actual diary – in contrast to most diary novels – but in the fictive frame this incoherence is transformed into a coherent image and story of an unhinged, insecure and fumbling individual who tries to find meaning in her life and achieves this goal on the very last pages.

As soon as an actual genre is transformed into a fictive frame, the fictive genre both employs certain variable characteristics of the actual genre, as a mimesis, and delineates itself from it when this is necessary for the fiction as a whole. Both the mimicry and the delineations are due to either formalistic, thematic or rhetorical considerations, specific to that particular work only, and therefore provide an essential generic understanding of how genres are put to use. In this process the reader, the student, or the scientist becomes aware not only of the uses of genres in the particular work, but, on a more general level, of how we use genres – both in fiction and real life – to convey meaning in different contexts.

The central place held by literature within genre studies is to some degree historical. Since genre was a major concept in literary studies at a much earlier point than in other studies, a lot of the basic assumptions – and a lot of the basic mistakes – have been made within literary studies. Even today literary theory is still vital to the study of genre – though indispensable work in genre theory has been made in a number of other fields, especially linguistics and rhetorics (such as Swales (1990) and Miller (1984, 1994)). Though rhetorics has had a long genre tradition, it has focused less on a theoretical or analytical understanding of genres, instead primarily employing a didactic approach, e.g. how is a good sermon, speech, letter, poem, etc. written. The basic, and very tentative assumption here is that since literature holds a central place in genre studies, and since genre holds a central place in culture, then studying literature, and especially studying genre in literature, is, by and of itself, conducive to our understanding of culture. And as literature is best studied by actually studying literature – and by now we are knee deep in platitudes – we really need to do just that, whether we study literature as a means to acquire cultural knowledge or, if you will, competence, or as an aim in itself. Hence, as is shown in the different examples given above, the line between fiction and fact is permeable – no matter what signposts, rhetorical situations or other characteristics are available to help us distinguish one from the other. There is a constant osmosis going from one to the other and back again; you cannot understand one without competence in the other and vice versa. This demonstrates that the ability to comprehend literature is by no means isolated. In many respects, the meaning-making taking place in our comprehension of literature is a specific form of a meaning-making that takes place all the time in our general interaction with the culture or cultures in which we participate. This is true not only of fiction, but also of other kinds of literature.

Turning back to genericity, we can see that much of our cultural competence is cast in generic form. As in so many other fields within the humanities, the study of genericity is marred by vagueness, by concepts whose meaning suddenly transmogrifies, by problems of demarcation between areas, etc. David Hume's attack on the human sciences in the introduction to *A Treatise of Human Nature* applies here as much as anywhere.[9] But, as is

9   Hume 1984, 41-46.

also the case elsewhere, this has more to do with the ambiguous character of the subject matter we are attempting to analyse than with any inherent shortcoming in the humanities. What is more: ambiguous and vague meaning-making is at the very heart of genericity. Generic knowledge is, so to speak, knowledge of the not known. If I enter a book store and go to the shelf with "Poetry" written on it (Oh, happy book store that has such a shelf), I know beforehand, without even having seen the books on the shelf, much less opened them, something of what to expect from them. Indeed, in all likelihood that is why I approach the shelf in the first place: I like poems and thus anticipate finding something I might like there. However, my generic knowledge is also knowledge of the not known as I would be utterly unable to recite even a single paragraph from the books there (unless, of course, it turned out that I knew some of the collections of poetry already); and, indeed, if I already knew what was in the books on the shelf I probably would not bother to approach it, but rather look for other books I did not know already. So generic knowledge is based on what may appear to be an inherent paradox at first glance: I approach the shelf because I know what I will find, but I also approach it because I do not know what is there. This is true not only of collections of poetry, novels or other kinds of literature, but equally of other areas. You choose to watch a "Newscast" on TV for the exact same reason. You want "news", something you do not yet know, but you do know that you want it. Seen from this angle, generic knowledge has some of the central characteristics of the question as it is described by Gadamer (1990). It is open-ended; there is no telling what the answer will be, and in order to achieve a new understanding, one has to keep the question afloat for as long as possible. But at the same time, it is not without direction; it imposes certain restraints on the investigation and it sets a subject for it, thus allowing it to move forward without being constantly sidetracked.

It is surprising that genre theory took so long to move from a specifically literary tool to one directed at a broader cultural horizon. Once you begin to take notice, you will see genres everywhere. We have newspaper genres (letter to the editor, commentary, reportage, review, TV or radio program, obituary, editorial, etc.), we have TV genres (news, show, competition, commercial, documentary, mockumentary, etc.), we have genres in libraries (fiction, non-fiction, poetry, biography, history, etc.), and the new media have generated a number of new genres (web page, text message, facebook status update, blog, wiki, etc.), each with its own specific characteristics. What is more, you do not even have to move into the field of culture or media to find yourself in the midst of genres. People go to a "consultation" at the doctor's, train for a "job interview", and children get confused when their parents tell them "we are not arguing, we are having a discussion" as all indications point to the communicative genre being an "argument" and not a "discussion".

Moreover, generic understanding is tacit to a very high degree. It is also active when we are not aware of it, even if we are unaware that such a thing as competence in genre actually exists. Most members of "our" culture are able to master the explicit and implicit rules governing the generic social situations described above without needing to reflect on the fact that they are actually dealing with genres. Despite being vague, ambiguous and hard to define, generic competence is a necessary and nuanced tool in our understanding of the cultural landscape surrounding us.

As indicated above, genericity is more than just expectations guiding our choice of book/TV program/movie, etc., it is also an open-ended set of regulations which governs our interpretation of works or situations. This has been unfolded in a number of different studies and needs no further elaboration here. The "laws" of a genre are clearly not fixed and immovable, and multigenericity, genre bastardizations, genre breaks and genre mixtures are prolific. This is clearly demonstrated in the works of, for instance, Fowler (1982) and it is recurrently evident in any extensive studies of generic structures; it is evident in Croce's refutal of genre as a concept, in a number of details in Frye's work with genre as rhetorical structures, in Bakhtin's distinction between primary and secondary genres, and in Hans Robert Jauss' lucid discussion of the medieval genres.[10] Even at the time of writing the article, Derrida (1980) was evidently flogging a dead horse when he made a display of discovering that genres actually do mix. But still, as my example from the video rental store demonstrates, we have a very clear understanding of what is implied by different genres, and we are able to register the significance of even minor juxtapositions within genres.[11]

---

10 Croce 2000 [1902], Frye 1968 [1957], Bakhtin 2000 [1979], and Jauss 1982 [1972].

11 From this intertwining of literary studies and a broader cultural horizon the question may arise whether the beneficiary effects from literary studies described here are really just a local form of beneficiary effect achievable through cultural studies in general, and thus whether literary studies might as well be replaced by cultural studies. The question, however, seems slighty flagellantic, and somewhat meaningless as it presupposes that it detracts from the result if two different approaches lead to it. Literature remains worth studying for these reasons even though the same reasons might be given in favour of other approaches within the humanities.

Let me return to the opening question of this article. Is literature studied as an aim in itself or as a means to achieve some other purpose? Two dangers are inherent in this question. If, on the one hand, we argue too vehemently for literary studies on the grounds that we achieve something else through them, I believe we have lost the game before it even begins, as this "something else" will most likely always be better achieved by aiming directly at it. Moral philosophy is best studied by studying moral philosophy, language by studying language, history by studying history, and if you want to solve personal issues, consulting a psychologist or psychiatrist is probably the right thing to do. What is more, no matter how seriously we study literature in order to achieve other aims, we are in one important sense not studying it at all. Lewis (1961), using a soccer metaphor, describes it like this:

> The man who plays football for his health is a serious man: but no real footballer will call him a serious player. He is not whole hearted about the game; doesn't really care. His seriousness as a man indeed involves his frivolity as a player; he only 'plays at playing', pretends to play.[12]

On the other hand we must not become so purist that we are unable to accept the beneficial effects of reading literature as intrinsic to the study of literature. Arguments along the line that art serves its own purpose and needs no further justification are tantamount to argumentative solipsism as they will convince nobody not convinced already. Oscar Wilde's famous "all art is quite useless" aphorisms at the opening of *The Picture of Dorian Gray* are wonderfully elegant and arrogant, of course, but they presuppose that the reader is able to appreciate literature without any help from the book, and anyone approaching the study of literature without this sense will get every possible prejudice he ever had about literature confirmed by the aphorisms.

It is, of course, worth noting that we will learn a lot of things about history, language, psychology, etc. by studying literature, and this fact does not diminish the value of literature or of literary studies. In fact, many "defences of literature" will at some point end up arguing along the lines of Tzvetan Todorov:

> If someone asks me why I love literature, the answer that I immediately think of is that literature helps me live. I no longer seek in literature, as I did in adolescence, to avoid wounds that real people could inflict upon me; literature

---

12 Lewis 1961, 11.

does not replace lived experiences but forms a continuum with them and helps me understand them. Denser than daily life but not radically different from it, literature expands our universe, prompts us to see other ways to conceive and organize it. We are all formed from what other people give us: first our parents and then the other people near us. Literature opens to the infinite this possibility of interaction and thus enriches us infinitely. It brings us irreplaceable sensations through which the real world becomes more furnished with meaning and more beautiful. Far from being a simple distraction, an entertainment reserved for educated people, literature lets each one of us fulfil our human potential.[13]

It is hard to imagine two critics more different than Todorov and Lewis, but here, as in Lewis (1961), we have a deep-rooted sense of the importance of literature to life very close to that expressed in the Great Books-tradition. At a later stage in his argument, Lewis also puts forward viewpoints on the "use of literature" quite similar to Todorov's. So the basic argument seems to be that there may be great benefits from spending a lot of time on literature, but that these benefits are best achieved by reading literature out of interest and for the sake of literature. In fact, the core of the argument might well prove to be that these benefits are intrinsic to the study of literature *as* literature, and cannot be achieved by studying literature as a means to an end.

Here, the study of genre offers a crucial opportunity. Genre is a vital concept at all levels of the study of literature, so in working with genre we are at the heart of literary studies, and we are thus studying literature as an aim in itself. There is plenty of room for the Lewisian reader who reads literature to admire it as such, who studies it to become more receptive to the manifold and all-consuming experience of reading, who reads out of a passion for literature.

But as we have seen even *within* the field of literature, the factual plays an important role, and as readers we will repeatedly need to have recourse to information taken from the realm of the factual in order to understand what we read. Moving from the fictional to the factual realm, we will constantly need to have recourse to different kinds of fictive genericity in order to find our way. So we cannot study literature from a generic perspective without at the same time entering the factual world. There may be "signposts" (Cohn) or rhetorical considerations (Walsh) telling us when we cross from one realm to the other, but there is no such thing as an isolated literary understanding of genre. Even in the case of Fowler (1982), a literary scholar if ever there was

---

13   Todorov 2007, 17.

one, the principles guiding his understanding of literary genre are relevant in numerous other contexts, as witnessed by Swales (1990).

Consequently, as soon as you take up the study of literary genericity, you will end up studying not *just* literary genericity, but genericity in a much broader context. Seen from this perspective, a clear distinction between studying literature as an aim in itself or as a means to an end *could* be seen as a misunderstanding, since studying literary genericity in order to understand literature will by itself give you a deeper understanding of a much broader cultural horizon – which will prove beneficial in regions far beyond literary studies. But, in fact, this can only be achieved in a satisfactory manner by studying literature with the aim of studying literature – not just reading it for the sake of your health.[14]

Written with the assistance of Christel Sunesen.

REFERENCES

Atwood, Margaret. 2000. *The Blind Assassin*. London: Virago Press.
Bakhtin, Mikhael. 2000 [1979]. The Problem of Speech Genres. In *Modern Genre Theory*, ed. David Duff. Edinburgh: Pearson Education Ltd.
Boer, Ronald. 1999. *Novel Histories. The Fiction of Biblical Criticism*. Sheffield: Sheffield Academic Press.
Booth, Wayne, C. 1988. *The Company We Keep. An Ethics of Fiction*. Los Angeles: University of California Press.
Bredella, Lothar. 1996. How can Literary Texts Matter? In *Why Literature Matters*, eds. Rüdiger Ahrens and Laurenz Volkmann, 101-115. Heidelberg: Universitätsverlag C. Winter.
Cohn, Dorrit. 1999. *The Distinction of Fiction*. Baltimore. The Johns Hopkins University Press.
Croce, Benedetto 2000 [1902]. Criticism of the Theory of Artistic and Literary Kinds. In *Modern Genre Theory*, ed. David Duff. Edinburgh: Pearson Education Ltd.
Derrida, Jacques. 1980. The Law of Genre. *Critical Inquiry* 7/1: 55-81.
Eliot, T.S. 1968 [1933/1964]. *The Use of Poetry and the Use of Criticism*. London: Faber and Faber.
Fielding, Helen. 1998 [1996]. *Bridget Jones's Diary*. London: Picador.
Fleming, Bruce E. 2000. What is the Value of Literary Studies? *New Literary History* 31/3: 459-476.

---

14 The author wishes to thank The Genre Research Group at The Institute for Scandinavian Studies and Linguistics at The University of Copenhagen and – for language revision – Rita Rosenberg.

Fowler, Alastair. 1982. *Kinds of Literature. An Introduction to the Theory of Genres and Modes*. Cambridge: Harvard University Press.

Frow, John. 2006. *Genre*. New York: Routledge.

Frye, Northrop. 1968 [1957]. *Anatomy of Criticism*. New York: Atheneum.

Gadamer, Hans-Georg. 1990 [1960]. *Wahrheit und Methode*. Tübingen: J.C.B. Mohr (Paul Siebeck).

Gumbrecht, Hans Ulrich. 2008. Shall We Continue to Write Histories of Literature? *New Literary History* 39/ 3: 519-532.

Hale, Dorothy J. 2006. *The Novel. An Anthology of Criticism and Theory, 1900-2000*. Malden: Blackwell Publishers.

Hume, David 1984 [1739-1740]. *A Treatise of Human Nature*. London: Penguin Books.

Ishiguro, Kazuo 1996 [1989]. *Remains of the Day*. London: Faber and Faber.

Jauss, Hans Robert. 1982 [1972]. Theory of Genres in Medieval Literature. In *Towards an Aesthetic of Reception*. Translated by Timothy Bahti, 76-109. Brighton: The Harvester Press Ltd.

Karla, Grammatiki A., ed. 2009. *Fiction on the Fringe. Novelistic Writing in the Post-Classical Age*. Leiden: Brill.

Lewis, C.S. 1961. *An Experiment in Criticism*. Cambridge: Cambridge University Press.

Miller, Carolyn. 1984. Genre as Social Action. *Quarterly Journal of Speech* 70: 151-76.

Miller, Carolyn. 1994. Rhetorical Community: The Cultural Basis of Genre. In *Genre and the New Rhetoric*, eds. Aviva Freedman and Peter Medway, 67-78. London: Taylor and Francis.

Smyth, Gerry. 2008. *Music in Contemporary British Fiction. Listening to the Novel*. New York: Palgrave Macmillan.

Swales, John M. 1990. *Genre Analysis. English in Academic and Research Settings*. Cambridge: Cambridge University Press.

Todorov, Tzvetan 2007. What is Literature For? *New Literary History* 38/1: 13-32.

Veel, Kristin. 2009. *Narrative Negotiations. Information Structures in Literary Fiction*. Göttingen: Vandenhoeck & Ruprecht.

Walsh, Richard. 2007. *The Rhetoric of Fictionality. Narrative Theory and the Idea of Fiction*. Columbus: Ohio State University Press.

Wilde, Oscar. 2006. *The Picture of Dorian Gray*. New York: Oxford University Press.

MODELS AND THOUGHT EXPERIMENTS

Brian McHale

MODELS

Why study literature? Among the most compelling reasons is one that derives from the work of the contemporary Israeli cultural theorist, Itamar
Even-Zohar. In Even-Zohar's view, the most valuable product of the literary
system is not texts as such but the cultural models from which texts are
constructed, and which they in turn help to maintain and circulate. "The
most consequential socio-semiotic product of literature", Even-Zohar writes,
"lies ... on the level of images, moods, interpretation of 'reality', and options
of action. The products on this level are items of cultural repertoire: models
of organizing, viewing, and interpreting life" (Even-Zohar 2004). If we adopt
this view of literature's cultural function, its cultural work, then one reason to
study literature is that literary study provides extraordinary, privileged access
to a culture's models of reality, enabling reflection on culture's world-making
and world-maintaining functions. Literary study allows us to glimpse how
a culture organizes itself and the non-human world around it, and this
applies not only to historically or geographically distant cultures, whose
models of reality might be alien to us, but also to our own contemporary
culture, whose models might pass unnoticed, taken-for-granted, pitched
below the threshold of our attention, without the salience or foregrounding
that literature imparts to them.

Far from being a mimetic theory of literature, Even-Zohar's approach is
a thoroughly *semiotic* one. Literature gives us access not to raw, unmediated
reality (whatever that might be), but to prefabricated reality, ready-made
reality, reality filtered through and shaped by a culture's grid of categories
and structured according to its system of relations.[1] By this account, literature mirrors, not the world, but *world-models*, the world as mediated by
a culture's modeling systems, beginning with the fundamental modeling
system of language itself. In this respect, Even-Zohar's approach has much
in common with other semiotically-oriented theories of literature and culture that emerged in the later decades of the 20th century, especially the

---

1   See Itamar Even-Zohar [1990] 2009. "'Reality' and Realemes in Narrative".

work of the Tartu-Moscow semiotic circle around Jurij Lotman, but also the literary-sociological approach of Pierre Bourdieu and certain aspects of recent cognitive poetics. There are even affinities between Even-Zohar's approach and that of new historicists such as Stephen Greenblatt (though Even-Zohar is generally wary of the impulse toward ideological critique that is a feature of much new historicist work).

Cultural models of reality, and consequently their literary reflections, vary widely in kind and scale, ranging from micrological details of language and behavior right up to worldviews and cosmologies. Toward the micrological end of this range, for example, fall our everyday, working models of linguistic variety, of the way language varies with respect to user and situation – what David Crystal once called our "linguistic stereotypes", as distinct from the expert knowledge of *actual* linguistic reality painstakingly acquired by professional linguists and dialectologists.[2] Literary texts, even the most verisimilar of novels, typically make use of such linguistic stereotypes to represent real-world speech. For instance, 20th-century novelists typically represent children's language not through transcriptions that reflect children's actual, real-world speech behavior, but rather by using a conventionalized linguistic stereotype of children's language. Novelists use not child-language, but *baby-talk*, the special variety of language that adults employ when *talking to* children (and sometimes to pets and lovers, too). The baby-talk model stands for, and *stands in* for, children's language in these novels; baby-talk *models* child-language for writers and readers alike, indeed for everyone except child-language specialists, who have a different, professional apprehension of children's speech.[3] Here, then, is one small-scale example of why we might study literature: in order to catch a glimpse of cultural models, such as the baby-talk model of child-language, that might otherwise escape our notice. It serves to illustrate why Even-Zohar's semiotic approach to literature and culture seems so compelling.

Compelling, but also limiting in at least one important respect. Approaching literature as a modeling system enables us to think about the ways that literature serves to reflect, maintain and recycle its culture's models, but it does not give us tools for thinking about the possibility of literature *exceeding* those models. Literature, viewed through this semiotic lens, can yield valuable insights into the *given* of culture, but what about literature's

2   See David Crystal 1973. "Objective and Subjective in Stylistic Analysis".
3   See Brian McHale 1994. "Child as Ready-Made: Baby-Talk and the Language of Dos Passos's Children in *U.S.A*".

putative capacity to produce the *new*? The cultural-semiotic approach constructs literature as a vehicle for *re-cognition*, for reminding us of what we already know (perhaps without fully knowing that we knew it); but does this preclude the possibility of grasping literature as a vehicle of *cognition*, of knowing something new? It is not clear that Even-Zohar's approach – any more than that of Lotman or Bourdieu, or of the cognitivists or new historicists for that matter – is particularly well-equipped to give a theoretical account of the possibility of literary *innovation*, and insofar as it fails to address innovation, it leaves unaccounted-for one of our strongest intuitions about literature's capacities. The various theories of literature as modeling system all treat literature's cultural work as essentially *homeostatic*: they account well for how literature helps *conserve* a culture, but not for how it could conceivably help *renew* one.

This seems to be the point of Terry Cochran's contribution to a recent special issue of *New Literary History* that posed the question, "What Is Literature Now?" – clearly a question akin to the one posed by the present volume, *Why Study Literature?* Cochran chooses to respond indirectly, by calling into question the monopoly that historical understanding holds over the study of literature now. Historicism is something like the default setting of literary understanding today, entailing a number of more or less unexamined assumptions about how literature means and how it is to be comprehended – namely, historically. When we *historicize* a text, that is, when we seek to restore it to the interpretative context of its time – and this even includes texts of our own historical moment when we seek to historicize them – we operate on the assumption that the text can know only as much as its historical moment knows, and no more. If we assumed otherwise, we would be opening the door to anachronism, to *untimeliness*, which is expressly prohibited by our historicist preconceptions. Cochran objects that, under the contemporary institutional regime of historicism, "literature … has been stripped of its powers to evoke the unknown, the unknowable, the unforeseen, or even the unthinkable" (Cochran 2007, 129). Now, theories of literature as modeling system are essentially historicist theories, and so Cochran's objection applies here, too. Insofar as we historicize literary texts as mirrors of their cultures' models, and the literary system as homeostatic, does that not effectively preclude any genuine innovation – any knowing of the unknown, seeing of the unforeseen, thinking of the unthinkable?

Certainly, that was what the 20th-century avant-gardes suspected: that the literary institution – business-as-usual literature – was the enemy of innovation and of the future, that its cultural work was profoundly conservative.

The avant-gardes, committed to the principle of aesthetic and cultural innovation, to "making it new", were for that very reason antagonistic toward literature's homeostatic function of maintaining and recycling cultural models. That antagonism took various forms in the course of the 20th century, from sly, subversive parody to appropriation and *détournement*, from estrangement to acts of literary vandalism and sabotage, from outright denunciation to silence and refusal. The avant-garde attitude rooted itself especially firmly in the French intellectual tradition, where literature's homeostatic function was assimilated to the Aristotelian concept of *doxa*, variously associated (depending upon the context) with "public opinion, verisimilitude, commonsense knowledge, commonplace, *idée reçue*, stereotype, cliché" (Amossy 2002, 369) – with the prefabricated, the ready-made, the already-given and already-known, all anathema to avant-garde aesthetics.

It is this avant-garde revulsion against *doxa* that animates, for instance, Roland Barthes' analytical masterpiece, *S/Z* (1970), which demystifies "classic" realism by reducing its cultural work of maintaining and circulating reality-models to the recycling of toxic clichés. Belonging to the same tradition, though less overtly demystificatory, is Michel Riffaterre's semiotics of poetry. According to Riffaterre, poetic text-production is only a kind of periphrasis-machine: ready-mades of various kinds – kernel words, clichés, "descriptive systems", intertextual fragments – are fed into the input end, certain operations of expansion and conversion are performed, and a poetic text emerges at the output end.[4] Riffaterre's unmasking of poetry's reliance on clichés, stereotypes, and second-hand language – on *doxa* at the verbal level – is every bit as damaging to the prospects of innovation in literature as Barthes' autopsy of a Balzac story. There seems to be as little hope for true innovation in Riffaterre's poetics as there is in Barthes' – no way out of the dead end of homeostasis: literature will only ever repeat the given and the same, although with variations.

Innovation, the literary quality that I perceive to be unaccounted for in modeling-system approaches, needs to be distinguished from *deviation*. Deviation from received cultural models can be accommodated unproblematically by all these approaches, Barthes' and Riffaterre's as readily as Even-Zohar's or Lotman's. Indeed, without *some* deviation there would be no possibility of text-production at all. For instance, in Riffaterre's *doxic* semiotics of poetry, periphrasis in the form of expansion and conversion is required to produce a text that is a *variation* on received materials, and

----

4   See Michael Riffaterre 1978. *Semiotics of Poetry.*

not merely verbatim repetition. Similarly, in cognitive narratology, cultural scripts are given in advance and recycled by texts, but the *tellability* of any particular narrative depends upon its deviation from the received script; if there were no deviation, there would be no story, or at least no story worth telling (which amounts to the same thing).[5] In the same spirit, but adopting the long view of a transhistorical typology of culture, Lotman distinguishes between an "aesthetics of identity" and an "aesthetics of opposition". In the aesthetics of identity, satisfaction derives from the perfect correspondence between the text and the cultural models that it evokes. Its province is folk art, medieval art, *commedia dell'arte*, popular formula fiction, and all the varieties of "classicism". By contrast, the aesthetics of opposition, which values deviation from cultural models, is more typical of modern literary genres since Romanticism. Lotman gives the example of movie-going, where one approaches a film with

> a certain expectation based on advertisements, the name of the studio, the direc-
> tor and the actors, the film's genre, [the] opinions of your acquaintances who
> have already seen the film, and so on .... [I]f the entire work fits the *a priori*
> structure of your expectation, you leave the theatre with a profound sense of
> dissatisfaction. The work brought nothing new to you; the author's model of
> the world proved to be a cliché. ... [But if] the real course of the film and your
> idea of its necessary course enter into conflict, [then] this conflict destroys the
> old model of the world, which is sometimes false, sometimes merely familiar,
> representing knowledge that has been gained and transformed into a cliché. A
> new, more perfect model of reality is created (Lotman 1977, 288-9).

Lotman's account here of expectation and disappointment in movie-viewing is certainly compelling, yet his conclusion seems mistaken. The film's deviation from "your idea of its necessary course" seems very *un*likely to "destroy the old model of the world" and create a new one. Isn't it much more likely to *foreground* the old model, to render it salient, and implicitly to *corroborate* it? As with the deviation from a script that ensures tellability, here it is the deviation from received models that creates interest and aesthetic satisfaction. What it does *not* create is a new model, any more than a story renovates the script upon which it depends for its tellability. The script survives intact, as does the old world-model. Genuine innovation is not so easily achieved.

---

5   See David Herman 2002. *Story Logic: Problems and Possibilities of Narrative.*

MODELING-FOR, OR, THOUGHT EXPERIMENTS

Is there any way to reconcile a modeling-system approach to literature with our intuitions about literature's capacity for innovation? In other words, can we somehow preserve the advantages of theorizing about literature as modeling system while at the same time making room for the possibility of innovation in world-modeling? Yes, we can, on condition that we acknowledge the inherent doubleness of the very concept of *model*. Already more than thirty years ago, the anthropologist Clifford Geertz observed that *model* has two senses, "an 'of' sense and a 'for' sense". *Modeling of* involves manipulating signs in such a way as to capture a pre-existing reality, while *modeling for* involves manipulating reality in order to bring it into line with a semiotic template. Geertz gives the example of developing a flow-chart or a theory of hydraulics to capture how a dam works – *modeling of* – and then constructing a new dam using the specifications implied in the flow-chart or the hydraulic theory – *modeling for*.[6] When literature performs its homeostatic function of maintaining and circulating cultural models, this is analogous to what Geertz calls *modeling of*. Given the built-in doubleness of the concept of *model*, the question immediately arises, whether there is any sense in which literature can be understood as a *model for* reality, not just as a *model of* it, and if so, to what degree does this *modeling for* function allow for the possibility of innovation?

A version of the *modeling for* function is already a feature of both Even-Zohar's and Lotman's approaches to literary modeling systems. Even-Zohar's approach explicitly accommodates both passive and active modeling, both the use of models as tools of understanding and their use as programs for operating in actual life, the former corresponding to something like Geertz's *modeling of*, the latter to *modeling for*. Lotman, once again adopting a culture-typological approach, associates the *modeling of* and *modeling for* functions with different eras in the history of culture. In certain eras – the era of 19th-century Realism, for instance – art, including literature, derives its models from reality – it circulates *models of* reality. In other eras, however – the Baroque era, the Romantic era, and again at the beginning of the modernist era – art *supplies* models for everyday behavior; life literally imitates art.[7] Only a theory of literature as *modeling for* reality adequately

---

6   See Clifford Geertz 1973. *The Interpretation of Cultures: Selected Essays*; see also Wolfgang Iser 2007. "Culture: A Recursive Process".

7   Jurij Lotman 1984. "The Theater and Theatricality as Components of Early Nineteenth-Century Culture".

explains, for instance, the otherwise incoherent behavior of the rebel officers of the Decembrist uprising in St. Petersburg in 1825.[8] The Decembrists were Romantics, and they acted out their Romantic literary models in real life, literally to the end – as far as Siberia, or even the gallows.

But is *modeling for* identical with innovation? Not necessarily, it appears. The case of the Decembrists, for example, appears to be more an instance of the *recycling* of cultural models, rather than the production of new ones. A more compelling example of innovative *modeling for*, which Lotman mentions by way of contrast with the Decembrists, might be the case of Turgenev, celebrated for his capacity to identify in the social life around him the emergence of new models of consciousness and behavior before anyone else did, and for capturing those models in fictional characters.[9] But does Turgenev's sensitivity to new models constitute innovation, or only a kind of prescience – a *modeling of* an emergent reality, rather than a *modeling for* a projected one? If we need an even stronger case, it might be that of Dante who, a century or more before the fact, according to Lotman, anticipates the model of the "Renaissance man" in his characterization of Ulysses. Lotman writes,

> [I]n this image of the heroic adventurer of his time, of the seeker, of the one who is inquisitive in all areas except that of morals, Dante discerned … not just the features of the immediate future, the scientific mind and cultural attitudes of the modern age, [but] the coming separation of knowledge from morality, of discovery from its results, of science from the human personality [...] Standing on the threshold of the modern age, Dante saw one of the greatest dangers of the future (Lotman 1990, 184).

If Lotman is right, then Dante's Ulysses would constitute a case of genuinely innovatory *modeling for* – the projection of an unprecedented future model of human identity and behavior.

Evidently we need to distinguish between cases such as Dante's Renaissance man before-the-fact and other, less innovatory instances of *modeling for*, such as the Decembrists' Romantic self-fashioning or Turgenev's emergent social types. It might help to have a separate category, and perhaps a fresh metaphor. Terry Cochran, in the article from *New Literary History* that

---

8   Jurij Lotman 1984. "The Decembrist in Everyday Life: Everyday Behavior as a Historical-Psychological Category".

9   *Ibid.*, 87.

I cited earlier, proposes just such a category. Cochran, it will be recalled, wants to rescue literature from the domination of historicism, and to re-empower it to evoke "the unknown, the unknowable, the unforeseen, or even the unthinkable" – to reclaim, in other words, its epistemological rights. To accomplish this, he proposes to associate literature with the notion of *thought experiment* (*Gedankenexperiment*), borrowed from theoretical physics.[10]

Thought experiments abound in the history of physical science. Galileo imagining what would happen if he dropped weights from the Leaning Tower, Newton imagining a bucket rotating at the end of a rope, Maxwell imagining his Demon violating the Second Law of Thermodynamics: these are all thought experiments. Thought experiments also abound in philosophy; in the discipline of history they go by the name of *alternate history*, while in political science they are called *counterfactual reasoning*. In some cases, at least, thought experiment aspires to produce new and unpredictable knowledge, and not just to expose the limitations of our conceptual apparatus (see Kuhn). It is thus an instance of *modeling for*, and one with the potential to innovate, not merely to recycle models. Cochran quotes the physicist and philosopher of science Ernst Mach, who as long ago as 1897 recognized the kinship between scientific thought experiments and other kinds, including literary kinds. Mach wrote:

> The planner, the builder of castles in the air, the novelist, the author of social and technological utopias is experimenting with thoughts; so, too, is the respectable businessman, the serious inventor and the researcher. All of them imagine conditions, and connect with them their expectations and conjecture certain consequences: they perform a thought experiment (Mach 1976, 136).

Physicists' thought experiments are essentially exercises in literary fiction, Cochran argues – little narratives. He writes:

> Schrödinger's cat, locked in a fictional box, eternally both dead and living, may allow for thinking the consequences of relativity theory, but it is above all a

---

10 See also Catherine Z. Elgin 2007. "The Laboratory of the Mind". In a similar spirit, John Gardner, the novelist and critic, once wrote, "True moral fiction is an experiment too difficult and dangerous to try in the world, but safe and important in the mirror image of reality in the writer's mind"; Gardner 1978. *On Moral Fiction*. Despite his having devoted an entire book to defining it, "moral fiction" remains basically an honorific category; it means, in effect, "Fiction that I value".

LOCALITY AND TEMPORALITY

work of literature, modest in length but powerful in suggestiveness (Cochran 2007, 139).

As it happens, Cochran is mistaken about the object of Schrödinger's thought experiment, which was *not* to illuminate the consequences of relativity theory but rather to expose the absurdity of the Copenhagen interpretation of quantum indeterminacy (about which Schrödinger was skeptical). Nevertheless, Cochran's point about the affinity between the imaginary cat experiment and literary narrative is compelling.

If physicists tell stories in order to think about the world – if they use literature to *model for* reality – then why shouldn't the converse be true? Why shouldn't literature be credited with the power to conduct thought experiments? There is at least one genre of literary narrative that consciously performs thought experiments; indeed, doing so is part of this genre's very definition. As Cochran observes, when Mach mentions "the author of social and technological utopias" in his list of thought experimenters, he is referring to science fiction. Lacking the term "science fiction" (which at the turn of the 20th century had yet to be coined), Mach nevertheless already recognized how intimately this genre is connected with thought experiment. Not all literary thought experiments are science fictions, of course, but all science fictions are by definition thought experiments, so I want to begin with this genre before moving on to consider literary fiction more generally.

Science fiction is of course a genre of "formula fiction", meaning that it depends to some extent on familiar, ready-made, prefabricated motifs and models; in Lotman's terms, it belongs to the aesthetics of identity. As with other formulaic genres (detective stories, romance novels, Westerns, slasher movies, *etc.*), readers come to science fiction partly to indulge in the comfortable pleasures of recognition and repetition: we *re*-cognize, with satisfaction, its motifs and materials, having seen them before, maybe many times before. Nevertheless, paradoxically enough, science fiction also depends for its generic identity on the principle of *newness*. Every science fiction, to qualify as science fiction at all, must posit something *new*: a place, thing, type of being, or state of affairs that is *not* to be found in our contemporary reality, but can be imagined to exist or occur in some *future* or spatially *distant* reality. Darko Suvin, science fiction's greatest theorist, calls this kernel of novelty the *novum* (Suvin, 1979).

Every science fiction asks, in effect, "What if?" What if beings lived on Mars? What if we could travel faster than the speed of light? What if all human reproduction occurred *in vitro*? What if all books were banned? This ontological proposition constitutes its *novum*, and around this kernel, or sometimes a number of such kernels, science fictions build their worlds. By definition, science fiction is a *world-building* genre. Of course, so are all other fictional genres, to some greater or less extent; if they did not undertake world-building at all, but relied entirely on the "givens" of received reality, they would not even qualify *as* fictional. World-building in science fiction, however, is *foregrounded* – conspicuous, spectacular, carried out in plain sight. It is a main source of science fiction's distinctive interest and pleasures, counterbalancing and complicating the pleasures of recognition that science fiction shares with other genres of formula fiction. To put it another way, science fiction conducts thought experiments. It "tries on" or "tries out" an ontological proposition – "What if?" – and then builds a scale-model world in which to develop some of the possible consequences of that proposition.

Science fiction thought experimentation – the building of scale-model worlds to develop the consequences of "what if" questions – is not the same as *forecasting*, with which it is sometimes confused. In fact, only rarely – much more rarely than science fiction's apologists would like to admit – does a science fiction accurately forecast some real-world innovation or turn of events. It is almost always wrong in what it forecasts (*e.g.,* lunar settlements at the beginning of the 21st century), and it almost always fails to predict the great transformative innovations (*e.g.,* personal computing). Successful forecasting (*e.g.,* Jules Verne's submarine, H.G. Wells' tanks, Arthur C. Clarke's communications satellite in geosynchronous orbit, William Gibson's cyberspace[11]) is no more than a kind of lucky accident, a minor side-effect, and not at all intrinsic to science fiction's poetics of thought experimentation.

What *is* essential to science-fiction poetics is the production of *alternative reality-models*. Science fiction enables us to think of the world as *otherwise than it currently is*. It projects a reality that is in some *systematic* way different from our own – different, that is, in its *models*, not just in its *individuals*.[12]

---

11 See Carl Freedman 2000. *Critical Theory and Science Fiction*. Of these "accurate" forecasts, cyberspace is perhaps the most interesting, since it is a true instance of *modeling for*: the developers of the internet were actually influenced by Gibson's vision of what cyberspace could be like. See also John Clute 2003. "Science Fiction from 1980 to the Present".

12 Even the most verisimilar contemporary realism – or "mundane" fiction, as science-fiction theorists sometimes rather invidiously call it – posits *individual* differences from received reality (people who never existed in the real world, places that cannot be found on the map, *etc.*), leaving the world-model intact; science fiction, by contrast, posits the kinds of difference that imply a different world-model.

LOCALITY AND TEMPORALITY

Science-fiction thereby throws our own reality-models into high relief; it *estranges* them, and encourages us to reflect on them. For this reason, Suvin defines science fiction as the fiction of *cognitive estrangement* – estrangement of received reality that leads potentially to new cognition, and not just *re*-cognition.[13] Projecting alternatives to received reality, science fiction serves the valuable function of enabling us to think of reality-models not as inevitably given, but as merely one set of possibilities among a range of other such possible models, and in that sense relativizes them. Moreover, it does so even if its "what if?" extrapolations never come to pass, or perhaps *especially* when they fail to materialize.[14]

Consider, for instance, a relatively straightforward case of science fiction thought experimentation: Alfred Bester's *The Stars My Destination* (1956), a superior example of the kind of science fiction novel being written in the United States in the mid-1950's. Undeniably colorful and inventive, yet in many respects conventional and formulaic, *The Stars My Destination* is often identified as a favorite science fiction novel by *other* science fiction novelists. It projects a future in which human beings have acquired the ability to travel instantaneously from place to place simply by the force of thought – by teleportation, or what in the novel itself is called *jaunting* (after the name of its fictional discoverer). Teleportation or jaunting is this novel's primary *novum*, though far from its only one, and Bester develops

---

13 The distinguished science fiction writer, Ursula LeGuin, in the 1976 introduction to her classic novel *The Left Hand of Darkness* (originally published in 1969) characterizes science fictions as "thought experiments" whose purpose is "not to predict the future ... but to describe reality, the present world"; "Introduction", in *The Left Hand of Darkness* (LeGuin 1976, n.p.). I would rather say, not that science fiction *describes* present reality, but that it estranges and relativizes it.

14 As a number of its theorists, including Jameson and Freedman, have observed, science fiction functions analogously in this respect to historical fiction. Historical fiction produces worlds that are always versions of the present, but the present *alienated, estranged* by historical distance; science fiction accomplishes the same thing, but typically by displacing its worlds in the *opposite* direction, toward the future. The two genres' compatibility of purpose is corroborated by the existence of a *hybrid* genre, that of *alternative history*, where science fiction's "What if?" premises are projected into the historical past: What if the Confederacy had won the American Civil War? What if the Axis powers had triumphed in the Second World War? What if Charles Babbage's steam-powered computer had been perfected in the 1820's? These are the premises of, respectively, Ward Moore's *Bring the Jubilee* (1953), Philip K. Dick's *The Man in the High Castle* (1962), and William Gibson's and Bruce Sterling's *The Difference Engine* (1991).

in considerable detail and with striking ingenuity some of the many consequences of this *novum* in various areas of human life: its consequences for labor and consumption, for personal security and sexual mores, for crime and punishment, for housing, urban design and everyday life, for the politics of war and peace. The multiple plots of this eventful narrative (including a revenge plot based on *The Count of Monte Cristo*) function as little more than pretexts, motivating devices enabling exploratory "grand tours" of a world transformed by jaunting.

Teleportation, it need hardly be said, is not yet a reality of our world, and it is unlikely ever to become one, so the value of *The Stars My Destination* as forecast would seem to be about nil; nevertheless, its value as a thought experiment is considerable. What teleportation produces – directly for inhabitants of this future world, and vicariously for Bester's readers – is the experience of drastically foreshortened space and time. Thanks to their powers of teleportation, these people of the future can circumnavigate the globe in a matter of hours, if not minutes – shadowed, of course, by ourselves as readers. At one point, Bester's criminal anti-hero, Gully Foyle, masquerading as a rich playboy, skips from one New Years Eve party to another, following midnight around the planet, from Canberra to Shanghai to Rome, and ending up in New York. Later on, in a cinematic chase-scene, Foyle stays one step ahead of his adversaries as he teleports himself from New York to San Francisco to Nome, Alaska, then to Tokyo, Bangkok, Delhi, Baghdad, Paris, and finally London, leading his pursuers, as the novel puts it, "three-quarters of the way around the world in fifty minutes" (Bester 1996, 253). Surely no-one could fail to hear in that phrase the echo of Jules Verne's title, *Around the World in Eighty Days* (1872), confirming what many readers would already have guessed: that Bester's motif of foreshortened space updates Phileas Fogg's 19th-century circumnavigation of the globe. Just as Verne's novel anticipates the "shrinkage" of the world that the new transportation technologies of the early 20th century would bring about, (Freedman 2000, 52) so Bester anticipates the even more drastic shrinkage of the planet that was imminent around the year 1956. Jaunting models the experience of *space-time compression* that David Harvey would come to associate with the postmodern condition of the late 20th century[15] – models it *before the fact*, since in 1956 the first commercial transatlantic jet service was still three years off, and other world-shrinking technologies of trans-

---

15 See David Harvey 1989. *The Condition of Postmodernity: An Enquiry into the Origins of Cultural Change.*

portation and communication (jumbo jets, communications satellites, the internet, *etc.*) lay even further in the future.

In this sense, Gully Foyle's jaunts around the world are literally prescient. More profoundly, by exploring some of the implications of his *novum* of jaunting, Bester produces a model of what, in the post-1989 world, we would come to call *globalization*: the *networking* of the planet through rapid transportation and speed-of-light communication; the economic and cultural consolidation of the world into a single market and something approaching a single monoculture; the recognition, for better or worse, of our planet-wide implication in each other's existences. *It's a small world, after all*: like Verne before him, Bester uses a science fiction *novum* to literalize that cliché.

Of course, Bester in 1956 could hardly have *known* that globalization was coming. His speculative model of a world reduced to unity by the speed and ease of travel was no doubt mainly conceived as an *alternative* to the world-model he himself experienced directly as reality – the polarized mid 1950s world of superpower confrontation, of East *versus* West, divided by an Iron Curtain. His projection of this alternative, cosmopolitan or globalized world (as we would later call it) gave himself and his contemporaries a tool for reflecting on their own Cold War world, offering a counter-model to "official" Cold War reality; it *relativized* that Cold-War-era reality. But, as it happens, Bester's alternative to the received world-model of 1956 actually anticipates later developments of that world-model, somewhat in the same way that Dante's image of Ulysses (according to Lotman) anticipates the Renaissance man. Bester's globalized world-model converges with our own; his thought experiment produces, not so much a *model of* reality, in Geertz's sense, as a *model for* it.[16]

---

16 Bester's model of globalization amounts to planetary "Americanization", perhaps unsurprisingly, since an "Americanized planet" has been the default setting for most Anglophone science fictions that have speculated about the unified "small world" of the future (Clute 66). Interestingly, however, in recent decades science fiction alternatives to that Americanized future have begun to appear, in which other cultures play the lead role that used to be automatically assigned to the United States. In the 1980's one could glimpse anticipations of a "Japanized" future in American science fiction. In the 1990's, with the cooling of the Japanese economy, that "Japan-centric" model gave way to other alternatives: "Islamicized" futures, "China-centric" futures, and so on. Thought experiments about globalization continue; but that is the subject for a different paper.

What, then, do we learn from science fiction? We learn that, at least under certain circumstances, literature is indeed capable of conducting thought experiments and producing innovative world-models – or at least that *one* genre of literature is capable of doing so. Moreover, for this particular genre, conducting thought experiments is not incidental, but a defining characteristic. The question then is, how generalizable are these insights – how applicable are they to literature more generally? What about genres that are not, as it were, bound by definition to undertake thought experiments?

"All fiction is, in a sense, science fiction", writes the science fiction theorist Carl Freedman. This is a bold claim. Freedman means by it that all fiction projects alternative worlds; that all fictional worlds diverge more or less widely from their cultures' world-models; that all fictions practice some degree of cognitive estrangement. "It is even salutary", Freedman continues, "sometimes to put the matter in deliberately provocative, paradoxical form, and to maintain that fiction is a subcategory of science fiction rather than the other way around" (Freedman 2000, 16).

So, putting the matter provocatively and paradoxically, let us try thinking about fiction as a subcategory of science fiction. Freedman relates an anecdote, perhaps apocryphal, told by the distinguished science fiction novelist Samuel R. Delany. According to Delany, a certain historian of his acquaintance who had become a regular reader of science fiction in his spare time began to worry that he would never be able to appreciate classic realist fiction again. So he tried the experiment of rereading Jane Austen's *Pride and Prejudice*, and found it interestingly transformed. The historian reported:

> "Before, I used to read novels to tell me how the world really was at the time they were written. This time, I read the book asking myself what kind of world would have had to exist for Austen's story to have taken place ..." (Delany 1984, 99).[17]

The historian, we might say, had ceased to read *Pride and Prejudice* for its *modeling of* the given nineteenth-century world, and had begun to read it for its *modeling for* a world. He now reads Jane Austen's fiction not as a mirror

---

17 See Freedman 2000. *Critical Theory and Science Fiction, 21,* citing Paul Alkon 1990, *Gulliver* and the Origins of Science Fiction" in *The Genres of* Gulliver's Travels, ed. Fredrik N. Smith, 163.

held up to a historical reality, but as an exercise in world-building – a kind of thought experiment. "As far as I can tell", Delany concludes, "this man has started to read Austen as if her novels were science fiction". *All* literary fiction, this anecdote suggests, is, like science fiction, a kind of thought experiment, in the sense that it projects a world rather than merely modeling a received one – or at least, it could fruitfully be read that way. Apocryphal nor not, Delany's anecdote provokes some interesting reflections. To what extent are other genres of fiction indeed susceptible of being read as science fiction, and what insights might such a reading yield?

I do not propose to try replicating the findings of Delany's historian friend by undertaking here to reread *Pride and Prejudice* as science fiction. To do so would involve reading Austen's novel pretty aggressively against the grain; moreover, I suspect *Pride and Prejudice* was chosen for this anecdote precisely because it was the unlikeliest candidate for this sort of reading, not because that reading would have been particularly productive or worthwhile. In any case, there are other novels in the realist tradition that might yield more interesting findings when read this way – novels that are, let's say, less character-centric than Austen's, and more *world-oriented*.[18] One candidate might be Cervantes's *Don Quixote*. Of course, *Don Quixote* can be read, and has been read, in character-centric ways that foreground characters' speech, behavior and interactions – in particular, those of the protagonist and his sidekick, Sancho Panza; but, unlike *Pride and Prejudice*, it also readily yields

---

18   The science fiction critic John Clute, somewhat more circumspectly than Carl Freed-
     man, claims not, as Freedman does, that all fiction is science fiction, but only that
     "any novel that is about the world shares a structural identity with the most overt
     tale of [science fiction]"; "Science Fiction from 1980 to the Present" in *Cambridge
     Companion to Science Fiction,* 2003, eds. Edward James and Farah Mendlesohn
     (Cambridge: Cambridge University Press), 78. "*About the world*" is a problematic
     qualification, of course – aren't all novels "about the world", more or less by defini-
     tion? – but I think we can intuitively grasp the distinction Clute is trying to make.
     In many types of fiction – Austen's novels are a good example – the "world" is pretty
     decisively relegated to the background, while (for instance) the speech, behavior,
     social interactions and inner lives of characters are pulled into the foreground. One
     could read Austen's novels for their modeling of, say, the human ecology of the
     English countryside, or even of Great Britain's overseas empire – and such readings
     have been undertaken, of course – but to read them this way is to read against the
     grain, which would not be the case with the type of novel that Clute characterizes
     as being "about the world".

itself to readings that emphasize the novel's *world*. This is the sort of reading that I propose to sketch here.[19]

Valued, and rightly so, for its representation of the concrete particulars of 16th-century Spain – inns and roadside encounters, herdsmen and criminals, agricultural labor and urban workshops – *Don Quixote* does not just record piecemeal the disparate data of its world; it also *models* its world globally. It is not so much *a* text, in the singular, as a *plurality* of texts, a textual *manifold*; and its world is accordingly plural rather than singular, not a universe but a *multi*verse. The primary narrative of Don Quixote's adventures is frequently interrupted by inset narratives belonging to other genres – pastoral, picaresque, a "Moorish novel" (*novela morisca*), a novelized honor play in the manner of Lope de Vega, *etc* (Cascardi 2002, 65) – each inset seeming to derive from a different world, or what Martínez-Bonati calls a different "region of the imagination" (Martínez-Bonati 1992, 39-67).[20] Some of these inset narratives intersect with Quixote's, while others are entirely or almost entirely disconnected from Quixote's story. Moreover, almost all of the inset narratives stand in some analogical relation to parts of Quixote's own story: they function as partial *mises-en-abyme*. In Part Two, narrativized theatrical spectacles replace Part One's inset narratives: a wedding masque, a puppet-show, and several elaborately staged hoaxes, which Quixote and Sancho mistake for reality, but which the aristocratic onlookers enjoy as theatrical entertainments – court masques, in effect, in which Quixote and Sancho are inadvertent masquers. These theatrical insets continue to function, much as the narrative insets did in Part One, as partial *mises-en-abyme* of *Quixote* itself, for instance in the case of Master Pedro's puppet-show (Part Two, chapter 26), which Don Quixote metaleptically interrupts, mistaking fiction for reality (not for the first or only time).

The world of *Quixote* appears to be simultaneously single and multiple,

---

19 Recall Shklovsky's characteristically perverse and brilliant interpretation of *Quixote*, which argues that the character of Don Quixote was only developed in order to motivate the novel's stringing together of diverse, heterogeneous materials – in other words, that character here is at the service of world (Shklovsky 1991). In the analysis of *Quixote* that follows, I paraphrase and occasionally quote from an earlier essay, "*En Abyme*: Internal Model and Cognitive Mapping" (McHale 2007).

20 Compare Cascardi: "The world of the *Quixote* is formed as if from sheaves of language" and "[t]he characters in *Don Quixote* are drawn as if from other fictional worlds" (Cascardi 2002, 62).

LOCALITY AND TEMPORALITY

integrated and heterogeneous, centripetal and centrifugal.[21] There is as a primary plane, that of Quixote's adventures, but that plane is frequently interrupted or punctuated by a variety of inset or recessed secondary planes, each inset mirroring, to some lesser or greater extent, the primary world of *Quixote* itself. A world of diverse micro-worlds, *Quixote* is unified by a network of analogies; it is a total system, but at the same time an unruly assemblage of semi-autonomous "regions of the imagination".

As with other works of cognitive estrangement, including science fiction novels like *The Stars My Destination*, the world-model produced by *Don Quixote* diverges from the received world-model of its era, and relativizes it. "Official" reality in Spain of the Hapsburgs, a regime intolerant of racial, religious or ideological difference, was monolithic, unified under a single monarch and a single Church; but this is not the model of the world that we find reflected in *Quixote*, where totality coexists with diversity. *Quixote*, we might say, conducts a thought experiment about ontological plurality in an era of enforced ontological unity; it imagines an alternative reality, a multiverse, and in that respect can be read as a work of science fiction.[22]

Don Quixote innovates a world-model, but it also might be said to *anticipate* one, just as Bester anticipates globalization, or Dante (according to Lotman) anticipates the Renaissance man. In this case, however, what Cervantes anticipates is *his own world*, but his world modeled as only a 20th-century historian could model it. The world of *Don Quixote* is not the monolithic universe of the Catholic Church and the Hapsburg monarchy, but something more like "the Mediterranean world in the age of Philip II" – in other words, the Mediterranean world as it would be modeled more than three centuries later by the great 20th-century historian, Fernand Braudel. Braudel's model of the 16th-century Mediterranean is neither single (the world of orthodoxy and monarchy) nor double (Christian West *vs.* Islamic East, a "clash of civilizations"), but complex, simultaneously one

---

21 Compare Cascardi again: "As the reader makes his or her way through the text, there is a temptation to become fully absorbed in each one of the interpolated stories, but there is likewise a requirement to see that each is but one part of a multi-layered whole" (Cascardi 2002, 75).

22 Leo Spitzer, in his classic essay, "Linguistic Perspectivism in the *Don Quixote*" (1967 [1948]), sees the multi-perspectivism of *Quixote* as subordinate to a unifying theistic world-view. Cervantes, he argues, herds all of the many voices and perspectives of his world under a single Catholic "big tent". This is no doubt what a novelist of that authoritarian and orthodox era *ought* to have done; I wonder, though, whether it is actually what Cervantes *did* do.

and many, a "self-contained universe" that is at the same time a mosaic of micro-worlds. (Braudel 1976), 387).[23] Unified geographically and climatologically, Braudel's Mediterranean world is also multiple, a collection of distinct enclaves – peninsulas, island micro-worlds, a mosaic of semi-autonomous micro-economies. While the civilizations of Islam and the Christian West certainly do clash in the Mediterranean world of Braudel's model, the antagonists are not hermetically sealed off from one another, but spring leaks: trade, cultural goods, and individuals percolate back and forth across their permeable frontiers.[24]

One and many, whole and partial, Braudel's complex Mediterranean world-model is also Cervantes'. Just as Braudel's Mediterranean world comprises a single "universe" broken up into micro-worlds, where each micro-world and micro-economy partially mirrors the greater Mediterranean unity-in-diversity, so *Quixote* the novel comprises a single plane punctuated by insets, and unified by partial analogies. The two models, Braudel's and Cervantes', though separated by three centuries, coincide almost perfectly.

From a historicist perspective – the default setting of contemporary literary study, we recall – this is sheer anachronism. What could be more ahistorical than to imagine that Cervantes could have seen his own world as Braudel would see it in retrospect from his 20th-century vantage point? Lacking a 20th-century historian's resources – access to archives, statistical methods, the long historical perspective of over three hundred years, explanatory frames unknown in his own time, and so on – how could Cervantes possibly have constructed a Braudelian model of his world, one so radically at odds with the monolithic "official" world-model of his own era?

Various hypotheses might be advanced to explain, or explain away, this apparent anachronism,[25] but none seems more attractive than the possibility that Cervantes was simply better placed than almost anyone else in his era to see his own world, "the Mediterranean world in the age of Philip II", as Braudel would later come to see it. Consider his personal history: exposure to Renaissance Italy, still at that time the cultural hub of the Mediterranean

---

23 See also B.W. Ife 2002. "The Historical and Social Context".
24 See also Carroll B. Johnson 2000. *Cervantes and the Material World*.
25 For instance, one might try arguing that Braudel was actually inspired by Cervantes – that he found his model of the Mediterranean world in *Don Quixote*, and used the novel's world-model as his template. No surprise, then, that the two models coincide: the Braudelian model is really just a Cervantine model (or better, a Quixotic model) after all!

LOCALITY AND TEMPORALITY

world (De Armas 2002, 32-57); service in the decisive sea battle of Lepanto (1571), where the history of the Mediterranean clash of civilizations was literally written on his maimed body; then five years of captivity in Algiers, regarded by many critics as something like the "primal scene" of Cervantes' writerly vocation (De Armas 2002, 33),[26] where he was immersed in the Mediterranean world in all its polyglot, multi-cultural complexity (Cascardi 2002, 62). Not coincidentally, Cervantes' recasting of his own captivity experience as the "Captive's Tale" in *Quixote* Part One forms the epicenter of the novel's whole system of inset narratives and structures *en abyme*. Arguably, then, nobody was better qualified than Cervantes to model his Mediterranean world from the inside – to make a cognitive map of it, as Fredric Jameson might say. In any case, however we choose to explain its apparent anachronism, its *untimeliness*, it seems clear that *Don Quixote's* innovative world-model is a *model for*, not just a *model of* reality; a literary thought experiment; something like a work of science fiction.

So what *do* we learn from science fiction? For one thing, we learn how to read *Don Quixote* as a thought experiment in world-modeling. More generally, however, we learn how to begin answering our *other* question: "Why study literature?". One reason for studying literature is that, as Terry Cochran puts it, literature can be used for "producing thought" – for *modeling for*, not just *modeling of*; for innovation, not just maintenance and recirculation; for *cognition*, not just *recognition*.

REFERENCES

Alkon, Paul. 1990. *Gulliver* and the Origins of Science Fiction. In *The Genres of Gulliver's Travels*, ed. Fredrik N. Smith, 163-178. Newark: University of Delaware Press/ London: Associated University Presses.

Amossy, Ruth. 2002. Introduction to the Study of Doxa. In *Poetics Today* 23, 3: 369-94.

Bester, Alfred. 1996 [1956]. *The Stars My Destination*. New York: Random House.

Braudel, Fernand. 1976 [1949]. *The Mediterranean and the Mediterranean World in the Age of Philip I*, vol. 1, translated by Siân Reynolds. New York: Harper and Row.

Cascardi, Anthony J., ed. 2002. *The Cambridge Companion to Cervantes*. Cambridge: Cambridge University Press.

 – 2002. *Don Quixote* and the invention of the novel. In *Cambridge Companion to Cervantes*, ed. Anthony Cascardi, 58-79. Cambridge: Cambridge University Press.

---

26 See also María Antonia Garcés 2002. *Cervantes in Algiers: A Captive's Tale*.

Clute, John. 2003. Science Fiction from 1980 to the Present. In *Cambridge Companion to Science Fiction,* eds. Edward James and Farah Mendlesohn, 64-78. Cambridge: Cambridge University Press.

Cochran, Terry. 2007. The Knowing of Literature. In *New Literary History* 38, 1: 127-46.

Crystal, David. 1973. Objective and Subjective in Stylistic Analysis. In *Current Trends in Stylistics,* eds. Braj B. Kachru and H.F.W. Stahlke, 103-113. Edmonton: Linguistic Research.

De Armas, Frederick A. 2002. Cervantes and the Italian Renaissance. In *Cambridge Companion to Cervantes,* ed. Anthony Cascardi, 32-57. Cambridge: Cambridge University Press.

Delany, Samuel R. 1984 [1979]. Science Fiction and 'Literature' – or, The Conscience of the King. In *Starboard Wine: More Notes on the Language of Science Fiction,* 81-100. Pleasantville NY: Dragon Press.

Elgin, Catherine Z. 2007. The Laboratory of the Mind. In *A Sense of the World,* eds. John Gibson, Wolfgang Huemer and Luca Pocci, 43-54. New York: Routledge.

Even-Zohar, Itamar. 2009 [1990]. 'Reality' and Realemes in Narrative. In *Polysystem Studies, Poetics Today* 11, 1: 207-18.

 – 2004. Culture as Goods, Culture as Tools. In *Papers in Culture Research.* http://www.tau.ac.il/~itamarez/works/books /ez-cr2004-toc.htm.

Freedman, Carl. 2000. *Critical Theory and Science Fiction.* Hanover NH: Wesleyan University Press.

Garcés, María Antonia. 2002. *Cervantes in Algiers: A Captive's Tale.* Nashville: Vanderbilt University Press.

Gardner, John. 1978. *On Moral Fiction.* New York: Basic Books.

Geertz, Clifford. 1973. *The Interpretation of Cultures: Selected Essays.* New York: Basic Books.

Gibson, John, Wolfgang Huemer and Luca Pocci, eds. 2007. *A Sense of the World: Essays on Fiction, Narrative, and Knowledge.* Routledge Studies in Contemporary Philosophy, 6. New York: Routledge.

Harvey, David. 1989. *The Condition of Postmodernity: An Enquiry into the Origins of Cultural Change.* Oxford: Basil Blackwell.

Herman, David. 2002. *Story Logic: Problems and Possibilities of Narrative.* Lincoln: University of Nebraska Press.

Ife, B.W. 2002. The Historical and Social Context. In *Cambridge Companion to Cervantes,* ed. Anthony Cascardi, 11-31. Cambridge: Cambridge University Press.

Iser, Wolfgang. 2007. Culture: A Recursive Process. In *A Sense of the World,* eds. John Gibson, Wolfgang Huemer and Luca Pocci, 318-31. New York: Routledge.

James, Edward and Farah Mendlesohn, eds. 2003. *The Cambridge Companion to Science Fiction.* Cambridge: Cambridge University Press.

Jameson, Fredric. 1982. Progress versus Utopia, or, Can We Imagine the Future? *Science-Fiction Studies* 9, 2: 147-58.

Johnson, Carroll B. 2000. *Cervantes and the Material World.* Urbana: University of Illinois Press.

Kuhn, Thomas S. 1977 [1964]. A Function for Thought Experiments. In *The Essential Tension: Selected Studies in Scientific Tradition and Change*, 240-65. Chicago: University of Chicago Press.

LeGuin, Ursula K. 1976. Introduction. In *The Left Hand of Darkness*. New York: Ace.

Lotman, Jurij. 1977 [1971]. *The Structure of the Artistic Text*, translated by Gail Lenhoff and Ronald Vroom. Michigan Slavic Contributions 7. Ann Arbor: University of Michigan Department of Slavic Languages and Literatures.

  – 1990 [1984]. The Decembrist in Everyday Life: Everyday Behavior as a Historical-Psychological Category. In Jurij M. Lotman and Boris A. Uspenskij, *Semiotics of Russian Culture*, ed. Ann Shukman, 71-123. Michigan Slavic Contributions, 11. Ann Arbor: Department of Slavic Languages and Literatures.

  – 1990 [1984]. The Theater and Theatricality as Components of Early Nineteenth-Century Culture. In Jurij M. Lotman and Boris A. Uspenskij, *Semiotics of Russian Culture*, ed. Ann Shukman, 141-64. Michigan Slavic Contributions, 11. Ann Arbor: Department of Slavic Languages and Literatures.

  – 1990. *Universe of the Mind: A Semiotic Theory of Culture*, translated by Ann Shukman. Bloomington IN: Indiana University Press.

Lotman, Jurij M., and Boris A. Uspenskij. 1990 [1984]. *The Semiotics of Russian Culture*, ed. Ann Shukman. Michigan Slavic Contributions, 11. Ann Arbor: Department of Slavic Languages and Literatures.

Mach, Ernst. 1976 [1897, 1926]. On Thought Experiments. In *Knowledge and Error: Sketches on the Psychology of Enquiry*, translated by Paul Foulkes, 134-47. Dordrecht: D. Reide.

Martínez-Bonati, Félix. 1992. *Don Quixote and the Poetics of the Novel*. Ithaca and London: Cornell University Press.

McHale, Brian. 1994. Child as Ready-Made: Baby-Talk and the Language of DosPassos's Children in *U.S.A.* In *Infant Tongues: The Voice of the Child in Literature*, eds. Elizabeth Goodenough, Mark A. Heberle and Naomi Sokoloff, 202-224. Detroit: Wayne State University Press.

  – 2007. En Abyme: Internal Model and Cognitive Mapping. In *A Sense of the World*, eds. John Gibson, Wolfgang Huemer and Luca Pocci, 189-205. New York: Routledge.

Riffaterre, Michael. 1978. *Semiotics of Poetry*. Bloomington: Indiana University Press.

Shklovsky, Viktor. 1991 [1929]. The Making of *Don Quixote*. In *Theory of Prose*, translated by Benjamin Sher, 72-100. Normal IL: Dalkey Archive Press.

Spitzer, Leo. 1967 [1948]. Linguistic Perspectivism in the *Don Quixote*. In *Linguistics and Literary History: Essays in Stylistics*, 41-85. Princeton NJ: Princeton University Press.

Suvin, Darko. 1979. *Metamorphoses of Science Fiction*. New Haven: Yale University Press.

LITERARY STUDIES IN INTERACTION

Anne-Marie Mai

Academic studies can be said to exist in a never-ending process of motivating their mission and subject field. If the critical questioning "Why study literature?" ends, it means the ending of the study itself. Literary studies in today's post-national cultural context are challenged by the fact that the traditional reasons for studying literature as part of building a national identity are changing. In the European countries, national identity today has a multi-cultural meaning very different from the situation in the mono-cultural era of the 19th century.

As part of this change, national literary studies have extended their subject field and been renewed in terms of method; they have also experienced a growing research interest in cultural studies. Today, literature within national philology in the democratic countries is not studied to consolidate a mono-cultural formation, but rather to contribute to a post-national renewal within the literary and cultural field. Among several others, the literary theorist Hans Ulrich Gumbrecht has described the changes in contemporary literary studies in the article "The Future of Literary Studies?".[1] In his view, literary studies should enter even further into an oscillation between academic disciplines. Literary studies should become a facilitator to both material oriented research of cultural canons and epistemological-oriented research of meaning construction, thereby changing their focus from literary interpretation to a broader epistemological and historical analysis.

As Professor Gumbrecht emphasises, the legitimacy and cultural importance of literary studies also become topics for discussion because of the development of new media and genres that have gained popularity among both artists and audience. Movies, music and digital cross-over artefacts have a far greater impact on a young audience than traditional novels or collections of poems.

In his discussion, Gumbrecht tones down the traditional modern defence of literary studies that underlines literature's specific aesthetic and linguistic

---

1   Gumbrecht 1995, 499-518.

value. He finds a new meaning in a self-substitution of literary studies with cultural and epistemological research.

But before discussing if Professor Gumbrecht is right, allow me to pursue a little further the modern idea that the linguistic specificity of literature justifies the relevance of literary studies.

MODERN LITERARY VALUES AND THE LITERARY OPPOSITION

To modernist understandings, literature is a special form of aesthetical knowledge and experience, one that displays the full range of language and demands interpretation. This line of thought has been part of the legitimization by modern societies of the importance of literature and the study of literature when a political decision has been taken to support an author's work, to guarantee research into literature and to disseminate literature to many readers.

The United Nations has underlined the significance of literature by introducing a World Poetry Day under the auspices of UNESCO. In 2001, the then chairman of the General Assembly, Harri Holkeri, declared:

> Poetry has always played an important role in the arts, and in recent years the public's interest in poetry has grown. Poets are our 'cultural clairvoyants' and 'porte-paroles' of truth. They have the insight and capability to express what are profoundly human sentiments. Poetry is more than just a form of self-expression – it is also a form of cultural consciousness and a vehicle for interpersonal and intercultural dialogue. And it is a way for the young to creatively express their thoughts.[2]

Harry Holkeri's French quotation and justification of literary significance resembles the 19th-century modernist ideas about poetic vision and literature as a counter discourse. The poetics of symbolism has indeed been very influential on the modernist notions of literature and the social role of the modern poet.

The French symbolist Paul Verlaine played a part in disseminating the reading of the most important modern poets of his age, basing his theory on the idea of poetry as unique insight into everything human when, in 1884, he published his essayistic anthology, *Les Poètes maudits*. Here the reader could discover whom Verlaine considered to be the best poets of

---

2   Quotation from: http://www.un.org/News/Press/docs/2001/gasm236.doc.htm.

his age, including Baudelaire, Mallarmé and Rimbaud. In Verlaine's view, these poets were not only classically good, true and beautiful; they were also modern, diabolically good, true and beautifully disquieting, because from an aesthetic, linguistic, social and human point of view they completely refused to compromise.[3] Verlaine's anthology about the accursed poets on the fringe of society who dealt with what other people found it difficult to confront in the world around them and within themselves was an effective launching platform and helped to make them known, in their own age and in posterity.

The idea of the poem as a very special and important social discourse and of the poet as a 'cultural clairvoyant' has served to legitimize the study of literature. In this understanding, literature is conceptualized as a valuable but enigmatic art that may be interpreted by specially trained literary researchers who are committed to disseminating their studies and giving a reading audience access to the literary treasure chest of humanistic and artistic values.

The modernist literature of Charles Baudelaire and Paul Verlaine underlined the specifically aesthetical values of poetry and abandoned the Romantic longings for the divine or the eternal. They made the body, movement, the impressions of the city and the senses the subject matter of poetic longings and poetic language. The poetry of modernity is linked to the moment, to the soul and the body and the poem itself. Here the spirit is enticed out of nature, as in Hans Christian Andersen's tale *The Dryad* (1867/1868),[4] and is allowed to gleam for a moment before it perishes. The modern signs of loss are still strongly inscribed in literature, and as such literature is an important interpretation of the life-space and forms of experience of the present age. The confrontation of modern literature, full of both anxiety and desire, with a fragmentary, flickering, reifying and constantly volatile modernity gives the reader a special experience and constitutes a distinctive form of criticism.

---

3   From the preface to the Verlaine anthology, Verlaine 1982, 19:
    "Ces Poètes Absolus qu'il fallait dire pour rester dans le calme, mais, outre que le calme n'est guère de mise en ces temps-ci, notre titre a cela pour lui qu'il répond juste à notre haine et, nous en sommes sûr, à celle des survivants d'entre les Tout-Puissants en question, pour le vulgaire des lecteurs d'élite – une rude phalange qui nous la rend bien. Absolus par l'imagination, absolus dans l'expression, absolus comme les Reys Netos des meilleurs siècles. Mais maudits! Jugez- en".

4   Hans Christian Andersen's tale, 'The Dryad', is published on the Internet site of the University of Southern Denmark: http://www.andersen.sdu.dk/vaerk/hersholt/TheDryad_e.html.

The foremost writers of modernity have responded to their own age with constantly new poetic interpretations of the subjective, with artistic criticism and counter discourse and with stories large and small about life under modern conditions.

Popular mass literature has dominated the reading of the large audience in the social and cultural formations of 20th-century modernity. Quickly-read crime novels and biographical entertainment are still at the top of the bestseller lists. But actually the publications of writers such as Albert Camus, Philip Roth, Günther Grass and Doris Lessing appear in one edition after another and are mediated to new generations of readers both in the critical conversations of the public debate and in teaching. Modern literary mediation through the educational system has given modernist literature an important role in society.

Literary studies, as Gumbrecht underlines, have legitimized themselves by claiming that through academic interpretation, mediation and public debate ethical and humanistic values can be extracted from modern literary texts.[5]

The concept of specifically ethical and critical values has suddenly given literature a democratic task. The philosopher Villy Sørensen formulated this task in 1965 in connection with the establishment of The Danish Arts Foundation, which administers official Danish support of the arts, as follows:

> Just as the dictatorship quite logically bans original art in order to maintain itself, it is also quite logical that the democratic state favours art – in order to maintain itself. The arts foundation act is official expression of the fact that the state has recognised artistic opposition, just as it has done so with political opposition.[6]

Villy Sørensen's line of argument could definitely still include much of present day modern and modernist literature in democratic countries. But literature has also changed; it is far harder to define and position in particular media and literary fields today than it was in the early 1960s.

One could argue that the concept of literature has become less essentialist and less linked to a definition of literature as a particular form of discourse, cognition and criticism. As the literary historian Denis Hollier wrote in the preface of *A New History of French Literature* (1989):

---

5   Gumbrecht 1995, 503.
6   Sørensen 1975, 186.

Literature is engrossed by what takes its place. The possibility of a history of literature is thus dependent on both literature's resistance to history and literature's resistance to literature. Literature wants to be everything – but beside itself. As a result, the question today is no longer, as it still was for Sartre, 'What is literature?' but rather, 'What is not?'[7]

This condition in fact makes it more difficult to answer the question: "why study literature?".

But it does not necessarily imply that, as Gumbrecht suggests, literary studies should divide into studies of post-colonial cultural canons and philosophically-designed studies of construction of meaning.

Literary studies could also choose to pursue their subject matter, the literary text, into a variegated artistic landscape where literature as a specific aesthetic discourse is present among other discourses and art forms and contributes to social dialogues.

Many modern literary texts are still Grecian urns,[8] but some of them are shaped as aesthetic fields of a complex interaction between the reader, the writer and the context. This concept implies that the reading and writing of the literary text have become the main themes of the text itself and an important feature of today's literature. Literary discourse still has its aesthetic specificity stemming from language experiments and artistic reflection. But unlike the more closed literary discourses of high modernism the discourses of today's foremost literature are marked by a concept of literature as an open interaction with the reader, the context, different art forms and the literary tradition. This literary interaction invites readers into a dialogue on both social and artistic values. Literature has not lost ethical dimensions, but these are related to a new literary interaction and this tendency dates back to changes in literature and literary culture during the 1950s.

The American poet Allen Ginsberg stresses that the American poetry of that period transformed into an open form, an entirely new kind of poetry, in constituting a new dialogue with society.[9] And Ginsberg's poetry as well as beat poetry and its poetics have been a strong beacon for European poetry and literature from the 1960s up to the present day.

---

7   Hollier 1989, xxv.
8   I would refer to John Keat's famous "Ode to a Grecian Urn" and its long tradition of academic interpretation.
9   Chowka 1995, http://www.english.illinois.edu/maps/poets/g_l/ginsberg/interviews. htm.

It was the departure from the high modernism of the 1950s and early 1960s that caused literature to broaden out in new directions. This marks an international re-orientation – in American beat poetry and minimalism, in French, Italian and German 1960s avant-garde, in such writers as Allen Ginsberg, Georges Perec, Umberto Eco, Helmut Heissenbüttel, and Nordic writers like Pentii Saarikoski, Dag Solstad, Eldrid Lunden, Per Olav Enquist, Peter Laugesen and Klaus Høeck.

The poetry of rock music and folk music, with poets like Jim Morrison, John Lennon and Bob Dylan, played its part in changing lyric poetry from being exclusively a narrow, written genre to one that is inclusive of more oral genres. In this new context, texts that would normally be labelled as difficult acquired a common reference and identity-creating form of expression for young people all over the world.

The reaction against high modernism is a breakthrough of form in which the nature of literature as being a linguistic and aesthetic field of interaction[10] between the reader, the writer and the context is thematized in new ways. The concept of form as an aesthetic interaction does not only refer to the fact that the reader participates in a co-creative activity in the sense of reader-response theories, since the reader fills in empty spaces or textual holes. It has to do with the fact that the text as an aesthetic form and way of seeing things enables the reader to alternate between empathizing and distancing himself or herself from and co-actively relating to the existential *modi* that the text formulates. The concept of form means that the work of the author deposits reflections concerning the reading possibilities of the text in the text itself, and that the relation to the outside world and context is the subject of constant reflection and textual testing.

The rupture with modernism is characterized by a coincidence between various literary trends and -isms: minimalism, modernism, various forms of realism, surrealism, concretism, political writing and performative biographism.[11] Traditional boundaries between genres, generations, high- and

---

10 My concept of form as an aesthetic matter is based on Roman Ingarden's definition of the literary work as an inter-subjectively intentional object, Ingarden 1931 and Paul Ricœur's concept of the mediations of the literary text in 'On interpretation' in Ricœur 1991.

11 The concept of performative biographism has been formulated by Jon Helt Haarder in connection with his studies of contemporary Scandinavian literature, which mixes fiction and (self-)biography. A number of articles have been published on Jon Helt Haarder's websites: http://www1.sdu.dk/Hum/jhh/.

low-brow literature are broken down, and literature spreads out into new media and genres.

A number of present-day international novels talk about the prerequisites, environments and main figures of this process. In European literature, an example would be the Swede Sara Stridsberg's outstanding novel *Dröm-fakulteten. Tilläg till sexualiteorin* (The Faculty for Dreaming. A Supplement to Sexual Theory, 2006). The novel is about the feminist Valerie Solanas, who tried to murder Andy Warhol and who in 1968 wrote the manifesto for SCUM, the Society for Cutting Up Men.

Stridsberg's novel not only deals with Valerie and her particular fragility but also with the artistic environment in New York with all its paradoxes, freaks and artists that express themselves across genres and media. The novel illustrates that human conflicts both within the avant-garde group and in the surrounding community still have relevance for contemporary artists like Stridsberg.

In the large, highly diverse literary landscape from the mid-1960s to the present day there are three relations[12] around which many literary texts circle.

Firstly, relations between text and reader are in focus, since the reader often acquires a more actively meaning-creative role than in traditional literature. The reader cannot simply sit back and enjoy a good story, but has to interact directly with the text in order to create meaning – and the reading itself becomes a theme.

The French avant-garde group OuLiPo worked with various new interactions between text and reader. Raymond Queneau constructed the sonnet machine *Cent Mille Milliards de poèmes* (1961), which consists of a set of 10 sonnets in which each individual verse line can be combined with the other to form new sonnets. This gives a total combination potential of 10^{14} (= 100,000,000,000,000) different sonnets that the reader might find.

---

12 My concept of 'relation' has been inspired by the French art critic Nicolas Bourriaud 2002 a and 2002 b. In *Touch. Relational Art from the 1990s to Now* he especially emphasises that unlike an object that is closed in on itself via a style and a signature, contemporary art shows that form can only arise in consequence of the meeting, the dynamic relation that an artistic utterance maintains with other formations, whether they are artistic or not. In *Postproduction* Bourriaud sees in present-day art a will to inscribe the work of art into a network of signs and meanings instead of regarding it as an autonomous and original form.

Present-day electronic texts offer many opportunities for handling Queneau's machine and playing with it.[13]

Secondly, relations between text and tradition are an important dimension. Many texts and works refer explicitly to earlier texts or use them directly as ready-mades. Charlotte Brontë's classic, *Jane Eyre* (1847) has served in this way as a model for Jean Rhys' new classic *Wide Sargassso Sea* (1966), while Samuel Richardson's *Pamela. Or Virtue Rewarded* (1740ff.) and Jane Austen's *Pride and Prejudice* (1813) haunt such popular chick-lit as Helen Fielding's *Bridget Jones's Diary* (1996). This feature of today's literature underscores the fact that a modernist aesthetic claim of a transcendence of tradition is overruled by an experience of the aesthetic possibilities of the literary past. The modernist concept of the importance of literary renewal is replaced by a postmodern concept of free access to literary tradition.

Thirdly, literature finds itself in calm waters in new relationships between art forms and media, since the electronic media create unimagined possibilities for media convergences that cut across genres and art forms. The American Brian Kim Stefan, for example, has worked innovatively with digital poetry and is known for his digital poem "The Dreamlife of Letters" (1999).[14] Stefan's poem is a kind of short film with effects in the tradition of concrete art and it is, in contrast to much of the subsequent digital poetry, not an interactive work. According to Stefan, Eugen Gorminger's concrete poems of the 1960s[15] are parallels to "The Dreamlife of Letters" and have inspired Stefan's work. More advanced and interactive digital poetry has been created by artists like Jason Nelson, who works with three-dimensional poetry puzzles, word architecture and word games.[16]

---

13 In a Danish context, Peter Adolphsen has used Queneau's method when publishing 1,000,000 stories (2007), which are also digitalised. One can play with Adolphsen's stories at the address: http://www.enmillionhistorier.dk/.

14 The poem can be found at this address: http://www.arras.net/RNG/flash/dreamlife/ dreamlife_index.html.

15 Poems by Eugen Gorminger can be found at this address: http://lyrikline.org/index.php?id=162&L=0&author=ego0&show=Poems&poemId =176&cHash=d9ae9fd77d.

16 Poems of Jason Nelson can be found at this address: http://www.secrettechnology. com/.

TEXT RAIN – AN EXAMPLE

The three mentioned relationships – with the reader, tradition, and other art forms – point to the fact that literature is deeply involved in a performative turn, where works of art take the form of action, execution, event and doing rather than as being, existence, closed form and essence. Camille Utterback and Romy Achituv's interactive installation, *Text Rain* (1999) can be interpreted as an example of a new poetic interaction involving the relation to the onlooker/reader, the media and the tradition.

In Utterback and Achituv's installation the onlooker sees himself or herself as a black and white figure on a large screen and experiences it with his or her own body image capturing letters from a poem that gently descends over the screen like a drizzle of rain. The onlooker can capture letters, play with them, push them up or down, play ball with them, or give them a hard kick. If one is physically alert, it is possible to get whole words and phrases from the poem to float around the screen. The words and letters come from the poem 'Talk, You' by Evan Zimroth from the collection *Dead, Dinner or Naked* (1993). The poem goes like this:[17]

Talk, You
I like talking with you, simply that:
conversing, a turning-with or-around, as in
your turning around to face me
suddenly, saying Come, and I turn
with you, for a sometime
hand under my under
things, and you telling me
what you would do, where,
on what part of my body
you might talk to me differently.
At your turning,
each part of my body turns to verb.
We are the opposite of
tongue-tied, if there were such an
antonym; we are synonyms
for limbs' loosening of syntax,
and yet turn to nothing: *It's just talk.* (40-41)

---

17 Zimroth 1993, 40-41.

The poem has to do with the body, with listening, turning towards each other, giving and receiving in an erotic relation. Moving in front of the scene and catching letters, the onlooker can recreate parts of the poem or variations on some of the lines of the poem.

Once I myself managed to capture the words "as in your turning around to face me", and I will never forget the words and the phrase that I caught with my body in the rain of text.

Camille Utterback, in a comment on the installation, stresses that language is a virtual reality that one manipulates with one's speech, thoughts and writings. In the installation one uses the body image in one's linguistic acting and experiences a direct relation between body and language that is always present but perhaps overlooked when one writes and speaks. With the installation, Utterback attempts to create an artistic reality in which the physical reality in which the body moves interacts with a virtual reality:

> The line between the physical and cerebral encounters is blurred. This blurriness is viscerally encountered by certain users who claim they actually 'feel' the letters landing on their shoulders and arms. As the physical act of catching and lifting is stretched into the virtual world a dialogue is created between the physical and virtual spaces.[18]

She mentions how those looking at the work also start to cooperate in holding onto letters and words, how they play with words and use themselves and each other in order to grasp the letters. Utterback and Achituv's installation is not one that can easily be shaken off. It is hard to stop oneself from trying out another shower of text-rain.

The material of the installation is the quoted erotic poem by Evan Zimroth, but the title "Text Rain" also connects the installation with rain poems of the literary tradition, especially Paul Verlaine's famous "Il pleure dans mon cœur" from his *Romances sans paroles* (1874). In Verlaine's poem the lonely, melancholy I finds comfort in listening to the music of the falling rain:

> O bruit doux de la pluie
> Par terre et sur les toits!
> Pour un cœur qui s'ennuie,
> O le chant de la pluie!

---

18 Utterback 2001, 23-24.

(Oh, sweet sound of rain
on the earth and the roofs!
For a heart dulled with pain,
oh, the song of the rain!) (p. 102)[19]

Utterback and Achituv's installation answers the reader's experience of the music of Verlaine's words with an experience of the visibility of words and a playful encounter with other readers/onlookers.

Does "Text Rain" itself belong to literature or is it a work of visual art or sculpture? Perhaps the question is not as interesting as the fact that it demonstrates a new interaction between artistic genres and shows how a specific literary discourse can appear in new artistic contexts. Perhaps the installation could be interpreted as a creative reading and writing of a poem by the artists and an offer to the onlookers to perform artistically and poetically.

One of the members of the Swedish Academy, Horace Engdahl, has discussed the change of literature from a different perspective than the one we have seen in relation to Utterback and Archituv's installation. He sees a change in relation to genres, but still stresses that the classical, narrow concept of literature is disintegrating. He talks of a change within literature and a mixture of literary texts:

> I believe that the traditional division, where literature is seen as fiction and poetry as opposed to non-fiction, is on its way out. We have had an extremely narrow concept of literature. But I have a feeling that literature in the world is in the process of breaking out of this. Take a writer like the Italian Claudio Magris – all his work consists of this type of mixed text. Or take a writer like Péter Esterházy in Hungary, who in his latest work mixes the historical documentary with elements of fiction. Günter Grass' 'Crabwalk' is a further example".[20]

Where does this broader concept of literature and the changed function of the author leave literature and the study of literature? In the middle of a world of tales, poems, monstrous novels, challenging installations and many kinds of writer performances and self-reflective digital art forms. Perhaps the winner of the Nobel Prize for literature in 2050 will be an experimental digital poet or a literary installation artist.

---

19 Verlaine 1948, 102.
20 Engdahl 2004.

One of the innumerable writers the world over who have been put forward for the Nobel literature prize is Bob Dylan.[21] If Horace Engdahl is not the only one in the Academy who has realized that the concept of literature has changed, Dylan may perhaps have a chance of being awarded this prestigious prize within the next decade. But it is also highly possible that the 18 members of the Academy will turn up their noses at Dylan the poet for a long time to come. The question, however, of whether one can take Dylan seriously as a poet points directly at the discussion of a renewal of both literature and the study of literature.

Bob Dylan's lyrics have been strongly inspired by modern literature, modern theatre and folk music. There are innumerable literary and mythical references in his poems, which are not only presented as songs but have also been published separately as poetic texts. Dylan himself constantly uses new melodies for his texts, and also gives word-painting a decisive importance in his universe. It is characteristic of his art that he has taken poetry back to its sources in the aesthetic and in the beauty of sound, yet at the same time he has made it an artistic form of expression that speaks directly to the present day. He is further developing experimental romantic and modernistic traditions in world literature, and uniting them with a popular mode of expression. He is a poet in the old tradition of the troubadour; he is a hymn writer and an epic writer, but he is also a modernist and contemporary poet with a strong link to Allen Ginsberg and beat poetry.

Poetic texts by Bob Dylan have a beauty and sound that immediately invoke music. A good poem is also a musical display, even though the voice is the only instrument, as Verlaine demonstrated in his poetry. Dylan's poetry reminds the present age that the mythological figure of poetry is and was the singer and player of the lyre, Orpheus. Dylan, when asked, never clearly states whether he sees himself as a poet or a musician. The question seems to him to be irrelevant, as if he had long since entered a world where art forms mix in new ways. "I'm listening to Billy Jo Shaver and I'm reading James Joyce", he says in the text of "I Feel a Change Coming On", from the album *Together Through Life* (2009), where both Dylan and the songwriter from *Grateful Dead*, Robert Hunter, are credited as the album's authors. The outlaw texts of American country-singer Billy Jo Shaver, about being born in the heart of Texas and abandoned by his father, and James Joyce's

---

21 I have drawn up a recommendation, at the invitation from The Swedish Academy 2009 and 2010.

modernism do not exclude each other; on the contrary. High modernistic imagery, biblical references and folk music pop-text all mix in Dylan. Romanticism, beat poetry and minimalism enter into new relationships, as in "Highlands" from the 1997 album *Time Out Of Mind*, while Brecht's theatre inspires new classics such as "Desolation Row" (1965), in which T.S. Eliot and Ezra Pound appear as some of the poem's many literary figures.

If one is to study how literature is broadening out in new directions and entering into a dialogue with various art forms, this calls for interdisciplinary collaboration. To understand all the references in Dylan's poetry requires, for example, a detailed knowledge of both American folk music history and modernist literature. The study of literature will be hard put to have solid academic competence within both Billy Jo Shaver's texts and James Joyce's works. So it will become increasingly important to cultivate core-subject competencies in combination with other such competencies. Interdisciplinary collaboration is today the be-all and end-all, and it can be better developed and used in more focused projects than it is at present. Literature studies have a future when they enter into a new oscillation between academic disciplines.

CREATIVE READING AND WRITING

The thematization of reading as a creative activity in today's most prominent literature finds a thought-provoking parallel in the growing interest in creative writing with contemporary readers. The internet has made it possible for non-professional writers to publish and distribute literary texts and form forums for the exchange and communication of texts to interested participants. There are countless open forums for different genres and writers, where literature is studied by writers who comment on each others' texts.[22]

Creative writing has a long history in an Anglo-Saxon context; the writer Ralph W. Emerson is said to have been the originator of the first definitions of creative writing in 1837 in his discussion of the close relation between reading and writing:

> One must be an inventor to read well. As the proverb says, 'He that would bring home the wealth of the Indies, must carry out the wealth of the Indies.' There is then creative reading, as well as creative writing. When the mind is braced

---

22 See for instance http://www.writingforums.org/ with nearly 20.000 members writing a large range of genres.

by labor and invention, the page of whatever book we read becomes luminous with manifold allusion. Every sentence is doubly significant, and the sense of our author is as broad as the world.[23]

Perhaps, under the influence of the open invitations of contemporary literature for interaction between reader and text, one could develop the ideas of creative writing as a part of literary studies. In the Anglo-Saxon context, the discipline of creative writing comes into being as a renewal of the study of literature, based on the idea that students will become better at reading literature by themselves writing literature. As the grand old man of American creative writing Norman Foerster stressed in 1931:

> One of the best ways of understanding imaginative literature is to write it, since the act of writing – the selection of materials, the shaping of them, the recasting and revising – enables the students to repeat what the makers of literature have done, to see the process and the problems of authorship from the inside.[24]

One can also argue for the relevance of studies in creative writing on the basis of ideas about strengthening the dissemination of research and the communicative competencies of the student, as Paul Dawson does in *Creative Writing and the New Humanities* (2005). Here, he explains that the personal work involved in writing literature – indeed, all literary work – can contribute to a development of all-round communicative competencies and understanding. In Dawson's opinion, society shows a growing interest in a specific communication competency that can only be achieved if you experience writing fiction and poems. Such a line of thought has many interested parties, not least people in present-day business life, who are always keenly on the look-out for innovative thinking in communication. Just think of the business success that narratology and storytelling have had in USA and Europe.

Against this background literary studies should seek renewal, focusing on the relation between academic study and artistic creativity itself. It could be an advantage for students to have the opportunity both practically to write and theoretically to study literature with the aim of enhancing their understanding of creative work and creative processes. Such studies of literature would promote greater cooperation concerning the educating of researchers

---

23 Emerson 1938, 189.
24 Foerster 1941, 26.

within the field of art programmes as well as that of literature. A number of measures within art education programmes in Norway and Sweden open up precisely this possibility,[25] since a high degree of theoretical reflection is here connected to artistic work. Theory and practice are more directly and closely linked together there than in the Anglo-Saxon tradition of creative writing, where theoretical reflection is less prominent an element of studies which aim to enable people to become professional artists rather than literary theorists.

A renewed relation between theory and practice in literary studies also responds to a growing interest among young writers to be inspired by theory and philosophy in their creative work. Today, literature wants to be everything and itself as well, as Professor Hollier puts it. And as such, literature becomes involved in the many ways people think, talk, write, understand, and experience. Today's foremost literary works and texts can be regarded as aesthetic fields of complex interaction where the reader and the writer are often difficult to distinguish from one another. This fact is a fine motivation for Gumbrecht's idea that traditional literary interpretation should be replaced by broader epistemological studies of meaning constructions. So Gumbrecht is of course right, but even in regard to meaning construction literary studies can contribute to a broader academic discussion of creative interaction and creative language. It is a convincing motivation for the study of literature that literature today is used in various social and artistic contexts, because literary discourse as a specific artistic discourse with its old traditions confronts us with questions we as yet do not realize it is possible to ask, and provides us with examples of ways of experiencing and acting that surprise us and give us knowledge.

---

25 See for example the research fellowship programmes on art in Norway: http://www. kunststipendiat.no/en, where it is stressed that this is an attempt to link theoretical reflection with artistic practice: "The objective of the programme shall be to produce an independent work of art at a high international level. The research fellow shall also study theory and method in depth in order to acquire greater depth and breadth of knowledge in his/her own field, while at the same time putting the discipline in a broader context. Through the programme, the research fellow shall also receive training in communicating and teaching at a high level in his/her field. The programme shall build new networks for the development of knowledge and competence as well as promoting qualified and critical debate at art education institutions and in society at large".

REFERENCES

Andersen, Hans Christian. 1867/1868. The Dryad: http://www.andersen.sdu.dk/vaerk/ hersholt/TheDryad_e.html.

Adolphsen, Peter. 1997. *En million historier* (One million tales). http://www.enmillionhistorier.dk/.

Austen, Jane. 2006 [1813]. *Pride and Prejudice*. Cambridge: Cambridge University Press.

Bourriaud, Nicolas. 2002a. *Postproduction. Culture as Screenplay: How Art Reprograms the World*. Translated by Jeanine Hermann, New York: Lukas & Sternberg.

– 2002b. *Touch. Relational Art from the 1990s to Now*. San Francisco: San Francisco Art Institute.

Brontë, Charlotte. 2008 [1847]. *Jane Eyre*. Oxford: Oxford University Press.

Chowka, Peter Barry. 1995. Online Interview with Allen Ginsberg, http://www. english.illinois.edu/maps/poets/g_l/ginsberg/interviews.htm.

Emerson, Ralph W. 1838. *An Oration, Delivered Before The Phi Beta Kappa Society, at Cambridge*. August 31, 1837, Boston: James Munroe and Company.

Dawson, Paul. 2005. *Creative Writing and the New Humanities*. New York: Routledge.

Dylan, Bob. 1997. *Time out of Mind*. (CD): Columbia.

– 2009. *Together Through Life*. (CD): Colombia.

Engdahl, Horace. 2004. Modernismen er død (Modernism is Dead). Interview in *Weekendavisen* by Anders Ehlers Dam, Feb. 20 2004.

Fielding, Helen. 2001. *Bridget Jones's Diary*. London: Picador.

Foerster, Norman. 1941. The Study of Letters. In *Literary Scholarship Its Aims and Methods*, Chapel Hill: The University of North Carolina Press.

Gorminger, Eugen. 1995. Gedichte (Poems): http://lyrikline.org/index.php?id=162&L =0&author=eg00&show=Poems&poemId=176&cHash=d9ae9fd77d.

Gumbrecht, Hans Ulrich. 1995. The Future of Literary Studies? *New Literary History*, Vol. 26, No. 3, Baltimore: Johns Hopkins University Press.

Haarder, Jon Helt. 2005. Det særlige forhold, vi havde til forfatteren (The Special Relation We had to the Author). http://www1.sdu.dk/Hum/jhh/.

Holkeri, Harri. 2001. *Press Release*, March 21 2001, http://www.un.org/News/Press/docs/2001/gasm236.doc.htm.

Hollier, Denis. 1989. On Writing Literary History. *A New French History of Literature*, Harvard: Harvard University Press.

Ingarden, Roman. 1992 [1931]. *Das literarische Kunstwerk*. Tübingen: Niemeyer.

Nelson, Jason. Secret Technology. Net Poems: http://www.secrettechnology.com/.

Research fellowship programmes, Norway: http://www.kunststipendiat.no/en.

Richardson, Samuel. 1982 [1740 ff]. *Pamela. Or Virtue Rewarded*. Harmondsworth: Penguin.

Ricœur, Paul. 1991. *From Text to Action. Essays in Hermeneutics* II. Translated by Kathleen Blarney and John B. Thompson, Evanston: Northwestern University.

Stefan, Brian Kim. 1999. Dreamlife: http://www.arras.net/RNG/flash/dreamlife/ dreamlife_index.html.

Rhys, Jean. 1999 [1966]. *Wide Sargasso Sea*. New York: W.W. Norton.

Stridsberg, Sara. 2006. *Drömfakulteten. Tilläg till sexualiteorin* [The Dream Faculty]. Stockholm: Albert Bonnier.

Sørensen, Villy. 1965. Kronik. *Politiken*, 7/2 1965 (Feature in the newspaper *Politiken*). In *Dansk litterær debat. En antologi, 1950-75*, ed. Erling Nielsen. Copenhagen: Gyldendal, 1975.

Utterback, Camille. 2001. Between the real and the virtual – thin boundaries, room for discovery. In *Space and Spatiality*, Kolding: Kolding Design School.

Verlaine, Paul. 1948. *Selected Poems*. Translated by Carlyle Ferren MacIntyre, Berkeley: University of California Press.

– 1982. *Les Poètes maudits de Paul Verlaine*. Paris: Societe d'edition d'enseignement superieur.

Writing forum, at http://www.writingforums.org/ with nearly 20.000 members writing a large range of genres.

Zimroth, Evan. 1993. *Dead, Dinner or Naked*. Chicago: TriQuarterly Books.

HUMANITY

MAGNUS PERSSON
On the Differences between Reading and Studying Literature

DOROTHY J. HALE
Aesthetics and the New Ethics:
Theorizing the Novel in the Twenty-First Century

JAN ALBER
The Ethical Implications of Unnatural Scenarios

RICHARD WALSH
The Force of Fictions

ON THE DIFFERENCES BETWEEN READING AND STUDYING LITERATURE

Magnus Persson

Our time is often described as a period of transition from a text culture to a media culture. Literature's position as a privileged educational tool has been undermined and its competition from newer forms of media is enormous. Literature neither can nor wants to play the role of the bearer of a national spirit or a connective force in culture. The German philosopher Peter Sloterdijk (1999) describes the situation as post-humanistic and post-literary. But this hardly means that literature is dead. The market for books is booming and the number of books published is increasing steadily, often thanks to, and not despite, new media technology. There are many signs of this continued interest in literature and reading: within academia, there has been an expansion of literary theory in the last few decades; outside academia, there have been many reading campaigns, such as World Book Day, and a boom in guides on how to read literature (Persson 2008). These phenomena can be viewed not only as proof of the health of literature, but also as a symptom of the fact that people no longer understand, how and why they should read literature.

In these times, the reading of literature has to be *legitimized* in a new way (Persson 2007). In this debate, people often forget to contextualize their reasoning and arguments. An important example of this is the often im-plicit – use of the basic distinction between reading and studying literature. This distinction is far from as obvious and innocent as it may seem. Dealing with it includes more or less invisible valuations and ideas about what it really means to be able to read a literary text.

In this chapter, I will problematize a couple of the recurrent concepts and dichotomies within current literary theory that often arise in discussions about the practice of reading: e.g. naive/critical reading, consumption/reflection, and notions of "subjective" responses to literature. A central question is: how are the differences between "regular" and professional readers characterized and valued? The goal of this analysis is to emphasize the need for increased theoretical attention to the relationship between reading and studying literature. The presuppositions underlying the use of this distinction must be scrutinized. The traditional characteristics attributed respectively to ordinary and professional readers are inadequate. Ordinary readers lack the literary competence that is necessary to do justice to a literary work, it is claimed. They are only interested in pleasure. And conversely, studying literature means suppressing desire and subjectivity and instead focusing entirely on the meaning of the work. This is unproductive and uncreative, both in theory and in practice. In a time when the status of reading literature is far from clear, we have everything to gain by trying to understand, and also in some circumstances actively weaken, the borders between reading as it is practiced within and outside the academy.

In order to identify and clarify some of the issues at stake, I first discuss literary sociologist John Guillory and his useful (but not entirely unproblematic) outline of the differences between what he calls lay reading and professional reading. With his typology in mind, I then turn to Jonathan Culler's seminal text on literary competence from 1975. There are, of course, countless other examples one could have chosen to demonstrate how literary theory privileges certain ways of reading, but Culler's is certainly one of the most influential. His basic distinction between linguistic and literary competence, persuasive as it may seem, sets other distinctions into motion. These distinctions carry with them deeply problematic assumptions about, and conditions for, what it means to be able to read literature. In the third and final part, I try to make the case for a new way of treating the standard dichotomies of reading. I propose the concept and practice of creative reading, which is not simply a combination but rather an exploration and a working through of different ways of reading, "naive" as well as "critical".

LAY READING AND PROFESSIONAL READING

Guillory's (2000) characterization of the differences between professional reading and lay reading is especially useful in this context since it makes explicit the concrete and material conditions for different reading practices, aspects which are very seldom accounted for in mainstream literary theory. Professional reading broadly corresponds to what I call studying literature and lay reading to reading literature. Guillory's point of departure is that there is an "enormous gap" between how reading is practiced inside and outside of academia.

Professional reading in the academy is characterized by four distinct properties (31 f). First of all, reading is a sort of *work* that requires much time and many resources. This exertion, writes Guillory, is compensated for by payment. The second differentiating characteristic of professional reading is that it is a *disciplinary* activity. Reading is steered by research practices and conventions for interpretation that have been developed over a long period of time and require years for someone to master. The third characteristic is that it is *vigilant*. The pleasure of reading may not get the upper hand. Reading should not be distinguished by consumption but rather by reflection. The fourth characteristic is that professional reading is a *collective* practice. The reading of a researcher of literature is always in dialogue with other researchers and is aimed at a specific receiver (students in a classroom or readers of an academic journal where the results of the reading in question will be presented).

When Guillory then describes lay reading, he begins by claiming that it is very hard to engage in professional reading outside the academy. Certain of its aspects can, perhaps, be practiced, but for most non-professional readers, there is a lack of time and resources. These are serious limitations.

Lay reading is characterized by four qualities that, according to Guillory, are in direct opposition to professional reading (32). The first characteristic is that reading is practiced during one's *spare time*. If, during one's spare time, one should read the same work that is read within the academy, it is now disconnected from work. The second characteristic is that the *conventions* of lay reading are completely different, in terms of *where and when* the reading takes place (in bed before one is going to sleep, on the tube, in waiting rooms, on holiday, etc.). The third characteristic is that lay reading is primarily motivated by *desire*. Other reader interests (such as morals) can influence it, but the experience of desire/pleasure "will constitute the first and necessary motive of reading" (32). Finally, the fourth property is that lay reading is characterized by it being mainly a *solo* activity. One can argue against this, or at least make the picture more nuanced, by pointing out the current boom of informal book clubs and the growth of literary discussion and review forums for regular readers on the internet. But as a generalization of an important difference between professional and non-professional readers, Guillory's observation is nevertheless still correct.

Guillory believes that the divide between the two ways of reading is constantly getting larger in our culture. Guillory refers to Foucault when he tries to explain the divide. During early modernity, reading was an *ethical practice* for self-improvement through desire/pleasure. It was not a matter of wrapping the moral code of the literary text in a pleasurable package so that it may be easier to swallow, it was instead "the experience of pleasure itself that was to produce the improving effect" (41). The problem is that neither of the types of reading today admits or is conscious of "their identity as *ethical* practice" (42), as distinct, but of course never totally detached, from the moral and the political. Guillory writes that his usage of the term ethical practice "would conform more or less to the philosophical problematic descending from Socrates of 'how to live,' which is a question not reducible to adherence to moral law or 'obligation'" (38). It involves a care of the self and a choice between goods, not a choice between good and evil. The misrecognition of reading as an ethical practice has profound consequences:

> Reading emerged as an ethical practice of modernity only to be subsumed on the one side to mere consumption, and on the other to a highly serious, professionalized labor. In the context of mass-mediated pleasures, and of a strict division between work and leisure, lay reading tends to reduce the pleasure of reading to the immediacy of consumption, with no other end than momentary distraction. Professional reading by contrast tends to oppose its ascetic practice to pleasure, or to justify pleasure only as a means to a political end (43).

Guillory undeniably puts his finger on a central, perhaps the most central, aspect of the differences between reading and studying literature. But although Guillory is careful to write that his description of the two types of reading is a description of how they are in general, not of how they always are or should be, there is still something reductive about what is also a very elucidating typology. Can we be sure that all the effort made in literature classes in school to create conscious readers is just thrown away? Can we be sure that all the students who dedicate themselves to the professional type of reading in teacher training programmes and literature programmes stop practising it completely when they have finished their schooling? Are academic reading practices really always ascetic? And how can Guillory be so certain that it is the "wrong" kind of desire that dominates lay reading – that is, the simple and distracting kind rather than, for example, Foucault's "techniques of the self" or Barthes' subversive *jouissance*? Is not Guillory here rehearsing one of the most worn assumptions of traditional mass culture critique, i.e. that ordinary readers are cultural dupes?

I believe that the treatment of the dichotomy between desire and reflection is decisive for whether we can formulate productive and creative answers to the question of why we should study literature. The dichotomy must be weakened and problematized. One thing need not exclude the other and neither desire nor reflection has to be reserved for the domains of, respectively, spare time or the formal teaching of literature.

Guillory's sociological perspective helped us understand the dichotomy between professional reading (ascetic, distanced, collective, etc.) and lay reading (pleasurable, private, etc.). If we turn to reception theory, we can get many insights into how implicit or actual readers read, within and outside the educational system. My example is Jonathan Culler's now classic and enormously influential essay, "Literary Competence" from 1975, in which the dichotomy between linguistic and literary competence is set out. I will show how linguistic competence is framed as lay reading and literary competence as professional reading. How are these different reading practices characterized and valued?

Even if Culler's work is 35 years old, it is still an unusually clear example of how literary theory privileges certain ways of reading literature while other types are blatantly marginalized. In this regard, Culler's text can be viewed as representative of a tendency in literary studies that dominates today as well. A sharp dividing line is established between regular linguistic competence and literary competence. The latter is connected with educating people in the literary institution's distanced and analytical reading conventions. This dichotomy is also central for later reception theorists such as Rabinowitz (1998). One could also mention the striking recent revival of the concept of literary competence in, for instance, Scandinavian reception studies (Kåreland 2009, Thorson & Ekholm 2009, Torell 2002). Above all, it has been, and still is, a foundational idea in concrete literature training (Persson 2007).

The dichotomy between linguistic and literary competence has something immediately appealing and clear about it. In its simplicity, it sheds light on a number of central differences between being able to read a text and being able to read a text as literature. In order to understand William Blake's poem "Ah! Sunflower", all you need is to know English. But in order to understand the text as poetry, something beyond pure linguistic competence is required. One has to have learned a number of reading conventions that make it possible to "convert linguistic sequences into literary structures and meanings" (Culler 1975, 132).

Among the most important conventions for reading poetry is the rule of meaning, which stipulates that the text expresses an urgent opinion about some issue of human importance. The rule about poetic context is another central convention, permitting and, it might be added, in many cases requiring that the poem in question be compared to other poems or texts in literary history. Culler also names the rules of metaphorical context and thematic unity as other examples of powerful conventions (132 ff).

This perspective means that literary texts are not viewed as though they have intrinsic meanings. Culler's view turns such a common sense assumption upside-down and instead suggests that the poem "may be thought of as an utterance that has meaning only with respect to a system of conventions which the reader has assimilated" (135).

Culler advocates a semiotic poetics whose main goal should be to chart the origin, use and change of reading conventions within the literary institution. His essay has an obvious polemic perspective, aimed at what he calls interpretation-focused criticism. This criticism prioritizes interpreting specific works and often is based on assumptions about the text's autonomy and organic unity. Culler emphasizes that his poetics does not mean that interpretation should be excluded from the study of literature, but that it should have a secondary role. Instead, the goal is to explore the conventions that allow a literary work to have a number of meanings, but not just any meaning (138). The advantages of this approach are, according to Culler, increased consciousness about literature and reading's institutional mechanisms and an increased openness for more challenging and creative literary texts.

As mentioned before, Culler's theory is attractive. The dichotomy between linguistic and literary competence forces us to think about the differences between reading a text and reading it as literature. Obviously, the dichotomy is also a way of specifying the differences between reading and studying literature, even if Culler does not say this.

Culler defends himself against the objection that the concept of literary competence implies a distinction between competent and incompetent readers. Culler admits that texts can, of course, be appreciated for reasons unrelated to understanding and knowledge. A reader can misunderstand a text but nevertheless deeply appreciate it. But according to Culler, this is no argument against literary competence:

> Moreover, the claims of schools and universities to offer literary training cannot be lightly dismissed. To believe that the whole institution of literary education is but a gigantic confidence trick, would strain even a determined credulity, for it is, alas, only too clear that knowledge of a language and a certain experience of the world do not suffice to make someone a perceptive and competent reader. That achievement requires acquaintance with a range of literature and in many cases some form of guidance. The time and effort devoted to literary education by generations of students and teachers creates a strong presumption that there is something to be learned, and teachers do not hesitate to judge their pupil's progress towards a general literary competence (140 f).

Here, too, there is something immediately convincing about Culler's argument. The teaching of literature must, obviously, teach something, and this something is a special way of reading the type of textual production we call literature. It is hard to deny that this statement is true. However, Culler also seems to be implicitly saying that it could hardly be any other way. The major problem is that the *relationships* between linguistic and literary competence and between incompetent and competent readers are, even in the best-case scenario, unclear when the dichotomies are set in a concrete institutional context: the teaching of literature at a university. What happens to the ability to "just" read literature when instead one has begun to study it and thereby to learn the conventions and techniques of literary competence?

One deeply problematic but easily overlooked aspect of Culler's theory is that subjective responses to literature *ought* to be viewed as irrelevant to the serious study of literature. In other words, the very prerequisite for an ethical practice of reading "whose object is first of all oneself" (Guillory 2000, 43) is denied. The problem of subjectivity is touched on a few times by Culler, but only in passing and it is not theorized enough. Subjectivity is associated with idiosyncrasy and arbitrariness and is construed almost as an antithesis to literary competence. Or, to put it another way: gradually learning the reading conventions that characterize and are seen as necessary for literary competence is to correct and overcome subjectivity.

I shall give an example of this manoeuvre. Culler writes in one place about how what is needed is not a map of actual readers' behaviors but rather one of the tacit knowledge behind the way readers approach literature:

> The question is not what actual readers happen to do but what an ideal reader must know implicitly in order to read and interpret works in ways which we consider acceptable, in accordance with the institution of literature (144).

What Culler calls behavior or approach is clearly different from competence:

> [F]or behaviour can be influenced by a host of irrelevant factors· I may not have been paying attention at a given moment, may have been led astray by purely personal associations, may have forgotten something important from an earlier part of the text, may have made what I would recognize as a mistake if it were pointed out to me (143).

As a description of an existing practice – actually the dominating reading practice in literary studies – Culler's exposition is very clarifying. Learning to disregard personal, subjective and spontaneous reactions to literature is among the first things one learns as a new student of literary studies. However, it is deeply symptomatic, I believe, that Culler does not problematize this assumption, but rather simply moves from the descriptive to the normative: this is how it is – and how it should be. This makes it seem obvious because it is not explicitly articulated but rather carried out with the use of small, subtle, value-laden words such as "irrelevant". Subjectivity is arbitrary and personal – and therefore irrelevant.

Culler's theory has a number of flaws. First of all, literary studies' disciplinary aspects are made invisible. To study, as opposed to just reading, literature involves being taught to read in a certain way while also having to distance oneself from other – presumably more naive – reading practices, including the practice Guillory called lay reading. Terry Eagleton formulated this provocatively when he wrote that the first and most important aspect of teaching literature is to teach the student that she or he cannot read literature:

> In such a situation, Literature presents itself as threat, mystery, challenge and insult to those who, able to read, can nonetheless not "read". To be able to decipher the signs and yet remain ignorant: it is in this contradiction that the tyranny of Literature is revealed [...] Sited somewhere on the ground of familiar language, Literature entices only to refuse, appears complicit only to cold-shoulder. Literature is always somewhere else: that which, being literate, we have not read or cannot read. Literacy admits us to reading so that we can take the full measure of our exclusion: its effect is to display the secretive knowledge which is always possible but never possessed (Eagleton 1976, 165).

Eagleton's polemic tone can too easily be understood as a critique of Culler's dichotomy between linguistic and literary competence. Here, one can intervene and say that the teaching of literature, as with all teaching, has and must have disciplining elements, and (following Foucault) disciplining is not just repressive but also productive: new ways of producing knowledge about literature become possible. Despite this, it is noteworthy that Culler's theory, which explicitly claims to want to explore the literary institution, never discusses literary competence in terms of discipline.

Secondly, the theory of literary competence simplifies or ignores anything outside of it. Everything that is not about the reading conventions sanctioned by the literary institution is left in the theoretical shadow. What do categories such as the subjective, the personal and the unique really offer? All we are told is that they are arbitrary and irrelevant. However, as reception theorist Louise M. Rosenblatt (1995) and many others have pointed out, subjectivity is not just about private associations in a narrow sense but also about making connections between the text and one's own experiences. There can be many different types of connections, not least, as Guillory emphasised, existential and ethical ones. If this is a theory about *reading*, there are doubtless too many things ignored in Culler's text. The act of reading itself (or what Culler calls behaviour/approach) is also left untheorized. Central forces and mechanisms behind reading, such as empathy, identification, distance, getting lost in a text, desire, disgust and provocation are left untouched. Culler's theory is perhaps, then, more a theory of writing than one of reading. The professional readers' interpretations, as codified in writing, are the basis for the theory.

Thirdly, although Culler's theory is a critique of what he calls interpretation-focused criticism, it actually continues privileging interpretation. It is the professional interpretations of particular works that are the focus, but now as *given* objects of study which semiotic poetics approaches from a meta-perspective. When Culler describes reading, it is always in terms of sense, meaning and interpretations, rather than, for example, feelings, experiences and pleasure.

The disadvantages and blind spots of Culler's theory become clear when it is compared to Guillory's typology. The basic distinction between lay and professional reading is reproduced in the dichotomy between linguistic and literary competence. In Culler's defence one could argue that the reason he does not theorise concepts such as subjectivity and feeling is because he is analysing professional, and not lay reading. This line of defence could have worked, had Culler not made his move from the descriptive to the normative. His theory is not merely an outline of what constitutes literary competence, it is also a privileging of the very same competence. As a description of an existing practice the theory is convincing, as a prescription it is not. Guillory's four differentiating characteristics of professional and lay reading help us become aware of important – and problematic – obstacles to what he refers to as the ethics of reading. His, and my, ambition is to theorize and weaken the divide between these two different modes of reading – not to naturalize and strengthen it.

Culler belongs to a long literary theoretical tradition in which subjectivity is devalued and interpretation is seen as reading's highest and only purpose. In the tradition of New Criticism, this line of thought comes from I.A. Richards' (1929) picky catalogue of students' irrelevant responses to poems, via Wellek's and Warren's (1949) prohibition of extrinsic approaches to the study of literature, through Beardsley and Wimsatt's critique of the affective fallacy (Wimsatt 1954). Although more recent literary theoretical research has distanced itself from the idea of the literary text's autonomy and instead focused on the reader's active role, the privileging of interpretation is still common to almost all modern literary theoretical research, including reception theory. Karin Littau (2006) writes:

> In this respect, dispassionate analysis, whether it takes the form of a text-centered formalism or a reader-oriented will-to-interpretation, has a regulatory function: to put the intellect into control so as to bypass the unruly passions (156).

Or as Stanley Fish (1980, 355) writes in one of his famous slogans: "[L]ike it or not, interpretation is the only game in town". If Fish is right, this means that the opposition between reading and studying literature is naturalized and cemented. In the final section, I shall argue against this idea and instead suggest what can be called a third way of reading.

BRIDGING THE DIVIDE – TOWARDS A THIRD WAY OF READING

It cannot be the case that the reason and condition for studying literature is to stop reading it, can it? That getting literary competence has to take place at the cost of removing everything from reading except interpretation? Culler actually offers an explicit legitimization of literary studies at the end of his article: the aim is to question the self and regular social forms of understanding; the goal is an "expansion of self" (151). This is an interesting legitimization. Gaining literary competence is perhaps a necessary condition for this, but hardly enough. If the reader's psychological, emotional and physical reactions to literature are considered irrelevant, there is a risk of shrinking, rather than expanding, the self. What Guillory called the ethical practice of reading, a care for the self through pleasure, is blocked at the outset.

That modern literary theory so clearly privileges sense-making over sensations does not mean that it has always been thus. Viewed in a larger historical context, as Littau (2006) has explained, the relationship has in fact been the reverse. That new critics, and many others, trivialise the physical aspects of reading is easily recognised, but then there is a long tradition of thinking about reading that takes such aspects seriously:

When understood within the context of this broader history of criticism, bodily responses to literature cannot be written off as unsophisticated. The dictum from antiquity that the dramatic or poetic was to *move* its audience, to release pity, incite passion or fill with horror, is what major thinkers from Aristotle to Longinus, from Sidney to Burke, have all deemed to be a hallmark of great works of art (Littau 2006, 156).

Throughout her study, Littau works to construct dichotomies that show what modern literary theory ignores, devalues and leaves out. And there is a lot: the book as a physical object, the texture of a text, the reader's body, sensations, passion, the book as a springboard for feelings, readers of flesh and blood, warmth, nearness, passivity and materiality (154 ff). I believe that at best, a number of these characteristics and categories are forced into spare time and to what Guillory calls lay reading. There, they might be accepted, but not in professional reading, that is, in the *study* of literature. It is high time for literary studies to begin to take these excluded "others" seriously.

J. Hillis Miller (2002) is one of the few current literary theorists who actually agree with this. He believes that a skilful reader should try to read in two ways at the same time: naively and critically. Miller relates naive reading to the innocent and engaged reading of childhood, when the words on a page were windows to other worlds. The naive reader reads without suspicions and with maximum empathy and emotional engagement. "The relation between reader and story read is like a love affair. In both cases, it is a matter of giving yourself without reservation to the other" (120). The critical reader, on the other hand, is always suspicious. The reader does not look through the words but rather at them, in order to see which linguistic and narrative devices the author used to create the illusion of nearness and reality. Even though Miller views the idea of trying to read in both ways as very demanding, it is this double reading that he feels characterizes a truly talented reader of literature. In other words, Miller succeeds in valuing the naive form of reading, which literary theory and the teaching of literature views as their duty to counteract. At the same time, he also believes that critical reading is necessary to a deep and reflective reading.

Miller has taken some decisive steps towards what could be called a third way of reading, away from the sharp separation between naive and critical reading, lay reading and professional reading, linguistic and literary competence. I myself have worked further in this direction and in Persson (2007), I plead the case of what I call *creative reading*. This is characterized by an active exploration of the borders between categories such as "naive" and "critical", by a curiosity about *different* ways of reading, by reflecting on and problematizing one's own reading in dialogue with others. Categories such as subjectivity, emotion and physicality are not considered irrelevant or trivial. These categories are *accepted* as central dimensions in reading and the task of creative reading is to be able to describe such dimensions in as rich and nuanced a way as possible. This does not mean, of course, that the borders between, for example, the naive and the critical are erased, or that literary studies should suddenly stop teaching about the techniques of critical reading and only recommend subjective responses. Rather, this is about encouraging, noticing and training what Hans Robert Jauss considers the basic double nature of aesthetic experience: "understanding enjoyment and enjoying understanding" (1982, 32).

In the teaching of literature, naive reading needs the critical, and vice versa. As many pedagogues of literature have pointed out, teaching must recognize and use as its basis students' spontaneous and subjective reactions. Not least, readers' connections to personal experiences should be encouraged and not oppressed. At the same time, these should not just be accepted as they are, but rather should be items for discussion and reflection. And the literary text cannot be reduced to a springboard for personal introspection. It is the continual and increasingly more refined *interplay* between text and reader that should be sought after. Emphasizing the subjective basis does not mean that the aesthetic aspects of a text are ignored. On the contrary, intense attention should be paid to the text's form, or to what Derek Attridge (2004) calls literature's singularity – its character of radical "otherness" and unique experience. Rosenblatt expresses it well:

> When there is active participation in literature – the reader living through, reflecting on, and criticizing his own responses to the text – there will be many kinds of benefits. We can call this growth an ability to share discriminatingly in the possibilities of language as it is used in literature. But this means also the development of the imagination: the ability to escape from the limitations of time and place and environment, the capacity to envisage alternatives in ways of life and in moral and social choices, the sensitivity to thought and feeling and needs of other personalities (Rosenblatt 1995, 276).

There is no goal in this process in the form of a single true interpretation. The goal for creative reading is instead an ever more deepened and multidimensional experience and, in the long run, a development of aesthetic experiences and the literary repertoire.

Ideas about naive versus critical ways of reading have been central within both literary theory and literary pedagogy. But what do the concepts really mean and what is the relationship between them? What really characterizes the different types of reading and how are they valued and handled within the various arenas of teaching literature? Creative reading forces such questions out into the light. Creative reading, which could in principle be practised both in schools and in higher education, is not just a simple combination or synthesis of the naive and the critical. It is, rather, a practice and an exploration of *different* ways of reading, an activity that can very well lead to categories such as naive and critical having to be abandoned. Is it really so that the professional reader always tries to repress pleasure to the benefit of analytical chill? Or that the lay reader never reflects critically about his or her reading? It cannot be that simple – we can be sure of that. But these are empirical questions that demand empirical answers.

Implicit in Rosenblatt's account quoted above is a value which stretches far beyond the literature classroom. She actually connects reading with what could perhaps be called democratic virtues: a willingness to imagine Others and otherness. Guillory makes a similar point when he spells out the consequences of both lay and professional reading's failure to recognize their common identity as ethical practice:

> If the practice of reading is either lay or professional, either pleasure or labor, but never both, it is difficult to see how the public sphere is ever to be other than it is now, a massified sphere of entertainment, in which the discourse of the professionals is assimilated only in the most refracted and distorted form, as a threat to the pleasure of the people. The political public sphere depends finally upon the cultivation of an intermediate ethical practice, upon the development of the capabilities of private citizens through their individual practices upon themselves (Guillory 2000, 43 f).

Framed in this way, the relationship between reading and studying literature has profound political implications. The concept of creative reading becomes not just a question of how to read literature, but highlights why we should do it, inside and outside the academy. It draws our attention to the divide between lay and professional reading and urges us to explore and transgress it. There are no ready answers or fixed solutions – but the concept definitely puts the legitimization of reading on the agenda. We can no longer go on pretending it is business as usual – a lesson which of course also often can be learned from literature itself.

Not surprisingly, one can find strong arguments for creative reading in numerous works of literature. Many works encourage, or even require, the use of parallel types of reading. These can be from high culture or pop culture and they are not seldom, as in the following example, staged as an active interplay between ideas about what is considered "high" versus "low" and critical versus naive. The Argentine author Manuel Puig's novel *El beso de la mujer araña* (1976, English transl. *Kiss of the Spider Woman* 1991) is a deeply gripping tale about the distrust, friendship and love between two men who must share a prison cell, the homosexual Molina and the political activist Valentin. They seem to be each other's opposites. With an undistanced passion for romantic and melodramatic popular fiction, Molina represents feeling and the "female". He also represents naive reading. Valentin is the symbol of common sense and right and he views everything that cannot be fitted into the political struggle's domains as unimportant or even immoral. He represents "male" principles, and critical reading.

Valentin cannot understand Molina's taste for sentimental movies and accuses him of escapism, in a language similar to the mass culture critique of the Frankfurt School. Only "thinking about nice things" can be alienating and dangerous, claims Valentin, who continues:

> It can become a vice, always trying to escape from reality like that, it's like taking drugs or something. Because, listen to me, reality, I mean *your reality*, isn't restricted by this cell we live in. If you read something, if you study something, you transcend any cell you're inside of, do you understand what I'm saying. That's why I read and why I study every day (78).

Reading for Valentin is synonymous with studying, i.e. with work. And yet he is reluctantly seduced by the film plots Molina passionately retells him every night. Even for a man of strong principles and integrity, the pleasures of naive reading can apparently be activated. "Come on, tell me some more" (79).

Along with the dialogue between the prisoners, another discourse runs through the novel, very palpably. Footnotes begin to take up more and more room and they develop into long, academically distanced and psychoanalytically-colored essays about the nature of desire and sexuality. The reader has to make an impossible but necessary decision: to choose one of the discourses on the page at a time – *either* the main text's story about the collision between Molina's "sentimental" and unreserved tribute to desire and Valentin's strict, politically motivated but almost puritanical deprivation of urges *or* the footnotes' theoretical and analytical discussion of the problematic of desire.

The two different discourses comment on each other by thematizing the same problem, something that becomes clearer the more one reads. The conflict between the romantic view of love in Molina's favourite films and the analytical dissection of desire in the footnotes reflects the polarization of the two characters in the diegesis. Through this radical and literal juxtaposition of opposing discourses and ideologies (cf. the analysis of the novel in Collins 1989, 137 ff), the reader is also forced in a very concrete way to navigate different views of the relationships between life, fiction and politics. However, the opposing sides eventually get closer and want contact, just as Molina and Valentin gradually do, both intellectually and physically. When Valentin receives a letter he reflects, "Know something? There I was laughing at your bolero, but the letter I got today says just what the bolero says". (137) After reciting the bolero and identifying some of its counterparts in Valentin's real life, Molina concludes: "Listen, big man, don't you know by now, boleros contain tremendous truths, which is why I like them" (139).

The unrestricted power of the patterns of dichotomies is questioned in this novel. The naive and the critical are interdependent. Furthermore Puig shows us that these categories can never exist in pure forms.

> – I learned a lot from you, Molina …
> – You're crazy, I'm just a dope […]
> – It's kind of hard to explain. But you've made me think about so many things,
>   of that you can be sure … (261)

This is not only a novel *about* the relationship between the naive and the critical. It is a novel that forces not only Valentin but also the reader to question his own views on different ways of reading, and quite literally urges him to start reading creatively.

In recent years, several theorists have questioned literary theory's strong adherence to the politics of interpretation, with its bias towards studying rather than reading literature. In an article from 2006, reception researcher David S. Miall writes that Fish's slogan is still applicable: the literature researcher's job is and will continue to be to produce interpretations. Miall thinks there ought to be empirical studies of how regular readers read. There is nothing wrong with analyzing professional readers' interpretations, as Culler suggests, but it is an insufficient and misleading basis for new knowledge about how and why we really read:

No doubt the study of published interpretations has its own merit, but it is a poor answer to the question of how texts are actually read. Filtered out of printed interpretations are details of how a reader arrived at her understanding of the text; printed accounts are also likely to be subject to distortions and repressions of various kinds that misrepresent the act of reading. Above all, what is usually given in print is an interpretation, but this is not necessarily what a reader reading "non-professionally" is aiming to produce; thus a reliance on printed interpretations for a study of literary reading has little ecological validity (Miall 2006, 292).

We shall not stop interpreting literature, but it will not be the only thing we do. We have to develop a vocabulary that makes it possible to also talk about dimensions in reading that are not primarily about producing meaning. We need a new semantics of pleasure, emotion, sensation and affect. As Hans Ulrich Gumbrecht (2004) has pointed out, this is one of the largest and more important challenges facing the humanities today. With concepts such as intensity, complexity, epiphany and presence, he has himself begun constructing such a vocabulary.

We must give up the belief that there is just one legitimate way of reading literature. There is an almost endless array of reasons for reading literature (Felski 2008). An assignment for literary studies could be to begin mapping, describing and analyzing them instead of immediately classifying most of them as subjective and irrelevant. In this way, bridges can be built between the currently sharply divided practices of reading and studying literature.

REFERENCES

Collins, Jim. 1989. *Uncommon Cultures: Popular Culture and Post-Modernism.* London & New York: Routledge.
Culler, Jonathan. 1975. Literary Competence. In *Structuralist Poetics.* Routledge Classics Edition. 2002, 131-152. London & New York: Routledge.
Eagleton, Terry. 1976. *Criticism and Ideology.* 2006. London & New York: Verso.
Felski, Rita. 2008. *Uses of Literature.* Malden & Oxford: Blackwell.
Fish, Stanley. 1980. *Is There a Text in This Class? The Authority of Interpretive Communities.* Cambridge, Massachusetts & London: Harvard University Press.
Guillory, John. 2000. The Ethical Practice of Modernity: The Example of Reading. In *The Turn to Ethics,* eds. Marjorie Garber, Beatrice Hanssen and Rebecca L. Walkowitz, 29-46. New York & London: Routledge.
Gumbrecht, Hans Ulrich. 2004. *Production of Presence: What Meaning Cannot Convey.* Stanford: Stanford University Press.
Jauss, Hans Robert. 1982. *Aesthetic Experience and Literary Hermeneutics,* trans. Michael Shaw. Minneapolis: University of Minnesota Press.

Kåreland, Lena, ed. 2009. *Läsa bör man ...? – den skönlitterära texten i skola och lärarutbildning.* Stockholm: Liber.

Littau, Karin 2006. *Theories of Reading: Books, Bodies and Bibliomania.* Cambridge: Polity Press.

Miall, David S. 2006. Empirical Approaches to Studying Literary Readers: The State of the Discipline. *Book History* 9: 291-311.

Miller, J. Hillis. 2002. *On Literature.* London & New York: Routledge.

Persson, Magnus. 2007. *Varför läsa litteratur? Om litteraturundervisningen efter den kulturella vändningen.* Lund: Studentlitteratur.

– 2008. Boken om böcker i medieåldern. *Tidskrift för litteraturvetenskap* 3-4: 25-39.

Puig, Manuel. 1991. *Kiss of the Spider Woman*, transl. Thomas Colchie. London: Vintage.

Rabinowitz, Peter. 1998. *Before Reading: Narrative Conventions and the Politics of Interpretation.* Columbus: Ohio State University Press.

Richards, I.A. 1929. *Practical Criticism: A Study of Literary Judgement.* 1956. San Diego & New York: Harcourt Brace & Company.

Rosenblatt, Louise M. 1995. *Literature as Exploration.* Fifth Edition. New York: The Modern Language Association of America.

Sloterdijk, Peter. 1999. *Regeln für den Menschenpark: Ein Antwortschreiben zu Heideggers Brief über den Humanismus.* Frankfurt am Main: Suhrkamp.

Thorson, Staffan and Christer Ekholm, eds. 2009. *Främlingskap och främmandegöring: Förhållningssätt till skönlitteratur i universitetsundervisningen.* Göteborg: Daidalos.

Torell, Örjan, ed. 2002. *Hur gör man en litteraturläsare? Om skolans litteraturundervisning i Sverige, Ryssland och Finland.* Institutionen för humaniora, Härnösand. Rapport nr. 12. Härnösand: Institutionen for humaniora, Mitthögskolan.

Wellek, René and Austin Warren 1973 [1949]. *Theory of Literature.* Hammondsworth, Middlesex: Penguin Books Ltd.

Wimsatt, W.K. 1954. *The Verbal Icon.* Lexington: University of Kentucky Press.

AESTHETICS AND THE NEW ETHICS:

THEORIZING THE NOVEL IN THE TWENTY-FIRST CENTURY

Dorothy J. Hale

In the introduction to a 2002 special issue of *Diacritics* on ethics and inter-disciplinarity, Mark Sanders asks us to consider, "What points of contact, if any, are there between the current investment in ethics in literary theory, and the elaboration of ethics in contemporary philosophy?" (3). Yet the question behind this question – the one that motivates his selection of essays for the issue – is why literary critics and theorists have drawn their ideas about ethics from Emmanuel Levinas, Jacques Derrida, Michel Foucault, Giorgio Agamben, and Alain Badiou but have felt little or no need to consult past or present moral philosophers. As Sanders goes on to note, while "in North America and the Anglophone world generally, the tendency in ethics has been to bring moral reflection to bear on questions in political theory", there "has been relatively little attention among literary theorists to developments in disciplinary philosophy" (4).

Sanders's observation of this disconnect is particularly intriguing when we consider that the return to moral reflection in contemporary literary theory is in fact a double return: the renewed pursuit of ethics has been accompanied by a new celebration of literature, and it is in the imbrication of these endeavors – the revival of ethics leading to a new defense of literature that literary theory and moral philosophy find common ground in the twenty-first century.[1] No moral philosopher has been more enthusiastic or more vocal about the positive social value of literature than Martha Nussbaum. But the mere mention of the author of *Love's Knowledge* and *Poetic Justice* seems to take the mystery out of Sanders's question. Isn't Martha Nussbaum – self-described humanist, avowed liberal, public excoriator of

---

1   For recent work in moral philosophy on literary value, see Appiah; Diamond; Eagle-
    stone; Levinson; McGinn; Palmer; and Pippin. For new ethical literary theory, see
    Altieri; Attridge; Bernstein; Buell; Davis and Womack; Gibson; Glowacka and Boos;
    Harpham, *Shadows*; Helgesson; Huffer; J. Miller, *Ethics, Literature*; Newton; Rainsford
    and Woods; and Spivak, "Ethics", *Critique*.

Judith Butler's "defeatist" feminism (Nussbaum, "Professor", 37) – the prima facie evidence of moral philosophy's failure to get what is "new" about the new ethics? While literary theorists pride themselves on pursuing ethics and estimating literary value in the light of and in response to complex and difficult poststructuralist truths, Nussbaum in particular and moral philosophy in general seem to remain, as Andrew Gibson has said, "pre-Barthesian" (11). While Gibson identifies the pre-Barthesian as a throwback to mid 20th-century naive humanism (epitomized for him by Lionel Trilling, with whom he groups Nussbaum), others have found Nussbaum so retro as to be antiquity itself: "Nussbaum is defiantly Aristotelian and therefore pre-Enlightenment; her slogan might be 'Antiquity – An Incomplete Project'" (Harpham, "Hunger", 57).

Those hostile to Nussbaum find it fitting that the pre-Barthesian who unembarrassedly confesses her love of literature, who argues not just for the positive social value of literature but for the superiority of literature to other types of social discourse, and who even goes so far as to claim that "literary people" (authors and readers of literature) are "best equipped" to perform ethical inquiry would be in love with Henry James (Nussbaum, *Love's Knowledge*, 192). It is one thing for Trilling in 1948 to hold up the Jamesian novel as an ethical ideal, to see literature, and especially novels, as a moral corrective to what he calls the "cold potatoes" of social reform through government policies (22). After all, Trilling's defense of the social value of literature is rooted in a prestructuralist sense of the liberal individual, usefully defined from the post-Foucauldian perspective of D.A. Miller as "the subject whose private life, mental or domestic, is felt to provide constant inarguable evidence of his constitutive 'freedom'" (D. Miller, x). This is the kind of freedom invoked by Trilling when he argues that the imperialism of United States public policy can be checked only by the cultivation of the "free play of the moral imagination" and that "for our time the most effective agent of the moral imagination" has been a product of the literary imagination: "the novel of the last two hundred years" (27). For Trilling, the moral enterprise that is fiction – defined by its inutility, its anti-instrumentality, its inequivalence to state law – culminates in the work of an aesthete, Henry James.

But by 1990 shouldn't Martha Nussbaum have learned from literary critics the political lessons of Jamesian aestheticism? In *The Political Unconscious*, Fredric Jameson declares James's creation of an aesthetics of the novel to have such profound social consequences as to be "a genuinely historical act", a crucial cultural formation in the development of late capitalism (221). For Jameson, James's refinement and glorification of point of view – both as a narrative technique and as a philosophy of perspectival individualism – serve as a "strategic loc[us] for the fully constituted or centered bourgeois subject or monadic ego", enabling capitalism to "produce and institutionalize the new subjectivity of the bourgeois individual" (154). Since Jameson's claim, made nearly thirty years ago, literary critics have fleshed out the list of Henry James's political offenses. Many of these critics follow Jameson in their belief that James's formal practices – and the aesthetic value that James attributed to novelistic form – are the key to his bad politics. James's dedication to developing the novel into a high art form is understood as part of a more general effort by nineteenth-century white male writers to make up in cultural capital what they were losing in sales. The ideological production of the aesthetic as a "discrete entity", Michael Gilmore and others have proposed, was the "creation of white male fiction writers reacting against the commercial triumphs of the feminine novel" (Gilmore, 70-71).[2]

For post-Marxist and post-Foucauldian interpreters of the development of the novel, James is indeed a culmination of the last two hundred years, and that culmination does produce, as Trilling believed, the liberal imagination. But for these critics the belief in the liberal imagination is precisely the problem that needs political reform. It has been the work of literary studies to show that the "free play of the moral imagination" is anything but free: it is an agent of regulation, discipline, instrumentality, and ideological delusion. Through its affective power and strategic representation of society, the novel creates a reader who (to quote D. A. Miller again) "seems to recognize himself most fully only when he forgets or disavows his functional implication in a system of carceral restraints or disciplinary injunctions" (x). In a similar line of argumentation, Nancy Armstrong finds the novel's social power to lie in its genre strategies of "displacement", which transmogrify the "material body" as a social and political reality into a "metaphysical object" of "language and emotion" (Armstrong, *Desire* 6) – an aesthetic act of partitioning that leads individual subjects to think of themselves as universal subjects (*How Novels Think*, 10, 18).

Is Nussbaum's defense of literature in general and Henry James in particular anything more than the disavowal of her own social positionality? The literary values Nussbaum admires, notes John Horton, "openness,

---

2   See Blair; Freedman; Jacobs; and Porter for particularly powerful political critiques of Jamesian aestheticism.

subtlety of discrimination, a delicately nuanced understanding and a precisely graded emotional responsiveness [are] perhaps not surprisingly, the virtues of a liberal literary intellectual" (88). And, indeed, her conception of literature, and the novel as her privileged example, is predicated on the ethical value it confers on private emotion: literature, Nussbaum says, gives "ethical relevance" to "particularity and to the epistemological value of feeling" (*Love's Knowledge*, 175). The novel distinguishes itself as a genre by its "profound" commitment "to the emotions" (40). This means, for Nussbaum, that the novel both communicates its meaning through emotion and communicates the ethical value of certain types of emotion. One such ethical emotion is the feeling of possibility: novels, she tells us, engage "readers in relevant activities of searching and feeling, especially feeling concerning their own possibilities as well as those of the characters" (46). Our feeling of possibility is, according to Nussbaum, an outgrowth of a more foundational ethical feeling: love. To feel that we love is at once involuntary proof of our deepest values – what we authentically care about, what we can't not care about – and a means of developing better social practices, since our love for others allows us to make their cares, their values our own, extending our experience by widening our "range of concerns" (47). Nussbaum proposes that the art of the novel is first and foremost a performance of – and education in – the care we should have (and those of us who love literature do have) for alterity, particularity, complexity, emotion, variety, and indeterminacy.

For the cultural critic, "love's knowledge", the care that on Nussbaum's view is inspired by and enacted through novel reading, stands as strong testimony to the particular way the novel performs its ideological work, the way that novelistic aesthetics accomplishes the project of universalizing the individual subject. The novel as a producer and agent of care certainly fits into D.A. Miller's account of the way the novel administers the "regime of the norm" (viii). For the Foucauldian, readerly love becomes the basis for (in Miller's words) "the subject's own contribution to the intensive and continuous 'pastoral' care that liberal society proposes to take of each and every one of its charges" (viii). Nussbaum's notion that the problem of human flourishing is first and foremost a private and "practical" affair, a problem pursued through and solved in relation to our emotional experience of "life" and, most intensely, through our emotional experience of life as represented in novels (*Love's Knowledge,* 21), is for the political critic confirmation of the liberal subject's valorization of psychological interiority through its mystification.

A key moment in *Love's Knowledge* provides a powerful example of how novels might be said to lead Nussbaum herself into liberal disavowal. She quotes at length a passage from *David Copperfield* that describes the "comfort" David derives from the characters he meets through novel reading. The passage that Nussbaum cites ends with David's memory of "sitting on my bed, reading as if for life" (qtd. in *Love's Knowledge*, 230). In a chapter title and elsewhere in her book, Nussbaum restyles Dickens's phrase "reading as if for life" as "reading for life". Her substitution seems to perform the erasure of the materiality of social reality by the free play of the liberal imagination. To forget the "as if" is to equate reading with life, to disavow the ideological nature of reading, the particular social conditions that encourage Nussbaum to believe that there could be no significant difference between life and its fictional representation, between reading as a private and individual experience and reading as cultural work. To forget this difference is to project both life and the reader as mystified essences, metaphysical objects.

It thus may seem the logical conclusion of Nussbaum's liberalism that the political program she develops in *Love's Knowledge* locates the path to social reform in the consciousness of a fictional character, and a Jamesian consciousness at that. The first thing that contemporary literary critics should teach the world in order to improve it, Nussbaum declares, is how "to confront reigning models of political and economic rationality with the consciousness of Strether" (192). The man of the imagination is for Nussbaum the epitome of right ethical value, brought into being by James's own ethical act: the creation of a novel that models through its narrative structure the "finely aware and richly responsible" acts of perception (the phrase is James's [*Art* 62]) that are for Nussbaum the key to human flourishing (*Love's Knowledge*, 148). What do politicians and law keepers have to learn from James's representation of Lambert Strether's consciousness? That "the well-lived life is a work of literary art" (148). This sentiment's echoing of the villainous aesthete Gilbert Osmond's advice to Isabel Archer in *The Portrait of a Lady* – that "one ought to make one's life a work of art" (261) – seems to suggest the limits and dangers of living "for" life by living life "as if" it were no different from art. The desire to confront power with Strether seems to reveal Nussbaum's addiction to imaginary solutions to real political problems. In a postmodern world of pop culture, globalism, and multiculturalism, we might take it as a sign of our cultural distance from the "genuinely historical act" of high-capitalist subject formation that most readers today, academic and nonacademic, feel the spectacular irrelevance of the Edwardian aesthete, either Strether or his maker. We might take it as the end of disavowal that we can say with Cynthia Ozick, "The truth of our little age is this: nowadays no one gives a damn about what Henry James knew" (2).

But I want to argue that, even if no one thinks it matters what Henry James knew, the modern novel that James helped to invent and the tradition of novel theory that he inaugurated provide a foundational aesthetics for the novel that underlies both Nussbaum's ethical philosophy and the new ethical theory that has emerged, especially in the past decade, in the attempt to articulate a positive social value of literature for our postmodern age. To mention J. Hillis Miller, Gayatri Spivak, Judith Butler, Derek Attridge, Geoffrey Galt Harpham, and Michael André Bernstein is to invoke some of the most influential contributors to the new ethical defense of literary value. And while these theorists do indeed, as Sanders observes, derive their ethics from diverse political theorists (Foucault, Agamben, Adorno, Walter Benjamin, Levinas, and Derrida), what Sanders and others have yet to note is that the heterogeneity of these political influences has coalesced in a surprisingly unified account of literary value.[3] For these new ethicists and a wave of others, the ethical value of literature lies in the felt encounter with alterity that it brings to its reader. It is the untheorized understanding of the form of the novel as inherently politicized that establishes a bridge between the poststructuralist ethicists and the "pre-Barthesian" Nussbaum. The development in the 20th century of a novelistic aesthetics of alterity cannot be adequately explained (away) by the ideological notion of disavowal since the avowal of disavowal is part of what defines it as an aesthetics. I want to show how both ethical camps not only take for granted the achievement of alterity as the novel's distinctive generic purpose but also understand it to be accomplished through novelistic form. I then want to suggest how the aesthetics of alterity derives from James's acute awareness that the politicized struggle between art and its ideological instrumentality is constitutive of novelistic aesthetics itself.

* * *

We can begin to chart the connection between Nussbaum and the new ethicists by comparing her revision of Dickens's "reading as if for life" with the ethical value Butler finds in the phrase "for life, as it were". The phrase

---

3   For studies of the political theory underlying the new ethics, see Critchley; Marchitello.

that interests Butler is, importantly, James's – and it ends the last sentence of *Washington Square*, the novel that Butler has used to make her own case for James's ethical insights. Here's the full last line of James's novel: "Catherine, meanwhile, in the parlour, picking up her morsel of fancy-work, had seated herself with it again – for life, as it were" (qtd. in Butler 208). Since I've discussed Butler's new ethics elsewhere, I want to draw forward here just the point of comparison with Nussbaum.[4] Butler understands the conditional phrase "for life, as it were" as James's insight into the necessary condition of meaning making not just in literature but also in life. Because Butler sees all meaning making as an act of figuration, of the "as if" imposition of order and coherence onto experience, any act of knowing, not just reading, is, on her view, created through the restyling of "reading as if for life" as "reading for life". For Butler, human understanding comes into being through the oscillation between reading for life and reading as if for life. Reading for life, we ignore or forget the conditionality of our understanding. Reading as if for life, we are self-consciously aware that our certainty is all hypothetical: we understand that we create the meaning we think we find; we know that when we feel most certain we are taking for fact exactly what we pretend to be.

How are these moments of self-conscious apprehension achieved? As Butler describes it, we come to self-consciousness about our pretended certainty through the confrontation with alterity, an experience of the other that surprises us in its intractability, its refusal to conform to what we imagine we know – to fit into our personal "regime of the norm" (to use D.A. Miller's term), the expectations that we call knowledge. For Butler, *Washington Square* provides us with this confrontation with alterity by refusing to explain the motives that drive its heroine, Catherine Sloper, to reject her suitor and pick up her fancywork. In refusing to explain herself to the other characters, Catherine, according to Butler, defines her autonomy not through language but by "marking the limits of all speaking that seeks to bind her, that offers itself to her as a way of binding herself" (208). The reader's easy access to Catherine throughout *Washington Square* thus abruptly ends with her transmogrification from knowable point of view to unfathomable other. What Butler doesn't say, but what is nonetheless an important feature of her account of alterity, is that it is precisely Catherine's move beyond social binding that binds the reader to her. Catherine's refusal to explain herself – and James's refusal to explain to us *for* her – is experienced by the reader as an

---

4   See my "Fiction".

emotional upset that reveals the reader's own participation in the everyday binding we all perform on people we pretend to know. When James stymies our comprehension – in this case by substituting the ambiguating phrase "as it were" for the clarifying authorial judgment we expect and desire – Butler tells us "the reader is left, in a sense, exasperated, cursing, staring" (208). On Butler's view, this emotional response is the precondition for ethical knowledge and choice: we are put in a position to "understand the limits of judgment and to cease judging, paradoxically, in the name of ethics, to cease judging in a way that assumes we already know in advance what there is to be known" (208).

To cease judging is, in other words, to cease trying to understand Catherine and instead, to use Nussbaum's word, to "care" for her as other. To the degree that the reader's judgment can be converted into recognition of/for Catherine is the degree to which we read not just "for life" but, in an even more spiritual way, for "*a* life" (Butler, 214; emphasis added). Being bound (to the enigma that is Catherine, to the ambiguity that ends James's novel), the reader "has" (as James himself might say) her ethical experience: "we *undergo* what is previously unknown we learn something about the limits of our ways of knowing; and in this way we experience as well the anxiety and the promise of what is different, what is possible, what is waiting for us if we do not foreclose it in advance" (Butler, 209; emphasis added). Our experience of how literature binds us (binds us to characters, binds us to its emotional effects) is thus the happy psychological condition that frees us from our usual epistemological limits. The felt condition of our own binding makes possible, in other words, our knowledge of life "as it were". Incomprehension of the other yields knowledge of the self: we are made to recognize our operative interpretative categories as our own "regime of the norm". And this felt recognition of the limits of our ways of knowing opens up, for Butler, the possibility that we might change for the better, that we might actively try to judge less and undergo more.

But, of course, the psychological model that underpins Butler's theory means that this ethical lesson cannot be learned once and for all. Our capacity for undergoing is dependent on our continuing to judge: alterity can only be registered positively by our experience of its power to disrupt us, to leave us, in a sense, exasperated, cursing, staring. Our avowal of our epistemological limits is something that must be freshly performed, undergone again and again. Indeed, the hope of Butler's model lies in her belief that the ethical autonomy and significance of *a* life, of any one life, always exceed the social "system of carceral restraints or disciplinary injunctions" (D. Miller, x) by which we know it. For Butler, alterity is defined by the endless potential to resist comprehension, to trouble certainty. And it is precisely the endless possibility for psychological upset that creates the positive conditions for personal and social change. The end of the liberal subject's feeling of "constitutive 'freedom'" defined by private life begins with the individual's emotional experience of the private life as confounded, invaded. Vulnerability allows change. Anxiety, promise.

How does Butler's "as it were" help us to understand Nussbaum's erasure of Dickens's "as if"? For Nussbaum, the conversion of "reading as if for life" to "reading for life" is, as it is for Butler, grounded in two types of alterity: the reader's honoring of the characterological lives depicted in the novel and the work of literature as itself a "life". For Nussbaum, as for Butler, it is the encounter with alterity – what Nussbaum calls the human – that produces "pains and sudden joys" – emotions that are themselves ethical in this context (*Love's Knowledge*, 53). The narrative strategies of the novel – "complex", "allusive", and "attentive to particulars" – position the reader to care "about what happens" (3-4), to be "lucidly bewildered, surprised by the intelligence of love" into an openness to the new and different (53). Nussbaum says she learns from Strether the "willingness to surrender invulnerability, to take up a posture of agency that is porous and susceptible of influence" (180). "The life of perception feels perplexed, difficult, unsafe... But this life also seems to Strether – and to us – to be richer, fuller of enjoyment, fuller too of whatever is worth calling knowledge of the world" (181). Literary texts thus display to Nussbaum what Butler calls "values of difficulty". Nussbaum argues that novels engage the reader in "the complexity, the indeterminacy, the sheer *difficulty* of moral choice ... the refusal of life involved in fixing everything in advance according to some system of inviolable rules" (141-42). For Nussbaum, as for Butler, we negotiate between the "conceptions", the "rules and principles", the categories for judgment that we bring to the text and our willingness to be "in some sense passive and malleable, open to new and sometimes mysterious influences" (29, 44, 238). This vulnerability, she believes, "is a part of the transaction [with literary texts] and part of its value" (238). To be truly vulnerable, to have authentically risked, is to honor the power of the life of the other through the feeling of "surrender", "succumbing" (Booth qtd. in Nussbaum, *Love's Knowledge*, 237).

Nussbaum's account of the novel thus distinguishes itself from Trilling's – and does so in a way that complements the political critique of Trilling. For Nussbaum the reader's experience of the free play of moral imagination ends in the experience of social restraint, of binding and of being bound to the life of the other.[5] In *Poetic Justice*, Nussbaum comes even closer to Butler in her meditation on the way literary representation produces otherness through figuration. Nussbaum's term for figuration is "fancy", and her definition of fancy neatly glosses why, in the James passage that so interests Butler, Catherine Sloper's act of refusal is accompanied by the picking up of her fancywork. Nussbaum tells us, "[F]ancy is the novel's name for the ability to see one thing as another, to see one thing in another. We might therefore also call it the metaphorical imagination" (36). Nussbaum, like Butler, believes that figuration enables us not only to apprehend alterity (to see one thing as another, to see one thing in another) but also to inhabit the conditions of possibility that ensure a future different from our "now": that "other things [can be] seen in the immediate things" (36).

One reason the connection between Nussbaum and the new ethicists might be hard to see is that the name given by poststructuralists to their valorization of readerly experience is anything but "love". But to find this much common ground between Butler and Nussbaum puts us in a position to understand how the names poststructuralist theorists give to literary experience – names like "estrangement", "defamiliarization", and "difficulty" – are, like Nussbaum's "love", an attempt to answer Foucauldian and Marxist subjective functionalism by offering an alternative theory of private interiority. Instead of being the "constant inarguable evidence of constitutive 'freedom'", our interiority is, for Nussbaum and poststructuralist ethicists alike, the constant inarguable evidence of our constitutive sociality, a sociality felt as self-restraint. The disavowal of social positionality entailed by reading "for life" is countered by the avowal of social positionality necessitated by reading for life "as it were". The psychological necessity of oscillating between disavowal and avowal is, for both Butler and Nussbaum and in new ethical theory generally, what makes possibility possible.

After noting the disconnect between literary theory and moral philosophy, Sanders declares, "Literature is an other-maker. It is to this activity that literary theory must attend" (4). But it seems that novel writers and readers have been attending to this definition of literature for at least a century. Sanders can take for granted that literature is an other maker precisely because in our cultural moment the novel and its aesthetics of alterity define the literary for most readers. The new ethics helps us recognize novelistic aesthetics as inherently politicized by showing how the novel form positions the reader to experience the self as "free" through the experience of being socially bound.

---

5   See Robbins on binding in Nussbaum and Butler, esp. 199-203.

The reader experiences the free play of his or her imagination as produced through a power struggle with a social other. The struggle to bind turns back on the reader, enabling the reader to experience the self as unfree, as in a constitutive relation with the other, who, in turn, binds him or her. And because the reader experiences his or her own binding as both a private and emotional condition, as a relationship with the lives represented by a novel and with the literary text as itself a life, the new ethicists theorize literature as conferring a felt encounter with alterity that is not simply compensatory for social positionality but outside systematic discipline. In the new ethical defense of literary value as the values of novelized form, reading produces not false ideology but a true experience of how possibility is produced in and through the operation of social constraint.

In new ethical theory, literature provides not just (or for some not even) the fictional imagination of social reform projected through the realist idiom of a story world. Novel reading does not yield a portable list of rules or tips to guide conduct. For the new ethicist, literature does not technically teach us anything at all, unless we understand learning as the overthrow of epistemology by experience, the troubling of certainty by an apprehension that comes through surprised feeling. Ethical knowledge is the experience of irresistible encounter with what one does not try to know, what one cannot but know. It is knowledge that is beyond reason, that is of the emotions, and that is so intuitive as to seem a bodily knowing. To formulate this knowledge as epistemology, as we must do, is to register the moment when we move from being bound to binding and back again. But the felt conversion of knowing into knowledge is what enables the process to continue and to be felt as a progress. The reader feels he or she comes to know more each time his or her current knowledge is confounded. Knowing is made possible by every felt failure to know and made new through every repetition.

That the reader's ethical experience of alterity begins with the encounter with literary character is an aspect of poststructuralist ethics that provides the powerful link to James. The deep psychology James creates for his characters leads readers, and himself as rereader of his own work, to regard these characters as possessing an autonomy that encourages the cultural perception that fictional creations have a right to human rights. The centrality of characterological alterity to the modern novel has shaped its aesthetic problematic in two fundamental ways. First, the modern novel's commitment to the creation of autonomous characters positions any act of narration as a potential encroachment on the existential freedom of those characters. Second, the commitment to characterological autonomy positions literariness as itself inimical to novelistic mimesis. The new ethics helps us to see that the belief that characterological freedom should be honored and respected is made possible not just by the agency the story world accords characters but also through the aesthetic functionalism that the novel as an art form assigns them. Butler can talk about Catherine as if she were an actual person not because James's use of point of view bestows on her a full subjectivity indistinguishable from our own but because as point of view, and in other ways, Catherine seems subjected to the novel's form.

This is the ethico-political basis of novelistic aesthetics. The representation of character in the novel is never free of the threat of instrumentality, either from the subjective source of narration or from an objectification posed by literary design. Fictional characters are produced as "human" precisely by the perceived limitation from both sources that novelistic form places on their autonomy. Fictional characters can be felt to be no different from real human beings to the degree that their functional positionality seems like a restriction of their subjective potentiality, a limit to the full freedom that they have a right to enjoy beyond their representation by and in the novel. This double nature – character as a full psychology and character as an element of aesthetic form – has led, in the twenty-first century, to an understanding of novelistic narrative as inherently hegemonic. The all-too-visible incarceration of subjectivity by aesthetic form is decried as an abuse of representational power. The author who must more or less use a character for his or her expressive ends is felt to be exploitative. The reader who identifies with a character worries about emotional colonization. And the reader and author who feel only the aesthetic thrill of a character's fate carry the guilt of the voyeur. The doubleness of novelistic subjectivity (as person, as artistic instrument) is perhaps best emblematized by the novel's third-person narrator, whose subjectivity is constantly imputed as the more than or the excess beyond the functional role as storyteller to which he or she is bound.

The politics of ethical possibility that the new ethicists find in literature generally are at the heart of Henry James's anxious consideration, in his prefaces and elsewhere, of the lives bound up in his fictions. The new ethical defense of literary value thus casts new light on the development of novelistic aesthetics into the twenty-first century. The aesthetics of alterity allows us to understand, on the one hand, the untheorized privileging of novel form that undergirds the cultural critic's interest in the novel and, on the other, the unacknowledged ethico-political values that inform the formalistic practice of teaching fiction as a craft. To show and not tell, to write what you know – such creative-writing-workshop dicta are connected to a conception of the novel as a social discourse different from other social discourses, made different by the aesthetic effects and ethical dilemmas particular to it. New ethical theory thus helps us see that what I have elsewhere called the social formalism at the heart of the Jamesian tradition of novel theory – the belief that the novel instantiates social identity through its form (*Social Formalism*) – is not a logical confusion about the ontological status of literary form but an aesthetic effect of the novel as the genre has been developed through the 20th century and into our own cultural moment.

The article "Aesthetics and the New Ethics: Theorizing the Novel in the Twenty-First Century" has also appeared in PMLA *(Volume 124, Number 3, May 2009, pp. 896-905). I am grateful to Charlie Altieri, Robert Caserio, Nancy Ruttenburg, Cindy Weinstein, and my graduate students at the University of California, Berkeley, for the exchange of ideas that enabled this project. I also want to thank the Berkeley Consortium for the Study of the Novel, the Huntington Library, the Stanford Center for the Study of the Novel, the University of Memphis, the University of Tennessee, and Princeton University for the opportunity to share work in progress.*

REFERENCES

Altieri, Charles. 2003. *The Particulars of Rapture: An Aesthetics of the Affects*. Ithaca: Cornell University Press.

Appiah, Kwame Anthony. 2005. *The Ethics of Identity*. Princeton: Princeton University Press.

Armstrong, Nancy. 1987. *Desire and Domestic Fiction: A Political History of the Novel*. New York: Oxford University Press.

– 2005. *How Novels Think: The Limits of Individualism from 1719-1900*. New York: Columbia University Press.

Attridge, Derek. 1988. *Peculiar Language: Literature as Difference from the Renaissance to James Joyce*. Ithaca: Cornell University Press.

Bernstein, Michael André. 1994. *Foregone Conclusions: Against Apocalyptic History*. Berkeley: University of California Press.

Blair, Sara. 1996. *Henry James and the Writing of Race and Nation*. New York: Cambridge University Press.

Booth, Wayne. 1988. *The Company We Keep: An Ethics of Fiction*. Berkeley: University of California Press.

Buell, Lawrence. 1999. In Pursuit of Ethics. Introduction. In *PMLA* 114.1 (1999): 7-19.

Butler, Judith. 2003. Values of Difficulty. In *Just Being Difficult? Academic Writing in the Public Arena*. Eds. Jonathan Culler and Kevin Lamb. Stanford: Stanford University Press. 199-215.

Critchley, Simon. 1999. *Ethics, Politics, Subjectivity: Essays on Derrida, Levinas, and Contemporary French Thought*. New York: Verso.

Davis, Todd F. and Kenneth Womack. 2001. *Mapping the Ethical Turn: A Reader in Ethics, Culture, and Literary Theory*. Charlottesville: University Press of Virginia.

Diamond, Cora. 1997. Henry James, Moral Philosophers, Moralism. In *Henry James Review* 18.3 (1997): 243-57.

Eaglestone, Robert. 1997. *Ethical Criticism: Reading after Levinas*. Edinburgh: Edinburgh University Press.

Freedman, Jonathan. 1990. *Professions of Taste: Henry James, British Aestheticism, and Commodity Culture*. Stanford: Stanford University Press.

Gibson, Andrew. 1999. *Postmodernity, Ethics, and the Novel: From Leavis to Levinas*. New York: Routledge.

Gilmore, Michael T. 1991. The Book Marketplace, I. In *The Columbia History of the American Novel*. Emory Elliott, gen. ed. New York: Columbia University Press, 46-71.

Glowacka, Dorota, and Stephen Boos, eds. 2002. *Between Ethics and Aesthetics: Crossing the Boundaries*. Albany: State University of New York Press.

Hale, Dorothy J. 2007. Fiction as Restriction: Self-Binding in New Ethical Theories of the Novel. In *Narrative* 15.2 (2007): 187-206.

– 1998. *Social Formalism: The Novel in Theory from Henry James to the Present*. Stanford: Stanford University Press.

Harpham, Geoffrey Galt. 2002. The Hunger of Martha Nussbaum. In *Representations* 77 (2002): 52-81.

– 1999. *Shadows of Ethics: Criticism and the Just Society*. Durham: Duke University Press.

Helgesson, Stefan. 2004. *Writing in Crisis: Ethics and History in Gordimer, Ndebele and Coetzee*. Scottsville: University of KwaZulu-Natal Press.

Horton, John. 1996. Life, Literature, and Ethical Theory: Martha Nussbaum on the Role of the Literary Imagination in Ethical Thought. In *Literature and the Political Imagination*. Eds. Horton and Andrea T. Baumeister. New York: Routledge, 70-97.

Huffer, Lynne. 2001. 'There Is No Gomorrah': Narrative Ethics in Feminist and Queer Theory. In *Differences* 12.3 (2001): 1-32.

Jacobs, Karen. 2001. *The Eye's Mind: Literary Modernism and Visual Culture*. Ithaca: Cornell University Press.

James, Henry. 1962. *The Art of the Novel*. New York: Scribner's.

– 1995. *The Portrait of a Lady*. New York: Norton.

Jameson, Fredric. 1981. *The Political Unconscious: Narrative as a Socially Symbolic Act*. Ithaca: Cornell University Press.

Levinson, Jerrold, ed. 1998. *Aesthetics and Ethics: Essays at the Intersection*. New York: Cambridge University Press.

Marchitello, Howard, ed. 2001. *What Happens to History: The Renewal of Ethics in Contemporary Thought*. New York: Routledge.

McGinn, Colin. 1997. *Ethics, Evil, and Fiction.* New York: Clarendon.

Miller, D.A. 1988. *The Novel and the Police.* Berkeley: University of California Press.

Miller, J. Hillis. 1987. *The Ethics of Reading: Kant, de Man, Eliot, Trollope, James, and Benjamin.* New York: Columbia University Press.

– 2005. *Literature as Conduct: Speech Acts in Henry James.* New York: Fordham University Press.

Newton, Adam Zachary. 1995. *Narrative Ethics.* Cambridge: Harvard University Press.

Nussbaum, Martha C. 1990. *Love's Knowledge: Essays on Philosophy and Literature.* New York: Oxford University Press.

– 1995. *Poetic Justice: The Literary Imagination and Public Life.* Boston: Beacon.

– 1999. The Professor of Parody. In *New Republic* 22 Feb. 1999: 37-45.

Ozick, Cynthia. 1993. *"What Henry James Knew" and Other Essays on Writers.* London: Jonathan Cape.

Palmer, Frank. 1992. *Literature and Moral Understanding: A Philosophical Essay on Ethics, Aesthetics, Education, and Culture.* New York: Clarendon.

Pippin, Robert B. 2000. *Henry James and Modern Moral Life.* New York: Cambridge University Press.

Porter, Carolyn. 1981. *Seeing and Being: The Plight of the Participant Observer in Emerson, James, Adams, and Faulkner.* Middletown: Wesleyan University Press.

Rainsford, Dominic, and Tim Woods, eds. 1999. *Critical Ethics: Text, Theory, and Responsibility.* London: Macmillan.

Robbins, Bruce. 2002. Pretend What You Like: Literature under Construction. In *The Question of Literature: The Place of the Literary in Contemporary Theory.* Ed. Elizabeth Beaumont Bissell. New York: Manchester University Press, 190-206.

Sanders, Mark. 2002. Ethics and Interdisciplinarity in Philosophy and Literary Theory. Introduction. In *Ethics.* Ed. Sanders. Spec. issue of *Diacritics* 32.3-4 (2002): 3-16.

Spivak, Gayatri Chakravorty. 1999. *A Critique of Postcolonial Reason: Toward a History of the Vanishing Present.* Cambridge: Harvard University Press.

– 2002. Ethics and Politics in Tagore, Coetzee, and Certain Scenes of Teaching. In *Ethics.* Ed. Mark Sanders. Spec. issue of *Diacritics* 32.3-4 (2002): 17-31.

Trilling, Lionel. 1948. Manners, Morals, and the Novel. In *Kenyon Review* 10.1 (1948): 11-27.

THE ETHICAL IMPLICATIONS
OF UNNATURAL SCENARIOS

Jan Alber

Why do we study fictional literature? This is one of the most important questions of our discipline. My answers are simple and subjective. First, I think that one should study literary fiction because it allows us to transcend ourselves and to experience scenarios and situations which are strictly speaking impossible in the real world. As Jean-Marie Schaeffer has shown in *Pourquoi la fiction?* (1999), fictional literature widens our mental universe beyond the actual and the familiar, and provides important playfields for numerous (sometimes disconcerting) thought experiments. Second, I think that one should study literary fiction because its projected storyworlds urge us to look at ourselves and the world we live in from a new and different perspective. Either explicitly or implicitly, the counterfactual worlds of fictional literature make us aware of other, and possibly even better, worlds. In other words, literary fiction always involves ethical questions. For instance, Heinz Antor argues that "since pattern-building processes and the acts of self-creation they involve always imply value-judgments, taking a stand or [...] positionality, literature as a medium of such practices is *per se* situated in the realm of the ethical" (Antor 1996, 70).[1]

The aim of this essay is twofold. First, I present examples of what I call "unnatural scenarios and events" from selected periods of English literary history in order to illustrate that physical and logical impossibilities play

---

1   It is perhaps also worth noting that these two reasons can best be seen by a professional reader who engages in the systematic study of literature as a disciplinary activity. While a lay reader typically reads on his or her own and is primarily motivated by desire or pleasure, a professional reader collaborates with other researchers, has knowledge of different periods and genres, and is (ideally at least) more vigilant than the lay reader (Guillory 2000). While the discovering of unnatural scenarios demands familiarity with a wide variety of different texts (both canonized and non-canonized), the determining of ethical implications demands discussions and collaborations with other researchers.

a crucial (and hitherto neglected) role in fictional literature.[2] Second, I highlight the ethical implications of these impossible scenarios and events because for me, there is more to the unnatural than aesthetic pleasure or mere experimentalism for experimentalism's sake. Following Mary Louise Pratt, the basic premise that I use in my analysis is that no matter how odd the textual structure of a literary text, it is always part of a purposeful communicative act (1977, 170). In other words, I assume that certain intentions and motivations played a role in the production of the literary work, and I form hypotheses about them. Furthermore, I argue that these intentions and motivations involve the ethical. More specifically, I am interested in one aspect of what James Phelan calls "the ethics of the telling" (2007, 11): I speculate about the role of the unnatural scenario with regard to the text's overall ethical stance, thus engaging in what one might call "hypothetical intentionalism" (Kindt and Müller 2006, 172-78; Herman 2008, 248).[3]

In order to give readers a first sense of what I mean when I use the term 'impossible,' I would like to begin by presenting two impossible objects and one impossible painting. I am doing so because the impossibilities in this visual material are immediately visible and recognizable. These are two impossible objects:

---

2   The term 'unnatural' denotes "physically impossible scenarios and events, that is, impossible by the known laws governing the physical world, as well as logically impossible ones, that is, impossible by accepted principles of logic such as the principle of non-contradiction" (Alber 2009, 80). Furthermore, the unnatural is measured against the foil of the 'natural.' My use of the term 'natural' closely correlates with our knowledge of natural laws and other cognitive parameters derived from our real-world experience (Fludernik 1996, 10-11; 2003). Natural cognitive scripts and frames (concerning time, space, and human agents) are cultural forms of simulation or representation, i.e., second- order constructs in the sense of Paul Watzlawick (1976, 140-2).

3   The term "hypothetical intentionalism" denotes a cognitive approach in which "a narrative's meaning is established by hypothesizing intentions authors might have had, given the context of creation, rather than relying on, or trying to seek out, the author's subjective intentions" (Gibbs 2005, 248).

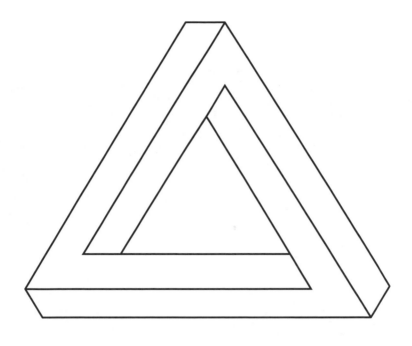

Figure 1: The Penrose triangle and the devil's tuning fork.

The first one is called the Penrose triangle and was first drawn by the Swedish artist Oscar Reutersvärd in 1934. Its combination of properties cannot be realized by any three-dimensional object. Lionel S. Penrose and Roger Penrose, two British psychologists, describe this object as follows: "Here is a perspective drawing, each part of which is accepted as representing a three-dimensional rectangular structure. The lines in the drawing are, however, connected in such a manner as to produce an impossibility" (1958, 31). The second geometrical object is called the devil's tuning fork. It seems to have three cylindrical prongs at one end which then impossibly transform into two rectangular prongs at the other end.

This is René Magritte's painting *Le blanc-seing*:

Figure 2: René Magritte *Le blanc-seing*, 1965. © Photothèque R. Magritte – ADAGP, Paris 2011.

This painting represents a physically impossible scenario: a tree that is located behind the lady on the horse blocks our view on this lady, while the space between two other trees makes her horse (and the lady's left hand) invisible. Ulf Linde argues that "if we wish to call the world the painting refers to a possible world we must [...] make an important limitation: the painting – and only the painting – makes that world possible" (1989, 312).

The general point that I am trying to make here is that the two objects and the situation in the painting would be impossible in the real world but they are possible in the paintings; they are possible in the world of fiction.

As I will show in what follows, English literary history is full of similar unnatural scenarios and events that radically deconstruct our real-world notions of human beings as well as temporal and spatial parameters (Richardson 2000, 2002, and 2006; Alber 2009). For me, this is, at least partly, what makes fiction interesting. The world of fiction is the only realm in which impossibilities can be represented. Furthermore, such impossible transformations are not ethically indifferent: they typically serve a moral purpose.[4] The unnatural scenarios that I will discuss in what follows relate to the four traditional narrative parameters of narrators, characters, time, and space (Chatman 1978, 26).

THE IMPOSSIBLE TEMPORALITY IN WALTER MAP'S *DE NUGIS CURIALIUM*

The earliest impossible temporality I have yet come across in the realm of English literature can be found in Walter Map's twelfth-century text *De Nugis Curialium* (in English *Courtiers' Trifles*). Map's medieval narrative presents us with an instance of time travel without a time machine and it verifies Ursula K. Heise's claim that narrative time is not necessarily dependent on the time laws of the real world (1997, 205).[5]

---

4   I am particularly interested in the ethical implications of narratives that project unnatural scenarios or events. Nevertheless, I would like to highlight that realist literature obviously has a moral function as well. Furthermore, I show that the unnatural is really everywhere: even realist novels contain unnatural elements such as the 'omniscient' (or telepathic) narrator. In this context, Monika Fludernik argues that "the 'omniscient' narrator function in fiction is [...] already a non-natural extension of the real-life schema of historical narration" (2001, 624). Finally, it is worth noting that I discriminate between unnatural scenarios that have already been naturalized (and turned into a cognitive category [Fludernik 2003, 256]) and unnatural scenarios that have not yet been naturalized. The former are physically or logically impossible scenarios that readers have come to accept as constituents of the projected storyworld (such as the speaking animal in beast fables or time travel in science fiction). Such scenarios can be found on Fludernik's cognitive *level III*, which "corresponds to the generic prototypes that determine our reading frames in literature" (Fludernik 2010, 15; 1996, 44-45).

5   Brian Richardson would speak of a 'differential' temporality in which a "character ages at a different rate than the people that surround him" (2002, 50).

More specifically, in *Courtiers' Trifles*, a pygmy king approaches the Briton King Herla and they agree to attend each other's weddings (Map 1983, 27). When King Herla leaves the pygmy's otherworld after the wedding, Herla discovers that he has actually spent "two hundred years" there, while in his own experience the lapse of time seems to have encompassed "but three days" (31). King Herla also realizes that he has lost his kingdom because the Saxons took possession of it. Upon Herla's departure from the otherworld, the pygmy presents him with a bloodhound and tells Herla that "on no account must any of his train dismount until that dog leapt from the arms of his bearer" (29). However, on their return to the human world, some of Herla's men forget the pygmy's orders, dismount, and immediately fall into dust (31). Finally, we are told that "the dog has not yet alighted" and that "King Herla still holds on his mad course with his band in eternal wanderings" (31). That is to say, he is doomed to wander around England forever.[6]

What is the function of these disparate time zones? I would like to suggest that Map's narrative uses the pygmy's time zone to critique leaders who are too restless, and hence do not pay attention to the demands of the actual world. In this context, it is worth noting that the narrator draws a link between the fictional King Herla and the real King Henry II, who ruled England between 1154 and 1189: "Recently, it is said, in the first year of the coronation of our King Henry", Herla and his men "ceased to visit our land in force as before [...] as if they had transmitted their wanderings to us" (31; see also 371). The narrator argues that Henry II shares the restlessness of Herla and is thus incapable of comprehending the problems of the real world. "We rush on at a furious pace; the present we treat with negligence and folly, the future we entrust to chance, [...] we are more than any man lost and depressed" (373). As Roseanna Cross has shown, the implication of Map's heterochronia is that all kings potentially face the danger of entering a different time zone, and thus of becoming oblivious to present concerns (2008, 170). The fact that some of Herla's men fall to dust, while others are doomed to eternal wanderings, clearly suggests that they have become ir-

---

6   The supernatural lapse of time experienced by King Herla is a conventional *locus communis* of folk tales, epics, and other canonical texts. The idea of the 'other time' has already been naturalized as a literary convention located on Fludernik's cognitive *level III* (1996, 44-45). I would like to argue that the supernatural lapse of time – which is clearly a precursor of time travel in science-fiction stories – is an unnatural scenario because the represented time lapse was as physically impossible in the middle ages as it is today. However, this unnatural scenario has been naturalized because it has become a common literary convention.

relevant to the human world. *Courtiers' Trifles* uses disparate temporalities to discriminate between restless leaders who fail to address the problems of the real world, and determined leaders who actually try to solve these problems. And to my mind, the narrative clearly argues in favor of the latter.

THE UNNATURAL NARRATORS OF THE 18ᵀᴴ CENTURY

Other literary texts play around with the figure of the anthropomorphic narrator. For example, the 18ᵗʰ century saw the production of numerous satirical narratives that confront us with non-human narrators. Some of these stories are told by *animals* such as fleas, cats, a horse, a lap dog, a louse, mice, a fly, and a jackdaw, while others are narrated by *inanimate objects* such as coins, a bank note, slippers, shoes, an umbrella, a coat, a coach, a watch, a sofa, a corkscrew, a bath tub, and believe it or not, even an atom.[7] Although such object narrators are impossible in the real world, they are of course possible in the world of fiction. Gérard Genette points out that in fiction, nothing prevents us from entrusting the role of the narrative agent "to an animal [...] or indeed to an 'inanimate' object" (1980, 244, n. 74). Marie-Laure Ryan also reminds us of the fact that "the narrator is a theoretical fiction, and that the human-like, pseudonatural narrator is only one of its many possible avatars" (2001, 152).

18ᵗʰ-century object narratives typically draw a link between their non-human narrators on the one hand and the general notion of authorship on the other. For example, the title page of *The History and Adventures of a Lady's Slippers and Shoes* (1754) reads as follows:

> So common now are Authors grown,
> That ev'ry Scribler in the Town,
> Thinks he can give Delight.
> If writers then are got so vain,
> To think they pleasure when they pain,
> No wonder Slippers write. Anon.

---

7   Tobias Smollett's novel *The History and Adventures of an Atom*, which is narrated by a speaking atom, was first published in 1769. Speaking animals and objects were as impossible in the 18ᵗʰ century as they are today. Nevertheless, these unnatural scenarios have become a literary convention in the context of it-narratives or circulation novels (see Flint 1998; Blackwell 2007).

Similarly, in Thomas Bridges's *The Adventures of a Bank-note*, the banknote speaks as the tale's author and compares its right to speak with the right of Dr. Samuel Johnson, the hyper-rationalist of the 18th century: "The author thinks he has as great a title to coin words as the great Doctor anybody [Samuel Johnson, J.A.]; and whether he takes his degree or not, he declares he will do it whenever he pleases" (1770, Vol. II, 42).

Another important feature of 18th-century object narratives is that the narrators pass from hand to hand, and we are presented with views of an atomized and fragmented society. For instance, in Helenus Scott's *The Adventures of a Rupee*, the rupee encounters all societal ranks, from a poor sailor to a princess in the royal family (1782, 92-93; 223-40). And it is worth noting that apart from the exchange of money, these diverse individuals do not have very much in common. In Charles Johnstone's novel *The Adventures of a Guinea* (1760-65), the narrator is even exchanged through transactions that involve bribery, corruption, and prostitution. At one point, the narrator of *The Adventures of a Bank-note* happily exclaims: "Who would not be a banknote to have such a quick succession of adventures and acquaintance?" (1770, Vol. II, 25). However, it is worth noting that the corrupt state of society in this novel obviously renders the bank-note's statement ironic.

How can we interpret these speaking objects that pass from one individualized owner to the next? For Liz Bellamy, such 'circulation novels' "provide a satirical vision of the atomized and mercenary nature of society within a commercial state" (2007, 132). That is to say, they critique the fact that the economic system and commercial values have come to define all relationships in 18th-century England. Indeed, the narrator of *The Adventures of a Guinea* argues that "when the mighty spirit of a large mass of gold takes possession of the human heart, it influences all its actions, and overpowers, or banishes, the weaker impulse of those immaterial, unessential notions called virtues" (Vol. 1, 7). Furthermore, these narratives comment on the objectification of human agents through commerce and trade. Among other things, they highlight that the commercialized circulation of books in the public sphere may turn authors into commodities so that inanimate objects sometimes become better storytellers than their human counterparts. In the words of Christopher Flint, "the narratives are, among other things, parables of textual and authorial objectification; the storyteller is not only transformed into an inanimate form but also compelled by a system of ownership to describe the experience of others, usually at the expense of internal or personal reflection" (1998, 221). That is to say, 18th-century circulation novels use speaking objects to make us aware of the fact that the principles of commerce and trade may gradually displace or perhaps even eliminate human qualities.

THE TRANSPARENT MINDS IN VIRGINIA WOOLF'S *MRS. DALLOWAY*

As Käte Hamburger (1973) first suggested, fictional literature is interesting because it can portray consciousness, particularly the consciousness of 'somebody else' from the inside. Indeed, in many Modernist[8] novels, the covert narrative medium provides us with access to the thoughts and feelings of its characters. In the real world, we cannot read other people's minds but in the world of fiction, we can read the minds of characters.[9] In this context, Marie-Laure Ryan speaks of "the supernatural ability of reading into foreign minds" (1991, 67). Similarly, in *The Distinction of Fiction*, Dorrit Cohn refers to what she calls "the unnatural power" of third-person narrators to see "into their characters' inner lives" (1999, 106).

The following passage from Virginia Woolf's novel *Mrs. Dalloway* (1925) uses narrative techniques such as psychonarration, free indirect discourse, and direct thought[10] to describe the deranged mind of Septimus Warren-Smith, a shell-shocked World War I veteran:

---

8 Brian McHale argues that "the dominant of modernist fiction is epistemological" (1987, 9). That is, Modernist fiction, such as the stream-of-consciousness novel, primarily addresses questions of knowledge.

9 The impossible insights into character interiority have also been naturalized because readers have come to accept them as elements of the projected worlds of literary Modernism. A more recent development is the 'omniscient' (or telepathic) first-person narrator, that is, a first-person narrator who can literally read the minds of other characters (Heinze 2008; Alber 2009) or knows significantly more than he could if he was a normal human being living under real-world constraints (Nielsen 2004).

10 The term 'free indirect discourse' refers to a third-person rendering of thoughts that stays close to the character's own oral syntax and diction except that tenses are shifted to the current narrative tense and pronouns are adjusted. The term 'psychonarration,' on the other hand, denotes a narrator's report of a character's conscious or unconscious mental states. Finally, stretches of direct thought convey what a character thinks without any narratorial mediation.

Men must not cut down trees. There is a God. (He noted such revelations on the backs of envelopes.) Change the world. No one kills from hatred. Make it known (he wrote it down). He waited. He listened. A sparrow perched on the railing opposite chirped Septimus, Septimus, four or five times over and went on, drawing its notes out, to sing freshly and piercingly in Greek words how there is no crime and, joined by another sparrow, they sang in voices prolonged and piercing in Greek words, from trees in the meadow of life beyond a river where the dead walk, how there is no death. There was his hand; there the dead. White things were assembling behind the railings opposite. But he dared not look. Evans was behind the railings! "What are you saying?" said Rezia suddenly, sitting down by him. Interrupted again! She was always interrupting (2000, 21).

When Septimus Warren-Smith experienced the death of Evans, his commanding officer, during the war, he must have lost the ability to feel and retreated into a private world of paralysis (Henke 1981, 15). Furthermore, Septimus shows clear signs of schizophrenia.[11] To begin with, he suffers from hallucinations. More specifically, he believes that the birds sing to him in Greek and that the dead Evans approaches him from behind the railings. Second, he is no longer able to clearly discriminate between himself and his surroundings. For example, he feels an "ecstatic connection with nature" (Crater 2000, 194), which is why according to him "men must not cut down trees". Third, he thinks that he has a mission, and throughout the novel tries to convince everyone of the idea of universal love (Henke 1981, 20). Fourth, he is talking to himself until Rezia, his wife, whom he experiences as a nuisance, interrupts him. Such passages allow the reader to experience thoughts, psychological problems, and mental illnesses he or she does not normally have access to. This particular passage is not unnatural because we are confronted with a schizophrenic character; rather, it is unnatural because the third-person narrator is somehow able to know and tell us what Septimus thinks and feels.

Interestingly, D.A. Miller and John Bender argue that tyranny surfaces in passages of free indirect discourse. According to Miller, free indirect discourse camouflages the abiding power of the "master voice" and "simultaneously subverts their [the characters', J.A.] authority and secures its

---

11 The term 'schizophrenia' describes a mental disorder characterized by abnormalities in the perception of reality such as auditory hallucinations, paranoid delusions, or disorganized speech and thinking (Sass 1992, 75-115). It differs markedly from another mental disorder known as 'split personality'.

own". In other words, the master-voice "continually needs to confirm its authority" (1988, 25). Bender even sees a link between free indirect discourse and structural attributes of the penitentiary. For him, "the penitentiary habilitates, in its own technical practices, devices parallel to those of free indirect discourse. The mode of literary production and the social institution present collateral images of one another" (1987, 203).[12] Cohn (1995) and Fludernik (1996, 368), on the other hand, argue that the use of free indirect discourse typically signals a willingness to incorporate and understand otherness rather than objectify and reify it. Indeed, in the character of Septimus Warren-Smith, Woolf's novel *Mrs. Dalloway* presents us with a "convincing portrait of schizophrenic breakdown" (Henke 1981, 13). Furthermore, the text illustrates how the demands of patriarchal society may drive a man crazy, and ultimately into suicide. In the words of Theresa L. Crater, Septimus Warren-Smith "is a failed hero. He has followed the prescription for becoming a *real man*, and the results are disastrous. He is mad, suicidal" (2000, 193; italics in the original). We are invited to sympathize with Septimus and perhaps even to understand his reasons for killing himself.[13] I do not feel that the master voice here continually needs to confirm its authority, and I also do not think that this is true with regard to other characters such as Clarissa Dalloway or Peter Walsh. Regardless of whether one feels that *Mrs. Dalloway* uses free indirect discourse to incorporate or objectify otherness, it is worth noting that narrative fiction is the only mode of discourse that allows us to get such inside views in the first place. Monika Fludernik describes the development of reflector-mode narratives such as *Mrs. Dalloway* or James Joyce's *Ulysses* (1922) as follows: "fiction at one point discovers that it can not only present another's mind by conjecture and a little bit of invention (by a stretching of the imagination, so to speak), but can present consciousness extensively as if reading people's minds" (1996, 48).

---

12 For a critique of the posited link between narrative structures and attitudes toward the prison see Jan Alber, *Narrating the Prison* (2007) and the collection *Stones of Law, Bricks of Shame: Narrating Imprisonment in the Victorian Age* (2009), edited by Jan Alber and Frank Lauterbach.

13 The novel also centrally thematizes the madness of the society Septimus lives in. In other words, *Mrs. Dalloway* asks whether the society Septimus inhabits might be considered to be insane in a metaphorical sense.

THE IMPOSSIBLE CHARACTERS IN CARYL CHURCHILL'S *CLOUD NINE*

The most striking examples of unnaturalness can be found in Postmodernist fiction.[14] Caryl Churchill's play *Cloud Nine* (1979), for example, contravenes real-world frames by presenting us with characters that display mutually incompatible features. More specifically, Clive's wife Betty "*is played by a man*" (1985, 251), while Clive's black servant Joshua "*is played by a white*" (ibid.). Furthermore, Clive's son Edward "*is played by a woman*" (252), whereas Lin's daughter Cathy is "*played by a man*" (289). In the words of Jim Phelan, the figures in *Cloud Nine* foreground "synthetic" as opposed to "mimetic" and "thematic" components of fictional characters (2005, 20)[15]; they foreground their own constructedness or artificiality.

These instances of cross-casting, which, for the reader or viewer, lead to logically impossible scenarios in which characters are simultaneously male and female (without being hermaphrodites) or both black and white (without being multiracial), serve various different purposes. According to Churchill, Betty is played by a woman because she "wants to be what men want her to be" (1985, 245). Indeed, at the beginning of the play she describes herself as follows: "I live for Clive. The whole aim of my life is to be what he looks for in a wife. I am a man's creation as you see, and what men want is what I want to be" (ibid., 251). According to Apollo Amoko, "this casting choice physicalizes and concretizes the occupation of her body and that of other women by patriarchy" (1999, 48). Similarly, the slave Joshua is "played by a white man because he wants to be what white men want him to be" (Churchill 1985, 245). Joshua introduces himself as follows: "My skin is black but oh my soul is white. I hate my tribe. My master is my light. I only live for him. As you can see, what white men want is what I want to be" (251-52). For example, he flogs other African workers, he happily sings a British Christmas carol (272), and he informs

---

14 According to Brian McHale, "the dominant of postmodernist fiction is ontological" (1987, 10). That is, postmodernist fiction self-reflexively problematizes the existence of the projected fictional world.

15 Phelan argues that "responses to the mimetic component involve an audience's interest in the characters as possible people and in the narrative world as like our own. Responses to the thematic component involve an interest in the ideational function of the characters and in the cultural, ideological, philosophical, or ethical issues being addressed by the narrative. Responses to the synthetic component involve an audience's interest in and attention to the characters and to the larger narrative as artificial constructs" (2005, 20).

on "the stable boys" who are "not to be trusted" because "they whisper", "go out at night", "visit their people", and "carry knives" (266).

In the case of Betty and Joshua, the cross-casting serves to critique the self-images of these characters: they are both so alienated from themselves and so much aspiring to be what white patriarchs and colonialists want them to be, that they do not value themselves for what they are and hence consent to their oppression.[16] In the cases of Edward and Cathy, on the other hand, the idea behind the cross-casting seems to be to accentuate their 'other' (i.e., feminine or masculine) side, and thus the potential discrepancy between one's biological sex and one's gender identity: men can of course be feminine, and women can be masculine.[17] Indeed, throughout the play, the male Edward fails to live up to his father's strict standards of masculinity. For instance, Edward is very fond of dolls (257, 274-75) and he is in love with Harry Bagley, a friend of his father's (269). At the beginning, Edward states that "what father wants I'd dearly like to be. I find it rather hard as you can see" (252). Furthermore, Churchill comments on Cathy's impersonation by a man as follows:

> [...] Cathy is played by a man, partly as a simple reversal of Edward being played by a woman, partly because the size and presence of a man on stage seemed appropriate to the emotional force of young children, and partly, as with Edward, to show more clearly the issues involved in learning what is considered correct behaviour for a girl (1985, 246).

While Edward is a rather feminine boy, Cathy turns out to be a rather a tough or masculine girl, who, for example, likes to play with guns (291).

The general point of the cross-casting in *Cloud Nine*, which, for the reader or viewer, leads to logically impossible scenarios in which characters are both male and female or both black and white, is clearly to critique the

---

16 As Amoko shows, this parallel between gender and racial oppression is not unproblematic: "These comparisons and equivalences are made despite critical material differences in the history of gender and sexual oppression within specific cultural contexts, and the history of colonialism and the peculiar history of gender and sexual oppression within colonialism. As a consequence, certain oppressed identities, for example white women, may have been provided with the prospect of empowering representation at the cost of consigning certain other identities, specifically African women, to further subjection and invisibility" (1999, 45).

17 The term 'gender identity' refers to the question of how one identifies one's gender (and associated roles) regardless of sex characteristics.

oppression of gender and racial identities. However, it is worth noting that the play highlights different facets of this repression. In the case of Betty and Joshua, we can literally see what their identities are dominated by, namely the ideas of white men, while in the case of Edward and Cathy, the play allows us to get a glimpse of the 'undesired' parts of their personalities that patriarchal (or heterosexist) society wants to do away with, namely Edward's femininity and Cathy's masculinity.

THE UNNATURAL SPACE IN BRET EASTON ELLIS'S *LUNAR PARK*

Other narratives radically deconstruct our real-world notions of spatial parameters. For instance, Bret Easton Ellis's novel *Lunar Park* (2005) confronts us with a transforming house in Midland, a fictional suburban town outside New York City. More specifically, Bret Easton Ellis, the first-person narrator, informs us that the house in which he lives with his wife Jayne Dennis, his stepdaughter Sarah, and his son Robby is "actually scarring on its own accord. Nothing was helping it. The paint was simply peeling off in a fine white shower, revealing more of the pink stucco underneath. It was doing this without any assistance" (222). We gradually learn that Ellis's house "was turning itself into a house that used to exist on Valley Vista in a suburb of the San Fernando Valley called Sherman Oaks" (254, see also 332), which is the house the narrator "grew up in" (270) as a child.[18] It is also worth noting that the furniture inside the house keeps rearranging itself in a particular manner. At some point, the narrator realizes that "the chairs and tables and sofas and lamps were arranged just as they had been in the living room of the house on Valley Vista" (223).

Other impossible things happen inside this house as well. For example, Ellis is repeatedly attacked by Terby, Sarah's bird doll. In one of the novel's most obscene scenes, the inanimate Terby enters Victor, the family dog, to attack the narrator: "When I lifted the dog's tail I tried leaping out of my mind. The dog's anus was stretched into a diameter that was perhaps ten inches across. The bottom half of the Terby was hanging out of the dog and slowly disappearing into the cavity, undulating itself so it could slide in with

18 Bret Easton Ellis, the author, tries to sell *Lunar Park* as an authentic tale ("all of it really happened, every word is true" [40]). However, I would rather like to classify the novel as a fictional autobiography. For some differences between Ellis's actual life and 'his' life in the novel see Holt and Abbott (2008).

more ease" (376). Also, throughout the novel, Ellis is haunted by his dead father. More specifically, he frequently sees his dead father or his cream-colored Mercedes 450 SL near the house; he finds his father's tombstone in the garden (128); and he receives an e-mail attachment that contains a film version of his father's death (231-37). Furthermore, at one point, the narrator and his son Robby are attacked by "a giant hairball" (316) from the woods, which "was covered with hair entangled with twigs and dead leaves and feathers" and "had no features" (307).

How can we make sense of the transforming house and the other "un-explained events" (334) in *Lunar Park*? At first glance, one might feel that we are presented with a ghost story and that we can explain the novel's unnatural elements as supernatural interventions.[19] However, it is worth noting that the novel frequently suggests that the narrator is hallucinating or suffering from delusional episodes due to his permanent drug abuse (39; 67; 388).[20] From my perspective, the best explanation of the unnatural scenarios and events is to see them as externalizations or materializations of the narrator's unconscious psychological processes, which do not only have an effect on him but also on his family.[21] Interestingly, when Ellis hires Robert Miller, who is both a "ghost hunter" and a "psychic researcher" (334), Miller tells the narrator "that these spirits might be projections from [his] inner self" (343). The house which transforms itself into the house of the narrator's childhood thus clearly suggests that Ellis travels – or has to travel – into his past. And this makes sense for two reasons. First, he has

---

19 In this case, the novel would be a "marvelous" text in the sense of Todorov, which means that we have to accept the supernatural as a given in the projected storyworld (1973, 41-42). As I have already shown, the supernatural has been naturalized through genre conventions. More specifically, we simply know that certain narratives (such as Gothic novels or horror movies) present us with ghosts or monsters and through our exposure to literature this does not strike us as being odd any longer.

20 If we kept oscillating between a supernatural explanation (ghosts) and a realist explanation (psychosis) up until the end of the novel, we would be confronted with a fantastic text in the sense of Todorov. According to Todorov, the fantastic obliges the reader "to hesitate between a natural and a supernatural explanation of the events described" and at the same time to "reject allegorical as well as 'poetic' interpretations" (1973, 33).

21 *Lunar Park* would then be an uncanny text in the sense of Todorov. Todorov argues that in uncanny narratives, seemingly supernatural events get explained as dreams or fantasies (1973, 41-42).

to confront himself with the memory of his dead father[22] and the fact that he did not spread his father's ashes according to his wishes (357). Second, he realizes that he superimposes the past over the present by repeating his father's ignorant behavior in his relation to his son Robby. Ellis experiences delusional episodes as he tries to overcome his feelings of guilt. At the end of the novel, Ellis notably spreads the ashes of his father according to his will and achieves some kind of inner peace (397-99). It is also worth noting that during the cleansing of the 'infested' house, we learn that the house is "not [...] the source of the haunting" (344); rather, Ellis himself is the "source" (344) while his son Robby is "the focal point of the haunting" (353). Within the context of my interpretation, this might mean that through these disconcerting and physically impossible events, Ellis is somehow trying to come to terms with his role as a father and he fails tragically.[23] To summarize, *Lunar Park* uses unnatural scenarios and events to critique its psychotic narrator who experiences delusional episodes as he fails to confront himself with his father's death and to relate to his son Robby as a father. In Ellis's hallucinations, the premonition of his failures gets mixed up with stories he wrote as a child, and this combination produces the phantasmagorias we are confronted with. More specifically, in the story "The Toy Bret", when the bird doll called the Terby enters the dog and makes it fly (367), while the story "The Tomb" is about a shapeless monster that breaks into the homes of families to eat their children (324-25).[24]

---

22 Among other things, Ellis tells us: "my father had blackened my perception of the world, and his sneering, sarcastic attitude toward everything had latched on to me. As much as I wanted to escape his influence, I couldn't" (7).

23 He only manages to find harmony with his son Robby when he meets him again several years after Robby had run away. At this stage, Ellis manages to say "I'm sorry" and he sees something in Robby "that suggested forgiveness" (397).

24 Throughout *Lunar Park*, Ellis also believes that Clayton, a student of his, impersonates Patrick Bateman, the first-person narrator of Ellis's novel *American Psycho* (1991). However, at the end, we are told that Clayton and the narrator "had always been the same person" (383). Also, toward the end of the novel, Ellis tells us that a man called Bernard Erlanger believed that he was Patrick Bateman and killed Ellis's lover Aimee Light in the Orsic Motel (389). However, since Erlanger presents himself to Ellis as "Detective Donald Kimball" (153), and "Detective Donald Kimball" (366) only exists in an unpublished manuscript version of *American Psycho* that he cannot possibly have read, we can presume that both Aimee Light and Bernard Erlanger are mere figments of Ellis's imagination as well.

CONCLUSION

According to Wolfgang Iser, literature allows us "to lead an ecstatic life by stepping out of our entanglements and into zones we are otherwise barred from". For him, "literature becomes a panorama of what is possible, because it is not hedged in either by the limitations or the considerations that determine the institutionalized organizations within which human life otherwise takes its course" (1996, 21; 19). Indeed, as my discussion suggests, literature moves beyond real-world possibilities in a wide variety of ways. For instance, literary texts allow us to experience the thoughts and feelings of characters. Furthermore, literature enables us to engage in thought experiments and experience other worlds in which sometimes even the physically or logically impossible is made possible. In this context, Ruth Ronen also highlights that "fiction can construct impossible objects and other objects that clearly diverge from their counterparts in the actual world" (1994, 45).

To my mind, the interesting question of literary studies is not to what extent the worlds of literary fiction reproduce the world we live in but rather to what extent they distort and deform the world as we know it. This question is interesting because unnatural scenarios and events fulfill numerous important functions. To begin with, by taking us to the most remote territories of conceptual possibilities, they significantly widen the cognitive horizon of human awareness; they challenge our limited perspective on the world and invite us to address questions that we do not normally address. Furthermore, the unnatural extends the limits of what readers can take to be the case so that the real becomes a zone of potentiality refusing reduction to any simplistic account of the way things are. Jerome Bruner also points out that innovative storytellers go "beyond the conventional scripts, leading people to see human happenings in a fresh way, indeed, in a way they had never before 'noticed' or even dreamed". And such innovations significantly shape "our narrative versions of everyday reality as well as [...] the course of literary history, the two perhaps being not that different" (1991, 12).

The unnatural closely correlates with a critical spirit that does not accept situations as given or 'natural' and potentially leads to the questioning of the status quo. Generally speaking, by confronting us with physical or logical impossibilities, unnatural scenarios attend to what the German philosopher Max Horkheimer called "die Sehnsucht nach dem ganz Anderen" (1970), a phrase used to describe the yearning for radical change, for a radically different society, caused by the fundamental split between the individual and society.

The unnatural also sheds new light on the old idea of the literariness or distinctiveness of fictional literature, that is, the question of how literature differs from other discursive modes.[25] I would like to suggest that the possibility of representing the impossible is one of the most crucial differences between fiction and other modes of discourse. It is only in the world of fiction that we can experience and ponder impossible narrators, characters, temporalities, and settings, and that we can gain unrestricted access to the minds of others.[26]

Moreover, there is an ethical dimension to the unnatural in so far as it allows us to address the question of whether we actually live in what the German philosopher Gottfried Leibniz called 'the best of all possible worlds' in his *Essais de Théodicée sur la bonté de Dieu, la liberté de l'homme et l'origine du mal* (1710). The worlds of fictional literature have always projected alternatives to the contemporary states of affairs and other ways of being. As I have shown, by criticizing restless leaders (as in *Courtiers' Trifles*), the commodification of authors (as in 18th-century object narratives), the demands of patriarchy (as in *Mrs. Dalloway*), the oppressive potential of identities (as in *Cloud Nine*), or the incapability of relating to one's child (as in *Lunar Park*), literature invites the possibility of changing the named conditions. Literature in general (and unnatural scenarios in particular) imply new ideas, other perspectives, and hence the potential questioning of things as they are or seem to be.

When reading literature, we enter the realm of the ethical through the experience of otherness. Both experimental and more realist types of literature confront us with the world views of others and invite us to reflect upon our own world views. I am of course not suggesting that literary critics look or have to look for some kind of greater good or Plato's perfect

---

25 Viktor Shklovsky and other Russian Formalists defined 'literariness' in terms of *ostranenie* (defamiliarization), i.e. "the technique of art [...] to make objects 'unfamiliar', to make forms difficult, to increase the difficulty and length of perception because the process of perception is an aesthetic end in itself and must be prolonged" (1965, 12).

26 Similarly, Pekka Tammi argues that "we should now ask whether it is not the capacity of literary fiction [...] to deal specifically with the impossibilities, the paradoxes and problems, of our human efforts to order experience" (2006, 29). Even though he talks about psychological impossibilities and problems (rather than physical or logical impossibilities), I think that our understandings of narrative converge in so far as we both argue that narratives are far less concerned with order, coherence, stability, and causality than most classical theorists would claim.

World of Ideas. Rather, I would like to argue that the process of comparing our world views with those of others is ultimately an ethical process in the sense of Emmanuel Lévinas. For him, the encounter with others implies responsibility and thus an ethical standpoint: "The Other precisely reveals himself in his alterity not in a shock negating the I, but as the primordial phenomenon of gentleness" (Lévinas 1969, 150). We always compare our horizons with those of others – characters, narrators, and literary texts as a whole – when we read and also when we discuss literature. Through the study of literature, we allow for the possibility that we might be wrong and others might be right. In the words of Heinz Antor, "we have to seek out what is different from us and compare our ways with those of others. We must get rid of any anxiety of influence and willingly embrace the unfamiliar" (1996, 73).

In *Fiction Sets You Free*, Russell A. Berman suggests that fictional literature and democracy are inextricably linked. For him, the study of literary fiction is a democratic enterprise because it implies and leads to a democratic system. More specifically, Berman argues that "literature is democratic because it calls forth a reader as an imaginative and thinking individual, invited into a process of interpretive freedom and reflection". Furthermore, literature "asks its readers to suspend disbelief and decide on other worlds, it encourages a suspicion toward the given [...]" (2007, 158; 167). This ethical dimension of fictional literature presumably explains why the rulers in dystopian novels such as Aldous Huxley's *Brave New World* (1932), George Orwell's *Nineteen-Eighty Four* (1949), or Ray Bradbury's *Fahrenheit 451* (1953) and actual totalitarian despots such as Hitler, Mao Tse-Tung, or Stalin were so scared of the free study of literature. they simply did not want to allow for the possibility that they might be wrong and others might be right.[27]

---

27 Interestingly, one of the first things that the Nazis did when Hitler was appointed chancellor of Germany on January 30, 1933 was to burn books by Jewish authors and other intellectuals. With regard to the Soviet Union, Edmund Wilson points out that "Lenin and Trotsky, Lunacharsky and Gorky, worked sincerely to keep literature free; but they had at the same time, from the years of the Tsardom, a keen sense of the possibility of art as an instrument of propaganda. [...] The administration of Stalin, unliterary and uncultivated himself, slipped into depending more and more on literature as a means of manipulating [the] people [...]. Even the fine melodramatic themes of the post-revolutionary cinema and theater, with their real emotion and moral conviction, have been replaced by simple trash not very far removed from Hollywood, or by dramatized exemplifications of the latest 'directive' of Stalin which open the night after the speech that has announced the directive" (2001, 1247).

Jean-François Lyotard argues that totalitarian states have a problem with experimental literature in particular:

> When power assumes the name of a party, realism and its neoclassical complement triumph over the experimental avant-garde by slandering and banning it – that is, provided the 'correct' images, the 'correct' narratives, the 'correct' forms which the party requests, selects, and propagates can find a public to desire them as the appropriate remedy for the anxiety and depression that public experiences (1999, 75).

To conclude, I would like to propose that unnatural scenarios of literary fiction are particularly well designed to make us more open and more flexible because they urge us to deal with radical forms of otherness or strangeness. And what could be more important for a democratic system than the competence to deal with radical and complex forms of alterity? This is, in a nutshell, why *I* think that one should study fictional literature.

REFERENCES

Alber, Jan. 2007. *Narrating the prison: Role and representation in Charles Dickens' novels, twentieth-century fiction, and film.* Youngstown, New York: Cambria Press.
– 2009. Impossible storyworlds – and what to do with them. *Storyworlds: A Journal of Narrative Study* 1.1: 79-96.
Alber, Jan, and Frank Lauterbach. 2009. *Stones of law, bricks of shame: Narrating imprisonment in the Victorian age.* Toronto: University of Toronto Press.
Amoko, Apollo. 1999. Casting aside colonial occupation: Intersections of race, sex, and gender in *Cloud Nine* and *Cloud Nine* criticism. *Modern Drama* 42: 45-58.
Anon. 1754. *The history and adventures of a lady's slippers and shoes. Written by themselves.* London: M. Cooper.
Antor, Heinz. 1996. The ethics of criticism in the age after value. In *Why literature matters: Theories and functions of literature*, eds. Rüdiger Ahrens and Laurenz Volkmann, 65-85. Heidelberg: Winter.
Bellamy, Liz. 2007. It-narrators and circulation: Defining a subgenre. In *The secret life of things: Animals, objects, and it-narratives in eighteenth-century England*, ed. Mark Blackwell, 117-46. Lewisburg: Bucknell University Press.
Bender, John. 1987. *Imagining the penitentiary: Fiction and the architecture of mind in eighteenth-century England.* Chicago: University of Chicago Press.
Berman, Russell A. 2007. *Fiction sets you free: Literature, liberty, and Western culture.* Iowa City: University of Iowa Press.
Blackwell, Mark. 2007. Introduction: The it-narrative and eighteenth-century thing theory. In *The secret life of things: Animals, objects, and it-narratives in eighteenth-century England*, ed. Mark Blackwell, 9-14. Lewisburg: Bucknell University Press.

Bridges, Thomas. 1770. *The adventures of a bank-note.* 2 Vols. London: Davies.

Bruner, Jerome. 1991. The narrative construction of reality. *Critical Inquiry* 18: 1-21.

Churchill, Caryl. 1985. Cloud nine. *Plays: One*, 243-320. New York: Methuen.

Chatman, Seymour. 1978. *Story and discourse: Narrative structure in fiction and film.* Ithaca and London: Cornell University Press.

Cohn, Dorrit. 1978. *Transparent minds: Narrative modes for presenting consciousness in fiction.* Princeton, New Jersey: Princeton University Press.

– 1995. Optics and power in the novel. *New Literary History* 26: 3-20.

– 1999. *The distinction of fiction.* Baltimore: Johns Hopkins University Press.

Crater, Theresa L. 2000. Septimus Smith and Charles Watkins: The phallic suppression of masculine subjectivity. *Journal of Evolutionary Psychology* 21.3-4: 191-202.

Cross, Roseanna. 2008. 'Heterochronia' in *Thomas of Erceldoune, Guingamor*, 'The tale of King Herla,' and *The Story of Meriadoc, King of Cambria. Neophilologus* 92: 163-75.

Ellis, Breat Easton. 1991. *American psycho.* New York: Vintage.

– 2005. *Lunar park.* New York: Vintage.

Flint, Christopher. 1998. Speaking objects: The circulation of stories in eighteenth-century prose fiction. *PMLA* 113.2: 212-26.

Fludernik, Monika. 1996. *Towards a 'natural' narratology.* London and New York: Routledge.

– 2001. New wine in old bottles? Voice, focalization, and new writing. *New Literary History* 32: 619-38.

– 2003. Natural narratology and cognitive parameters. In *Narrative theory and the cognitive sciences*, ed. David Herman, 243-67. Stanford, California: CSLI Publications.

– 2010. Naturalizing the unnatural: A view from blending theory. *Journal of Literary Semantics* 39.1: 1-27.

Genette, Gérard. 1980. *Narrative discourse: An essay in method.* Ithaca, New York: Cornell University Press.

Gibbs, Raymond W. 2005. Intentionality. In *Routledge encyclopedia of narrative theory*, eds. David Herman, Manfred Jahn, and Marie-Laure Ryan, 247-49. London: Routledge.

Guillory, John. 2000. The ethical practice of modernity: The example of reading. In *The turn to ethics*, eds. Marjorie Garber et al., 29-46. New York and London: Routledge.

Hamburger, Käte. 1993. *The logic of literature.* Bloomington: Indiana University Press.

Heinze, Rüdiger. 2008. Violations of mimetic epistemology in first-person narrative fiction. *Narrative* 16.3: 279-97.

Heise, Ursula K. 1997. *Chronoschisms: Time, narrative, and postmodernism.* Cambridge: Cambridge University Press.

Henke, Suzette A. 1981. Virginia Woolf's Septimus Smith: An analysis of 'paraphrenic' and the schizophrenic use of language. *Literature and Psychology* 31.4: 13-23.

Herman, David. 2008. Narrative theory and the intentional stance. *Partial Answers* 6.2: 233-60.

Holt, Karen, and Charlotte Abbott. 2005. A fact-finding tour of *Lunar park*. *Publishers Weekly* 252.27, July 11, 22-23.

Horkheimer, Max. 1970. *Die Sehnsucht nach dem ganz Anderen*. Hamburg: Furche.

Iser, Wolfgang. 1996. Why literature matters. In *Why literature matters: Theories and functions of literature*, eds. Rüdiger Ahrens and Laurenz Volkmann, 13-22. Heidelberg: Winter.

Johnstone, Charles. 1760-65. *Chrysal; or, the adventures of a guinea*. 4 Vols. London: Watson.

Kindt, Tom, and Hans-Harald Müller. 2006. *The implied author: concept and controversy*. Berlin: de Gruyter.

Lévinas, Emmanuel. 1969. *Totality and infinity: An essay on exteriority*. Pittsburgh: Duquesne University Press.

Linde, Ulf. 1989. Image and dimension. In *possible worlds in humanities, arts and sciences*, ed. Sture Allén, 312-28. Berlin and New York: de Gruyter.

Lyotard, Jean-François. 1999. *The postmodern explained*. Minneapolis and London: University of Minnesota Press.

Map, Walter. 1983. *De nugis curialium: Courtiers' trifles*. Oxford: Clarendon Press.

McHale, Brian. 1987. *Postmodernist fiction*. New York, London: Methuen & Co. Ltd.

Miller, D.A. 1988. *The novel and the police*. Berkeley: University of California Press.

Newman, Karen. 2002. Why literature now? *PMLA* 17.3: 501-3.

Nielsen, Henrik Skov. 2004. The impersonal voice in first-person narrative fiction. *Narrative* 12.2: 133-50.

Penrose, Lionel S. and Roger Penrose. 1958. Impossible objects: A special type of visual illusion. *British Journal of Psychology* 49: 31-33.

Phelan, James. 2005. *Living to tell about it: A rhetoric and ethics of character narration*. Ithaca, New York: Cornell University Press.

 – 2007. *Experiencing fiction: Judgments, progression, and the rhetorical theory of narrative*. Columbus: Ohio State University Press.

Pratt, Mary Louise. 1977. *Toward a speech act theory of literary discourse*. Bloomington and London: Indiana University Press.

Richardson, Brian. 1991. Pinter's *Landscape* and the boundaries of narrative. *Essays in Literature* 18.1: 37-45.

 – 2000. Narrative poetics and postmodern transgression: Theorizing the collapse of time, voice, and frame. *Narrative* 8.1: 23-42.

 – 2002. Beyond story and discourse: Narrative time in postmodern and nonmimetic fiction. In *Narrative dynamics: Essays on time, plot, closure, and frames*, ed. Brian Richardson, 47-63. Columbus: Ohio State University Press.

 – 2006. *Unnatural voices: Extreme narration in modern and contemporary fiction*. Columbus: Ohio State University Press.

 – 2007. Plot after postmodernism. In *Drama and/after postmodernism*, eds. Christoph Henke and Martin Middeke, 55-66. Trier: wvt.

Ronen, Ruth. 1994. *Possible worlds in literary theory*. Cambridge: Cambridge University Press.

Ryan, Marie-Laure. 1991. *Possible worlds, artificial intelligence, and narrative theory.* Bloomington: Indiana University Press.

– 2001. The narratorial function: Breaking down a theoretical primitive. *Narrative* 9.2: 146-52.

Sass, Louis A. 1992. *Madness and modernism: Insanity in the light of modern art, literature and thought.* New York: Basic Books.

Schaeffer, Jean-Marie. 1999. *Pourquoi la fiction?* Paris: Seuil.

Scott, Helenus. 1782. *The adventures of a rupee.* London: J. Murray.

Shklovsky, Viktor. 1965. Art as technique. In *Russian formalist criticism*, eds. Lee T. Lemon and Marion J. Reis, 3-24. Lincoln: University of Nebraska Press.

Smollett, Tobias. 1989. *The history and adventures of an atom.* Athens: University of Georgia Press.

Tammi, Pekka. 2006. Against narrative ('a boring story'). *Partial Answers* 4.2: 19-40.

Todorov, Tzvetan. 1973. *The fantastic: A structural approach to a literary genre.* Cleveland and London: The Press of Case Western Reserve University.

Watzlawick, Paul. 1976. *How real is real? Confusion, disinformation, communication*, London: Souvenir.

Wilson, Edmund. 2001. Marxism and literature. In *The Norton Anthology of Theory and Criticism*, ed. Vincent B. Leitch, 1243-54. New York: Norton.

Woolf, Virginia. 2000. *Mrs. Dalloway.* Oxford: Oxford University Press.

THE FORCE OF FICTIONS

Richard Walsh

I want to make a case based upon one kind of literary study, and confined to one kind (or mode) of literature, without prejudice in either respect to other possible affirmations of the value of what literary scholars do. The kind of study I mean emphasizes the continuity between literary artefacts and the broader domains of cultural discourse, scientific understanding and human cognitive faculties; it is the study of narrative theory, and my claim is that its central preoccupation with literary narrative is in no way at odds with the much larger scope of narrative in general as a distinct object of study. More specifically, my object is fiction, though I mean fictional narrative in a sense that accommodates not only the novel, but the drama (and indeed film), and a great deal of poetry too. *Literary* fiction, for my purposes here, is defined both etymologically (written fiction) and honorifically (fiction it is possible to credit as a significant contribution to culture, rather than just a symptomatic cultural product); at the same time, however, I situate this narrowly-defined object of study within a series of progressively more inclusive context – that is, fictions in general, narrative discourse in general, and narrative as a cognitive faculty. The recursive relationship between these contexts secures a significant continuity between literature and the broad reaches of scientific understanding, while the distinctive contribution of literary study is provided for by the re-inflection of the concept of narrative with each narrowing and refinement of the frame of reference. Finally, in speaking of the "force" of fictions I am proposing to make some play with the relation between the notions of "force" and "value", extrapolating somewhat from the framework of speech act theory in order to emphasize a performative quality of literary narrative, which arises out of the recursive logic I am proposing, and which can be extrapolated one step further, to the activity of study itself.

My thesis, then, is that the importance of literary fictions as objects of study can be understood to follow from the status of such fictions as the most highly elaborated instances of a mode of cognition that lies at the heart of what it is to be human (the human, I mean, as a social and transcultural construct, rather than simply the species homo sapiens, though I am interested in the relation between the two). In making that claim I am situating literary fiction at the apex of a hierarchical stratification of levels: above the dynamics or rhetoric of fictionality in general; above the discursive ubiquity of narrative in general; and above the fundamental place of narrative sense-making in cognition. That hierarchy, I think, exists only for the purposes of my argument, but it corresponds to a process of recursive stratification that *does* structurally inform the genesis of any given narrative, and that inheres in the emergence of narrative cognition as such. The engine of that process is reflexiveness, and it is as a token of such a cyclical, metadiscursive series of levels that the stages of my own argument are meant to stand. So in due course I shall be attempting to bring home my argument in relation to Samuel Beckett's *Watt*, which is (I hope) both unimpeachably literary and fairly resistant to easy explanations of its value as an object of study. But before that I shall be considering narrative discourse in general against the backdrop of Darwin's theory of evolution (not the most obvious context for Beckett, but a legitimate one, as it turns out). The main point of this stage of the argument is to throw into relief the cultural importance of narrative, by situating it in relation to a theory – natural selection – it is notoriously incapable of representing. The discussion will also, and not adventitiously, consider the place of narrative itself in human evolution, because before then I shall be talking about the intimate relation between narrative sense-making and human cognition.

To even begin talking about narrative at a cognitive level, however, I need to make a declaration of methodological principles. It is not currently feasible to describe the mind's actual cognitive processes, at least at the level I want to discuss, in terms that would be meaningfully accountable to empirical confirmation or falsification within the disciplines of cognitive science and neuroscience. Any attempt at such a description is bound to be largely conjectural, and I prefer to confine myself to a less ambitious but more accountable approach, in which the goal is to understand the mind in terms of its outcomes, its manifest effects – such as a certain behaviour, or a certain ability to respond to an environment; that is, to conceive a model that will sufficiently account for those effects in given circumstances. The question of the relation between such a model and any actual cognitive process is bracketed: in this respect it offers only the merits and limitations of an analogy or a heuristic. The strength of such a methodology is that it confines itself to extrapolation from manifest features – in the case of narrative cognition, behavioural interactions with a physical and social environment, and the pervasive cultural phenomenon of narrative as a mode of explanation and communication. In articulating an adequate account of these manifest features, such an abductive model can also shed light upon their internal logic.

What would it take, then, to produce the cognitive faculty of narrative sense-making? To begin with a proposition I shall subsequently retract, narrative emerges in the cognitive effort to articulate causal relations. One way to get at the distinctiveness of narrative is to contrast causal thinking with associative thinking as ways of negotiating with reality. Associative thinking is horizontal: its syntax is coordinate, of the form "circumstance a and circumstance b". Causal thinking involves the hierarchical subordination of a and b, as instances of a general rule, in the form of a syllogism: "circumstance a is an instance of cause A; cause A always has effect B; instance a will result in an instance of effect B". The hierarchy of conceptual levels introduced by causal thinking is crucial in several respects, which I'll discuss in turn, but which can be briefly enumerated as concerning, firstly, the relation between the explicit and the implicit (which I shall refer to as saying and doing); secondly, the relation between the particular and the general; and thirdly, the relation between the cognitive and the communicative, or social.

It is important to recognize that any behaviour oriented towards an anticipation of future events is already an implicit form of representation, in that it is falsifiably predictive of a state of affairs.[1] Associative thinking is implicitly representational in this way. So, my dog gets excited when I pick up my wallet – he expects to be taken for a walk. He has reasonable grounds for this: there's a good chance I have picked up my wallet because I'm going to the shop, and there's a good chance, if I'm going to the shop, that I'll take him with me. So, very often, he's right; but this impressive feat of understanding doesn't mean that my dog is particularly shrewd. In fact, my dog is particularly stupid: in twelve years he has still not grasped the basic canine fact that being on a lead means you can't go wherever you like. He certainly isn't capable of grasping the concepts of money, goods, shops, and the convenience of walking the dog at the same time as going to the shop, all of which would figure in a credible causal explanation for the association he has made. But neither does his association depend upon a naïve causal inference, such as "wallets make walks happen". He needs only to have responded to prior conditioning, in the form of the experience of the

---

1   For a suggestive discussion of representation in the context of emergence, see Bickhard 2000.

wallet being followed by the walk a number of times in the past. The most elementary difference between the associative and causal modes of understanding, then, does not concern the quality of the causal explanation but the bare fact that, as explanation, it involves an explicit representation of the circumstances – a modelling of them. Although associative thinking involves implicit representation, in that it projects a falsifiable state of affairs, it does not generate a hierarchy of levels as explicit representation does. The difference is brought out clearly when the expected circumstance *is* falsified, as it very well might be: I may be reaching for my wallet, for example, in order to buy off the kids – which, for even the most basic causal understanding would require a revision of the model, such as "wallets make walks happen, except when kids are around". An association involves no such revisionary moment, because it is merely cumulative. If a conditioned response is falsified on a particular occasion, then that occasion takes it statistical place in the ongoing series of such occasions, and the conditioning is weakened in proportion. Conditioning is additive: it is a behavioural response to the sum of experience, and as such it requires no explicit abstraction from, or synthesis of, the occasions that make up that experience. Conditioned behaviour is just doing it – even when the behaviour concerned is entirely mental, as in the association of ideas (or in modern parlance, the sort of cognitive processing that can be wholly accounted for in terms of connectionism). The explicit representation involved in causal understanding, on the other hand, is the saying of a doing, the articulation of a cognitive response; it is the reflexive product of a stratification of levels and of the relation between them. Saying, as speech act theory has taught us, is itself a kind of doing; the relation is recursive, a feature which has vast implications. One way of conceptualizing this dual aspect of saying-as-doing is to recognize that each explicit articulation of a specific instance is also the implicit permutation of a covering rule. That is to say, each cognitive act of causal thinking is a representation that instantiates a perceived or anticipated regularity; it is the articulation of the particular in terms of the general.

Narrative, as we have known since Aristotle, is fundamentally concerned with the relation between the particular and the general, but I want to stress the reciprocity between the two: the particular is understood in terms of the general, and the general is understood in terms of the particular. This is one of the reasons I want to retract my original proposition, that narrative emerges from the articulation of causal relations: there is a sense in which that proposition seems merely tautologous, in that the possibility of a concept of causal relations in itself already presupposes narrative thinking. The relation of the particular to the general in causal thinking, in other words, already participates in a discursive economy. It presupposes not only the availability of a general frame of reference within which to articulate the particular, but also the reciprocal contribution particular articulations make to the establishment and consolidation of that general frame of reference. As soon as we ask where the general comes from, it becomes clear that every causal articulation also participates tacitly in a communicative context, and the boundary between the cognitive and social frames of reference must be seen as permeable. We do learn from our own experience, incident by incident, yes – but that way of learning can be very expensive. One of the obvious advantages of causal thinking over associative thinking is that it allows us to short-circuit this process, to draw upon the collective legacy of representational paradigms, established idioms and tropes, folk wisdom, types, genres and masterplots that constitute the whole category of the general within which, and in terms of which, every specific narrative is articulated.[2]

The social nature of narrative understanding is fundamental to its importance and to its limitations as a mode of cognition, in a sense that is best illustrated by considering another quality of narrative that seems to disallow the equivalence with causal thinking I have proposed. According to this view, narrative thinking implies more than the mere articulation of causal relations, in that it is concerned not just with bare causal sequence, but with agency.[3] That is to say, narrative is more specifically concerned with the behaviour of people than with our whole physical environment, and this substantive focus upon agents and their acts is what really marks out the social orientation of narrative understanding. But the essential point here, that the horizons of narrative understanding are defined by specifically human concerns, is correct in a more fundamental sense than this formulation allows for, a sense that ultimately obliterates the distinction it seems to require between narrative understanding proper and causal understanding. Narrative does indeed deal in agency and purposive actions, and the adaptive value, for a social animal, of understanding the behaviour of others presumably accounts for those features of narrative in terms of human cognitive evolution. Narrative serves human needs, addresses human concerns, and expresses human values; but it does so in virtue not of its

---

2   Turner 1996 gives a good, wide-ranging sense of this continuity between the literary and the cognitive.

3   See, for example, Fludernik 1996, 12-13.

subject matter, but of the inherently anthropocentric scope of its frame of reference, which is the inevitable, only frame of reference for the articulation of any sequential explanation in human terms – no less so than human visual cognition is necessarily defined in terms of our apprehension of the visible spectrum. Narrative does not merely take human experience as its topic, but subordinates the flux of existence to human experientiality. So, there is an irreducible level at which every cause is an anthropomorphic agent, every effect the result of a purposive action, however muted and figurative its formulation may be. Narrative is anthropocentric not because of what it is about, but because of who it is for; it is not a belated cognitive faculty, but one that is coeval with our ability to reflect upon our environment and condition as temporal beings, and inescapably defines the terms in which we do so. Human cognition and narrative are mutually, recursively reinforcing; accordingly, narrative does not merely depend upon a general context of human values, it substantially constitutes that context with respect to the temporality of consciousness.

I have been trying to characterize the centrality of narrative to the conceptual frame of reference that marks the evaluative horizons of the human; and in doing so I have been circling around the difficult concept of emergence. Emergence, roughly speaking, defines the possibility of the appearance of anything really new, from helium to human culture.[4] In the pat phrase, it is the notion that the whole may be more than the sum of its parts. It is a live concept in fields as diverse as philosophy, theoretical physics, evolutionary biology and artificial intelligence, and I don't propose to get drawn into it here, beyond noting that the additive notion of the sum of parts is extremely unhelpful, and contributes to a somewhat misleading confrontation between emergence and the principles of reductionism; it isn't possible to approach a viable concept of emergence until we begin to think in terms of relations.[5] I have been circling around the concept because I think it involves, more specifically, the kind of recursive relations that I have been trying to articulate with respect to narrative. The development of narrative cognition is itself an example of emergence, that is to say of the appearance of something that is not intrinsic in the conditions prior to its appearance. Narrative cognition is also at the heart of the difficulty of the concept of emergence itself, because it is not a concept susceptible to nar-

---

4   Good general introductions to the concept of emergence include Holland 1998 and Johnson 2001.

5   See Holland 1998, 244-6.

HUMANITY

rative explanation, even though it is clearly temporal and developmental. Narrative is so fundamental to our grasp of reality that it is extraordinarily hard to even think things that do not fit its template; and yet the possibility of narrative cognition itself does not fit that template.

If narrative does not respond to something intrinsic in how the world works, but rather to the contingencies of human cognitive needs in an evolutionary context, then it is unsurprising that its limitations are exposed by complex developmental phenomena exhibiting emergence. The question of the limits of narrative understanding is what I want to pursue further in the context of a classic version of emergence, which is the concept of evolution itself – evolutionary biology being one of the fields in which emergence is most prominent as both an explanatory concept and a problem. The canonical model of evolutionary process, of course, is Darwin's theory of natural selection; among literary scholars the influence of Darwin upon narrative since the late 19th century is well known, as is the incompatibility between natural selection and any narrative account of it.[6] Porter Abbott has shown in detail that natural selection provides for no agents, and no purposive action, on which to pin a narrative explanation (Abbott 2003). He also shows just how resistant to understanding this makes the idea of natural selection, and also how hard it is to avoid traducing the theory by projecting agency and purpose onto it and subjugating it to narrative (both Darwin himself and such modern champions as Richard Dawkins occasionally indulge in such misrepresentation, as Abbott notes, and the fact that they make only figurative use of narrative explanation, by attributing agency to nature, or to the gene, does not at all diminish the significance of the expository need to do so). My point is that this and other non-narrative models of process are more fundamentally problematic than just because they challenge our habitual narrative way of thinking. That is, to the extent that such models of temporal process resist narrative explanation, they are experienced as not offering an explanation at all. Narrative cognition is so involved with what it is to be human, in other words, that an account of temporal process that does not work in narrative terms has failed to bring that process into relation with human experientiality; has failed to fully mediate between the implacably unfolding universe and the domain of human value.

Natural selection is a theoretical model of great explanatory power, yet its irreducible abstraction does not offer that sense of mastery over brute reality

---

6   Eminent studies of Darwin's influence upon literature include Beer 1983 and Levine 1988.

we gain by subordinating it to human meaning. This is a problem encountered whenever science, or theory, seeks to go beyond the scope of human experience as a literal or figurative frame of reference, and the intractability of emergence to narrative explanation can be seen in the larger context of debate about the nature of knowledge. One of the most vexed issues in the philosophy of science is the status of "scientific realism", to which the notion of explanation is crucial.[7] In quantum physics, for example, there are current mathematical models of subatomic phenomena which powerfully predict what can occur at this level in given conditions, but which offer no intelligible description of what is going on. From a realist perspective this amounts to an approach to quantum physics as a kind of magic, but although the scientific realist stance is adopted in the name of the real, as with all realisms what is actually at stake is the accessibility of the real from within the parameters of human understanding. There is some force to the argument that an abstruse mathematical model with predictive but not descriptive power falls short of scientific explanation, or anything we can recognize as explanation; but then there is no reason to suppose that reality is ultimately recognizable, that it is any more accessible to the human cognitive apparatus than subatomic phenomena are to the human sensory apparatus.

So it is with the resistance of natural selection to narrative explanation. As a model of temporal development, natural selection appears to invite comprehension in narrative terms; yet the independence of natural selection from any concept of agency or purpose, and the massively aggregate, recursive and statistically distributed nature of the model, put it beyond the human experiential horizons within which narrative sense-making operates. The inadequacies of narrative sense-making, however, only testify to its power. Narrative cognition can itself be understood as an adaptation produced by natural selection, but this doesn't lead to a cultural Darwinist view of the relation between narrative cognition and all the innumerable contemporary manifestations of narrative.[8] It is fairly clear that the adaptive advantages of narrative are exhausted at a relatively early stage in its development as a cornerstone of human culture: yes, for a social animal the ability to model and anticipate the behaviour of others offers improved

---

7 For a good overview of the issues, see the entry in the *Stanford Encyclopedia of Philosophy* (Boyd 2002).

8 The arguments for and against literary Darwinism have been aired recently in a special issue of *Style* (Knapp 2008).

chances of survival and enhanced reproductive prospects; an understanding of Beckett, on the other hand, will not appreciably improve your chances of perpetuating your genes. Beyond a basic level, the development of narrative understanding, and human culture in general, is an incidental bi-product, or spandrel, of evolutionary processes. The vast elaboration of narrative culture has not been sustained by evolutionary pressure; I am suggesting instead that its mechanism is reflexiveness (by which I mean representational recursiveness).[9] For this reason it is implausible to see the cognitive challenge of ideas like natural selection as part of some quasi-evolutionary development in human thought beyond the limitations of the narrative paradigm. The prejudicial value system to which narrative cognition so fundamentally contributes, and which constitutes the deep, inherent anthropocentrism of the human, cannot be simply sloughed off; it is non-negotiable, because it leaves no position from which to negotiate with it. But this state of affairs does not leave us oblivious to our limitations, and one of the most powerful functions of reflexiveness is indeed to continually expose those limitations, refining and qualifying the framework of our narrative understanding in the process. Perhaps the most important effect of this reflexiveness, one of enormous significance in the development of narrative culture, is the troping of narrative sense-making that we understand as fictionality. The rudiments of this reflexive strategy can be seen in a simple example of figurative language such as Dawkins's image of "the selfish gene" (Dawkins 1976). This is such an overtly fanciful notion that to take it in earnest and convict Dawkins of unreflective anthropomorphism would be to wilfully ignore its rhetoric. Figurative language, when it functions figuratively, draws attention to its conceit: it says, in effect, "this is not the case: this is a manner of speaking". The need to speak thus in Dawkins's case, as we have seen, arises because of the inaccessibility of natural selection to narrative understanding; but the conceit does not unthinkingly defer to that limitation.

Figurative language is fictionality in miniature. The figurative is akin to the fictive in that both present themselves as dealing in meanings first and foremost, and only via that discursive obliquity offering to describe the

---

9   In making this suggestion I am distinguishing my view from the account of culture offered by memetics, based upon Dawkins's concept of the meme as a cultural unit of natural selection, analogous to the gene (Dawkins 1976, ch. 11). Memetics tends to conflate the formal mechanism of natural selection with the biological terms of its instantiation in the evolution of the gene, and in doing so fails to ground cultural phenomena in their only meaningful domain, that of cultural value.

world. Fictive discourse is not distinguished by the ontological status of its referents, nor by the suspension of its illocutionary force, nor by any dissociation of the discourse from its author, but by its rhetorical orientation, which both deploys narrative indirectly and foregrounds that indirection.[10] Fictionality, then, is inherently a kind of reflexiveness. All narrative meaning is the product of a discursive economy, of the reciprocal negotiation between the particular and the general within the domain of representation, and we ignore the fact at our peril; but fictive meaning offers itself directly as an exploration within that discursive economy, and to ignore that is simply to fail to respond to it as fiction. I am not referring to metafictionality here; that concept covers a range of devices by which a specific fiction may internally redouble its discursive strategies (as we shall see with *Watt*), and in doing so may raise the principle of recursiveness to a higher degree. The fundamental reflexiveness of fictionality is inherent in its rhetorical orientation, in the bare fact of being offered and received as fiction, which is to say, as a second-degree exploration of the faculty of narrative sense-making that is our cognitive heritage.

I hope I have done enough to make the leap from evolutionary narratives to *Watt* seem less arbitrary than at first sight. Darwin does in fact get a mention in *Watt* when Mr. Magershon, in exasperation, tells the repetitive Mr. O'Meldon, "Go on from where you left off ... not from where you began. Or are you like Darwin's caterpillar?" (Beckett 1953, 193). Darwin's caterpillar, if interrupted in the process of building its cocoon and placed in another cocoon at the same stage of construction would nonetheless begin the cocoon-spinning process all over again. Its behaviour was genetically programmed, not responsive to the demands of its actual environment. In Beckett's hands, the example becomes a parable of a kind of formal compulsion, in which the dogged recitation of a form of words takes precedence over any accommodation to the communicative purpose that occasioned it, and the effect is one of frustration, in which the possibility of resolution, of sense, is endlessly deferred. This, of course, is very relevant to the experience of reading *Watt* itself, in which the narrative is repeatedly held up by attempts to permutate all the possible combinations of circumstances or attributes that might apply in the given situation. So, among many other instances, we are given an extended account of all the ways a committee of five may look at itself without ever achieving a reciprocal look, along with the correct procedure for ensuring that any such committee has fully looked at itself in

---

10 See Walsh 2007, especially chapter one.

the minimum number of looks (this takes 7 pages; 173-79); we are given all the permutations of Mr. Knott's remarkably unstable physical appearance with respect to variables of figure, stature, skin and hair (3 pages; 209-11); and we are given a scrupulous analysis of all the possible implications of Mr. Knott's edict that his leftovers should be given to the dog, given that there is no dog in his household (12 pages; 87-98). Is there anything to be gained from studying, or even reading, such a narrative? Even by fictional standards, it seems remote from our understanding of the real world. I want to argue, however, that Beckett's intensification of fictive reflexivity actually makes that relation more direct and overt, so that far from being marginal, it is exemplary of the pertinence of literary fiction.

Permutation and narrative are antithetical ways of knowing, the one offering exhaustive multiplicity, the other offering coherent singularity. The novel appears to set them up against each other, stalling the progress of the narrative at every opportunity to conjugate a paradigm. Watt's relentless permutation of possibilities aspires to an intellectual mastery of the real, but this goal can never be reached, and mockingly recedes before him. The effect is absurdly comic in the first instance, and the more so given that it is vitiated by error anyway, as a footnote confirms for us: "The figures given here are incorrect. The consequent calculations are therefore doubly erroneous" (101). The absurd comedy is ratcheted up a third degree as the text continues to pursue this exponential permutational logic nonetheless, beyond all communicative moderation and beyond all sublimity. The narrative frustration of all this can be offset to an extent by aestheticizing it, submitting to its incantatory rhythms and its purely formal resolutions. The text provides for this, most obviously with the frog chorus that Watt recalls (135-7), consisting of three frogs croaking Krak!, Krek! and Krik! every 8, 5 and 3 beats respectively (Beckett provides the score for 120 beats, the interval from unison to unison). The series 3, 5, 8 forms part of the Fibonacci sequence, in which each number is the sum of the preceding two, and the relation between each adjacent pair approximates the golden ratio; which is to say, the most pervasive and fundamental principle of formal aesthetic satisfaction in Western culture.[11]

Even the most patient reader, though, will sooner or later say, "Ok, I get it – can we please get on with the story?" At which point Beckett has you, because in doing so you have merely confirmed your preference for one formal satisfaction over another; you have chosen the synthetic illusion of nar-

---

11   Beckett's interest in mathematics is well documented; see Culik 1993.

rative coherence over the analytic folly of exhaustive permutation. As in the case of narrative representations of evolution, narrative itself here becomes a limitation, perhaps a consolation. If evolutionary narratives amount to a failure of narrative understanding, though, Beckett's novel is, more acutely, a narrative of the failure of understanding. Its overriding preoccupation is with the ways in which the real continually eludes the most determined efforts of articulation, explanation and comprehension. The paradigmatic instance of this elusiveness in the novel is the incident of the Galls, father and son, a phlegmatic duo who come to tune Mr. Knott's piano and engage in a brief dialogue about it. This, we learn, "was perhaps the principal incident of Watt's early days in Mr. Knott's house" (69), and it shares with all the others the properties, for Watt, of "great formal brilliance and indeterminable purport" (71). Watt, who would've been happy merely to achieve narrative sense, to be able to say to himself, "That is what happened then" (70), finds that under the scrutiny of his analytic intelligence the incident of the Galls "gradually lost, in the nice processes of its light, its sound, its impacts and its rhythm, all meaning, even the most literal" (69). Watt is distressed, in this case as in others, to confront an unbridgeable gap between sensory fact and sense; he is unable to accept that "nothing had happened, with all the clarity and solidity of something" (73). Worse, it emerges that the incident of the Galls is actually one of his relative successes, as its presence in the narrative testifies, for

> [...] he could never have spoken at all of these things, if all had continued to mean nothing, as some continued to mean nothing, that is to say, right up to the end. For the only way one can speak of nothing is to speak of it as though it were something... (74).

The radical doubt therefore remains: at the time of the incident's occurrence, "were there neither Galls nor piano then, but only an unintelligible succession of changes, from which Watt finally extracted the Galls and the piano, in self-defence?" (76).

In this respect, *Watt* has been seen as part of an abiding Beckettian project to confront and demonstrate the impossibility of achieved meaning and value; the impossibility, in fact, of its own compulsive aspirations.[12] As one of Watt's predecessors, Arsene, puts it in his 25-page leave-taking,

---

12 The range of recent *Watt* criticism is well represented by Ackerley 2004, Beausang and Galiussi 1996, Benjamin 1997, Hayman 2002 and Wall 2002.

"what we know partakes in no small measure of the nature of what has so happily been called the unutterable or ineffable, so that any attempt to utter or eff it is doomed to fail, doomed, doomed to fail" (61). The converse of this inability to articulate ineffable knowledge is the inability to penetrate to the reality beyond our cognisances. Towards the end of the novel, *Watt* appears to reconcile himself to the inaccessibility of the real and to accept the bounds of appearances as he impatiently waits to identify a distant figure on the road:

> Watt's concern, deep as it appeared, was not after all with what the figure was, in reality, but with what the figure appeared to be, in reality. For since when were Watt's concerns with what things were, in reality? (226).

At face value, this seems a kind of resolution, albeit a negative one – resignation to the inevitable failure of his quest for the real. Such a reading is undercut, though, firstly by a pointed revelation of the reality beyond appearance – the figure is receding, not approaching as Watt had thought – and secondly by the rather more enigmatic intimation that this obscure figure, with its highly distinctive gait (225), is Watt himself, whose gait was described in detail early in the narrative (28). Soon afterwards, Watt disappears from the narrative, having bought a train ticket to the end of the line. When his train arrives, it does not take up a single passenger (245). The book ends with the remaining characters looking at "nothing in particular" (246), and a series of fragmentary addenda. The suggestion of a kind of skew circularity at the end of the narrative has been foreshadowed in the picture of a broken circle and a dot that Watt contemplates at length in Erskine's room. It is there too in the nearly regular alternation of types in the series of men, Watt and Erskine among them, who serve first downstairs then upstairs in the household of Mr. Knott. And it is developed in the mirroring motif that characterizes Watt's relation with Sam, who receives and relates Watt's narrative. Watt, by this point, is doing everything in reverse, notably both walking and talking. The intimate reciprocity between Watt and Sam is enacted in the physical clinch in which they engage during Watt's inverted narrations, clasped together face to face in lock step, Sam going forwards and Watt going backwards (161). The fact that this relationship is itself the vehicle of the narrative transmission confirms the sense that all these cycles, repetitions and reflections are not closed loops, but hierarchical recursions that generate a series of levels. Or perhaps "degenerate" would be better: Watt's narration is relayed to us by Sam, despite the fact that, as he repeatedly acknowledges, he has understood little, remembered less, and reported still less of Watt's reversed speech (72, 124, 154, 163ff.). The status of the narrative information is further undermined in respect of Watt's own dubious role in the narrative transmission: we are told, for example, that Watt largely ignored Arsene's long elaborate farewell speech (77), which is nonetheless given in its entirety.

The problem of knowledge, then, is not confined to Watt's experience of Mr. Knott's household, nor to his competence to narrate it, nor even to Sam's competence to understand and retell Watt's narrative. Sam's role as narrator only emerges gradually as the novel unfolds, and indeed most of the time the narration gives every appearance of being omniscient, making no discernible effort to conform to the logic of the narrative transmission it offers as the whole basis of its own authority, however woefully inadequate. The opening scene, for example, is entirely outside Watt's experience, and Sam's doubly so: most of it precedes Watt's introduction into the narrative, and when he does first appear, "like a roll of tarpaulin" (14), it is not as the narrative's centre of focalization, but as a distant object of the speculative discourse of other characters. At the other end of the novel, one of the addenda tersely notes that "Arsene's declaration gradually came back to Watt" (248). It is a wry, absurdly inadequate concession to the logic of the narrative transmission that the novel has flouted in so many other ways. The novel's addenda – which are offered to the reader with the comment that this material "should be carefully studied. Only fatigue and disgust prevented its incorporation" (247) – these addenda themselves foreground the fictive text and its transcendence of the logic of narrative representation to which it ironically purports to defer. To the same end the main body of the narrative has been qualified by footnotes, as for example following the observation that Kate, one of the numerous Lynch family, is "a fine girl but a bleeder" (100), where the footnote adds, "Haemophilia is, like enlargement of the prostate, an exclusively male disorder. But not in this work" (100).

At such moments the fictionality of the text, and indeed its literary status, is itself made the object of our attention. To the extent that this meta-fictionality is continuous with the problematics of narrating and knowing that saturate the narrative itself, it is inevitable and appropriate that such moments are themselves drawn back into the thematics of the novel, as my own gloss has suggested, and as the text itself intimates, for instance when the incident of the Galls finally becomes for Watt "a mere example of light commenting bodies, and stillness motion, and silence sound, and comment comment" (70). Meta-discourse is one more in a series of levels, of cycles of reflexivity. In this respect fictionality is an epiphenomenon of the condition that informs Watt's own experience and the benighted state of human cognition, of consciousness, in general – the irreducible recalcitrance of the real. At the same time, the displacement of consciousness by self-consciousness, without transcending that problematic, frames it as itself an object of knowledge. Fictionality effects a reversal of the dynamics of narrative knowing that makes it possible to conceive the limits of knowing, and to imagine the real by negation as that which throws those limits into relief. The narrative imagination is therefore precisely, and paradoxically, the closest approach possible to that grasp of the real to which narrative always aspires. Towards the end of the novel, Watt passes a "strayed ass, or goat, lying in the ditch, in the shadow.... Watt did not see the ass, or goat, but the ass, or goat, saw Watt" (222). The ass, or goat, is the real. It also appears early in the novel as the only witness, apparently, when Mr. Hackett "fell off the ladder" as a child (14). And it is there again just after Watt's disappearance at the novel's end (245). The goat eludes Watt, and therefore eludes the whole logic of the narrative transmission, which is contingent upon his knowledge, and yet it is there; there, in an ironic reversal, by virtue of the narrative imagination, the trope of fictionality.

That is not, however, an adequate account of the force of fictionality. Everything I've said comes within the compass of the thematicization of fictionality, and of metafictionality, which is only one face of its reflexive dynamic – what each cycle of reflexivity *says*. But just as every reflexive cycle of narration, in trumping the one before, provides occasion to be itself trumped, so every interpretative recuperation leaves a remainder, itself available to interpretation but perpetuated rather than exhausted by it. This continual surplus results from the performative force of narrative representation, considered as an act itself susceptible to narrative representation. The best index of the effect in *Watt*, I think, is comedy. It is an extremely funny book, and we would have no trouble, if asked to identify the cause of our laughter, in picking out any number of comic incongruities in the text, which abounds in inversions, perversions, inflations and deflations of our common understanding of things. If we are asked about the tenor of our laughter, though, we would probably have greater difficulty, because although we are always laughing at *something*, the novel's reflexiveness continually subordinates the comic object to the comic routine, which is itself comical *as* routine, and so quickly establishes a generative mechanism for levels of comic dislocation that is in principle interminable. Within the novel, Arsene offers a kind of typology of laughter:

> The bitter laugh laughs at that which is not good, it is the ethical laugh. The
> hollow laugh laughs at that which is not true, it is the intellectual laugh. … But
> the mirthless laugh is the dianoetic laugh, down the snout – haw! – so. It is the
> laugh of laughs, the *risus purus*, the laugh laughing at the laugh, the behold-
> ing, the saluting of the highest joke, in a word the laugh that laughs – silence
> please – at that which is unhappy (47).

This is offered as a hierarchical series, and critics have understood the di-
anoetic laugh to be Beckett's own ultimate laugh, just as they have sought to
gloss his comedy in various ways: as absurd, stoical, nihilistic, and so forth.[13]
But Arsene's speech is only part of *Watt*, a discourse enclosed and qualified
by several more levels of discourse – and Arsene himself refers to his series
as "laughs that strictly speaking are not laughs, but modes of ululation" (46).
In the same way these evaluative critical interpretations of Beckett's comedy
confine it within a limited frame of reference, the sphere of thematics. They
make it mean something, but in the process they leave out what it does. The
very idea of the tenor of laughter reduces it to its evaluative import; it gives
the sense without the effect, just as the explained joke is not funny. This is
only to say that the comedy of Watt exemplifies the way in which the more
general reflexive movement enacted by all narrative, *a fortiori* by all fiction,
and most rigorously by literary fiction, is a creative force that always outlives
final signification. Here, that logic is played out in the oscillation between
thematics and affect; thematics is a form of reductionism, in the scientific
sense, oriented towards the sufficient cause of the representation, and this
orientation in itself generates the phenomenon of the emergent, the surplus
effect, which – temporally and conceptually – faces the other way. The laugh
itself is recursively generative: the fact that something is funny may itself
be funny, and most laughter is a more complex, layered response than interpretation generally allows. Laughter, indeed, is in itself both absurd and
infectious, and every laugh may be the occasion of a further, more inclusive
laugh. The ultimate haw has not been hawed.

The comic force of Beckett's novel exemplifies the same duality that I was
concerned with at the beginning of this essay, where I described narrative
sense-making in terms of a split between what it says and what it does.
Narrative sense-making, narrative discourse, fiction, literary fiction, are
characterized by this symbiotic but asymmetrical relation between saying
and doing, not once but recursively, over and over, and I equate these two

---

13   The classic studies are Kenner 1962 and Cohn 1962.

faces of narrative respectively with the notions of value and force. What narrative *says* is how it articulates a sense of the way things are from within the domain of human value: it cashes in value in order to achieve the resolution of meaning, however local, however fleeting. What narrative *does* is how it functions as a communication, or an articulation; how it changes the terms of reference, the value system, within which it was performed. What narrative does is its force, a force being what acts, rather than what is. Literature, which I have considered synecdochically as literary fiction, is the most elaborated exploration of these reflexive hierarchies that our culture has to offer, and its intricacies strive to articulate our fullest sense of the human – that is, both to express it and to produce it: continuously, simultaneously, reconceiving the entire space in which we live, and living in it. The study of literature is also the saying of a doing, then; the saying of this doing which is itself a saying, and which itself enfolds a hierarchy of doing and saying. Literary study specifies and articulates the operation of these negotiations of cultural value in literature, and it draws out the significant continuities between the literary and broader, more fundamental frames of reference such as those I have concentrated upon here. This in itself would be enough to justify its place in the academy, but it is not all; literary study also, necessarily, participates in the negotiations of cultural value it describes; it acts, it has force. The immediate manifestations of this performative dimension of literary scholarship are its interface with contemporary culture at large and its pedagogy. In both respects literary scholarship testifies to the impossibility, characteristic of the discipline, of disentangling its object of study from the act of engaging with it. I suspect this quality of literary study features prominently among the reasons its status is called into question, but it is no weakness – far from it; I have argued that it is principled, and essential to a recognition of the significance of its object.

REFERENCES

Abbott, H. Porter. 2003. Unnarratable knowledge: the difficulty of understanding evolution by natural selection. In *Narrative theory and the cognitive sciences*, ed. David Herman, 143-62. Stanford, California: CSLI Publications.

Ackerley, Chris. 2004. Samuel Beckett and the geology of the imagination: toward an excavation of *Watt*. *Journal of Beckett studies* 13: 150-63.

Beausang, Michael, and Valérie Galiussi. 1996. Watt: logic, insanity, aphasia. *Style* 30: 495-513.

Beckett, Samuel. 1953. *Watt*. Paris: Olympia Press.

Beer, Gillian. 1983. *Darwin's plots: evolutionary narrative in Darwin, George Eliot and nineteenth-century fiction*. London: Routledge and Kegan Paul.

Benjamin, Shoshana. 1997. What's Watt. *Poetics today* 18: 376-96.

Bickhard, M.H. 2000. Emergence. In *Downward causation*, eds. P.B. Andersen, C. Emmeche, N.O. Finnemann, P.V. Christiansen, 322-348. Aarhus: Aarhus University Press.

Boyd, Richard. 2002. Scientific realism. In *Stanford encyclopedia of philosophy*. http://plato.stanford.edu/entries/scientific-realism/.

Cohn, Ruby. 1962. *Samuel Beckett: the comic gamut*. New Brunswick, New Jersey: Rutgers University Press.

Culik, Hugh. 1993. Mathematics as metaphor: Samuel Beckett and the esthetics of incompleteness. *Papers on language & literature* 29: 131-51.

Darwin, Charles. 1859. *The origin of species*. Reprinted. London: Penguin.

Dawkins, Richard. 1976. *The selfish gene*. Oxford: Oxford University Press.

Fludernik, Monika. 1996. *Towards a "natural" narratology*. London: Routledge.

Hayman, David. 2002. Getting where? Beckett's opening gambit for *Watt*. *Contemporary literature* 43: 28-49.

Holland, John H. 1998. *Emergence: from chaos to order*. Oxford: Oxford University Press.

Johnson, Stephen. 2001. *Emergence: the connected lives of ants, brains, cities and software*. London: Allen Lane.

Kenner, Hugh. 1962. *Flaubert, Joyce, Beckett: the stoic comedians*. Boston: Beacon Press.

Knapp, John V., ed. 2008. Special issue on literary Darwinism. *Style* 42.2-3.

Levine, George. 1988. *Darwin and the novelists*. Cambridge: Harvard University Press.

Turner, Mark. 1996. *The literary mind: the origins of thought and language*. Oxford: Oxford University Press.

Wall, John. 2002. A study of the imagination in Samuel Beckett's *Watt*. *New literary history: a journal of theory and interpretation* 33: 533-58.

Walsh, Richard. 2007. *The rhetoric of fictionality: narrative theory and the idea of fiction*. Columbus: Ohio State University Press.

CONTRIBUTORS

Marie-Laure Ryan is Scholar in Residence at the University of Colorado, Boulder and for 2010-2011 a visiting scholar at the Johannes Gutenberg University in Mainz, Germany. She is the author of *Possible Worlds, Artificial Intelligence and Narrative Theory* (1991), of *Narrative as Virtual Reality: Immersion and Interactivity in Literature and Electronic Media* (2001) and of *Avatars of Story* (2006), as well as the co-editor, with David Herman and Manfred Jahn, of the *Routledge Encyclopedia of Narrative Theory* (2005). She has been the recipient of a Guggenheim fellowship, of a fellowship from the National Endowment for the Humanities, and has been a fellow of the Cornell Society for the Humanities. Her work on narrative, media, the theory of fiction, and digital culture has appeared in such journals as *Poetics, Poetics Today, Semiotica, Narrative, Game Studies,* and *New Literary History,* and it has been published in French, German, Czech, Spanish, Korean, Chinese and Japanese.

Werner Wolf is Professor and Chair of English and General Literature at the University of Graz in Austria. His main areas of research are literary theory (concerning aesthetic illusion, narratology, and metafiction in particular), functions of literature, 18th- to 21st-century English fiction, 18th- and 20th-century drama, as well as intermediality studies (relations and comparisons between literature and other media, notably music and the visual arts). His extensive publications include, besides numerous essays, *Ästhetische Illusion und Illusionsdurchbrechung in der Erzählkunst* (1993) and *The Musicalization of Fiction: A Study in the Theory and History of Intermediality* (1999). He is also co-editor of volumes 1, 3, 5 and 11 of the book series "Word and Music Studies" (1999-2010) as well as of volumes 1 and 2 of the series "Studies in Intermediality" (also published by Rodopi): *Framing Borders in Literature and Other Media* (2006), and *Description in Literature and Other Media* (2007). He is currently leading a project financed by the Austrian Science Fund (FWF) on 'Metareference in the media', in the course of which he has edited *Metareference across Media: Theory and Case Studies* (2009) as vol. 4 of the series "Studies in Intermediality", and is preparing the edition of yet another volume in the same series, namely *The Metareferential Turn in Contemporary Arts and Media: Forms, Functions, Attempts at Explanation.*

Morten Kyndrup, dr.phil. is Professor of Aesthetics and Culture at the Department of Aesthetics and Communication, University of Aarhus, Denmark. His work include books as *Det Postmoderne* (1986), *Framing and Fiction* (1992),

Riften og sløret (1998), *Den æstetiske relation* (2008) and numerous articles on art theory, aesthetics, narratology, and comparative arts studies. He is currently director of the Doctoral School in Arts and Aesthetics, University of Aarhus, chairman of the Nordic Society of Aesthetics and member of director's board, The New Carlsberg Foundation.

Svend Erik Larsen is Professor of Comparative Literature, Department of Aesthetics and Communication, Aarhus University. He is a member of the Academia Europaea and the chair of its section for Literary and Theatrical Studies. He serves as secretary for the literary history series Comparative History of Literatures in the European Languages under the Association Internationale de Littérature Comparée. He is co-editor of *Orbis Litterarum*, vice-president of the Danish Research Council for Culture and Communication and serves on several advisory boards for journals and research and funding bodies. His research interests cover literary and cultural history, world literature, literary historiography, urban culture, memory studies, semiotics, and literary didactics. He has authored and co-authored and edited and co-edited numerous books and articles, among others: *Signs in Use* (2002), *La rue – espace ouvert* (1997), *Nature: Literature and its Otherness* (1997). Recently, books in Danish on literature and globalization and a literary history for high schools. Current project on literature, remembrance and forgiveness.

Sune Auken is dr.habil. and Associate Professor of Danish Literature at the University of Copenhagen. He has written several books and a number of articles within his field among these his habilitationsschrift on N.F.S. Grundtvig. For obvious reasons most of these works are in Danish. Sune Auken is head of the PhD-committee at the Faculty for the Humanities at the University of Copenhagen and leader of the university's Research Group for Genre Studies. As a tenured employee at a Danish University, Sune Auken spends most of his time dodging administrative demands and trying to do his job in the mean time. In response to this he has written the book *Hjernedød* (*Brain death*), sketching out the disastrous results of recent Danish university politics. He is an often cited debater in the field and has been known to commit acts of free speech in forbidden places.

Brian McHale is Distinguished Humanities Professor of English at the Ohio State University. He was for many years associated with the Porter Institute for Poetics and Semiotics at Tel Aviv University in Israel, and was an editor of the international journal, *Poetics Today*. He is one of the founding members of Project Narrative at the Ohio State University, and president (2010-11) of the Association for the Study of the Arts of the Present (*ASAP*). The author of three books on postmodernist fiction and poetry – *Postmodernist Fiction*

(1987), *Constructing Postmodernism* (1992), and *The Obligation toward the Difficult Whole: Postmodernist Long Poems* (2004), he has also published many articles on modernist and postmodernist fiction and poetry, narrative theory, and science fiction. He is co-editor, with Randall Stevenson, of *The Edinburgh Companion to Twentieth-Century Literatures in English* (2006) and, with his Ohio State colleagues David Herman and James Phelan, of *Teaching Narrative Theory* (the Modern Language Association Press, 2010). He is currently editing, with Luc Herman and Inger Dalsgaard, the *Cambridge Companion to Thomas Pynchon* and, with Joe Bray and Alison Gibbon, the *Routledge Companion to Experimental Literature*.

Anne-Marie Mai is Professor at Institute for Literature, Culture and Media, University of Southern Denmark, Denmark. She is the author of several articles and books in Danish and Swedish on contemporary Danish literature and history of Nordic literature. Her dissertation, *Danske kvindelige forfattere*, I-II (Danish Women Writers, 1982), is on the history of Danish women's literature. She has edited the fourth edition of *Danske digtere i det 20. århundrede*, I-III (Danish Poets of the 20th Century, 2000-2002) as well as *Nordisk kvindelitteraturhistorie* (Nordic Women's Literary History, 1993-1998) and *Læsninger i dansk litteratur* I-V (Readings of Danish Literature, 1997-2000). She published *Hvor litteraturen finder sted. Bidrag til dansk litteraturhistorie*, I-II, 2010 (Where literature takes place. Contributions to the study of Danish literature I-II, 2010). Her publications in English include articles on literary history, 18th-century literature and culture, theory of literature, contemporary Danish and Nordic literature. She is a co-editor of *Nordic Light* (2007) and in 2011 *Nordisk kvindelitteraturhistorie* will be published in English, Swedish and Danish as free internet publication.

Magnus Persson is Associate Professor at the Department of Culture, Language and Media, School of Teacher Education, Malmö University. He has a PhD in Comparative Literature from Lund University. Persson is the author of articles and books in Swedish on reading, cultural theory, popular culture and pedagogy. His dissertation, *The Struggle for High and Low Culture. Studies in the Late Twentieth Century Novel's Relationship to Mass Culture and Modernity*, is an analysis of how a number of contemporary Scandinavian high cultural authors have approached, used and transformed popular culture from various perspectives. Persson is the author and co-author of a series of books dealing with literature, culture and aesthetics within the educational system. He is currently working on a book about the value of literature in a post-literary society.

Dorothy J. Hale is Professor of English at the University of California, Berkeley. She is the author of *Social Formalism: The Novel in Theory from Henry James to the Present* (Stanford UP, 1998) and editor of *The Novel: An Anthology of Criti-*

cism and Theory, 1900-2000 (Blackwell, 2006). Publications related to her current book project include "The Art of English Fiction in the Twentieth Century" in *The Cambridge Companion to the Twentieth-Century English Novel*, edited by Robert Caserio (Cambridge UP, 2009); and "Fiction as Restriction: Self-Binding in New Ethical Theories of the Novel", *Narrative* (2007).

Jan Alber is Assistant Professor in the English Department at the University of Freiburg in Germany. He is the author of *Narrating the Prison* (Cambria Press 2007) and has edited collections such as *Stones of Law, Bricks of Shame: Narrating Imprisonment in the Victorian Age* (with Frank Lauterbach, University of Toronto Press, 2009), *Postclassical Narratology: Approaches and Analyses* (with Monika Fludernik, Ohio State University Press, 2010), and *Unnatural Narratives, Unnatural Narratology* (with Rüdiger Heinze, de Gruyter, 2011). Alber has authored and co-authored articles that were published in such journals as *Dickens Studies Annual, The Journal of Popular Culture, Narrative, Short Story Criticism, Storyworlds*, and *Style*. He has also contributed to numerous edited collections as well as to the *Routledge Encyclopedia of Narrative Theory* and the *Handbook of Narratology*. In 2007, Alber received a fellowship from the German Research Foundation that allowed him to spend one year at Ohio State University as a visiting scholar doing research on his second book under the auspices of Project Narrative. His new project focuses on unnatural (i.e., physically or logically impossible) scenarios in fiction and drama. He has recently been awarded a Feodor-Lynen Research Fellowship for Experienced Researchers by the Humboldt Foundation to continue his research in this area.

Richard Walsh is a Senior Lecturer in English and Related Literature at the University of York, UK. He is the author of *Novel Arguments: Reading Innovative American Fiction* (Cambridge 1995) and *The Rhetoric of Fictionality: Narrative Theory and the Idea of Fiction* (Ohio State, 2007), which proposes a fundamental reconceptualisation of the role of fictionality in narrative, and in doing so challenges many of the core assumptions of narrative theory. He has published articles in *Poetics Today, Narrative, Style, Modern Fiction Studies* and *Storyworlds*, among others, and has contributed essays to edited volumes such as the Blackwell *Companion to Narrative Theory* (2005), *Toward a Cognitive Theory of Narrative Acts* (2010) and *Postclassical Narratology: Approaches and Analyses* (2010). His current research interests include narrative across media and narrative theory in interdisciplinary contexts, in particular the relation between narrative and the concept of emergence. He is the leader of the Fictionality Research Group, and director of Narrative Research in York's Centre for Modern Studies.

CONTRIBUTORS